A PRIMER OF TENNYSON

A PRIMER OF TENNYSON

WITH

A CRITICAL ESSAY

BY

WILLIAM MACNEILE DIXON
LITT. D., A.M., LL.B.

PROFESSOR OF THE ENGLISH LANGUAGE AND LITERATURE IN THE UNIVERSITY
OF BIRMINGHAM, AUTHOR OF " IN THE REPUBLIC OF LETTERS," ETC.

Routledge
Taylor & Francis Group

First published in 1901 by Methuen & Co. Ltd.

This edition first published in 2018 by Routledge
2 Park Square, Milton Park, Abingdon, Oxon, OX14 4RN
and by Routledge
711 Third Avenue, New York, NY 10017

Routledge is an imprint of the Taylor & Francis Group, an informa business

© 1901 Taylor & Francis

Publisher's Note
The publisher has gone to great lengths to ensure the quality of this reprint but points out that some imperfections in the original copies may be apparent.

Disclaimer
The publisher has made every effort to trace copyright holders and welcomes correspondence from those they have been unable to contact.
A Library of Congress record exists under ISBN: 29027747

ISBN 13: 978-1-138-55618-8 (hbk)
ISBN 13: 978-1-138-56367-4 (pbk)
ISBN 13: 978-1-315-12184-0 (ebk)

A PRIMER OF TENNYSON

WITH

A CRITICAL ESSAY

BY

WILLIAM MACNEILE DIXON
LITT. D., A.M., LL.B.

PROFESSOR OF THE ENGLISH LANGUAGE AND LITERATURE IN THE UNIVERSITY
OF BIRMINGHAM, AUTHOR OF " IN THE REPUBLIC OF LETTERS," ETC.

Routledge
Taylor & Francis Group

First published in 1901 by Methuen & Co. Ltd.

This edition first published in 2018 by Routledge
2 Park Square, Milton Park, Abingdon, Oxon, OX14 4RN
and by Routledge
711 Third Avenue, New York, NY 10017

Routledge is an imprint of the Taylor & Francis Group, an informa business

© 1901 Taylor & Francis

Publisher's Note
The publisher has gone to great lengths to ensure the quality of this reprint but points out that some imperfections in the original copies may be apparent.

Disclaimer
The publisher has made every effort to trace copyright holders and welcomes correspondence from those they have been unable to contact.
A Library of Congress record exists under ISBN: 29027747

ISBN 13: 978-1-138-55618-8 (hbk)
ISBN 13: 978-1-138-56367-4 (pbk)
ISBN 13: 978-1-315-12184-0 (ebk)

A PRIMER OF TENNYSON

A PRIMER OF TENNYSON

WITH

A CRITICAL ESSAY

BY

WILLIAM MACNEILE DIXON
Litt. D., A.M., LL.B.

PROFESSOR OF THE ENGLISH LANGUAGE AND LITERATURE IN THE UNIVERSITY
OF BIRMINGHAM, AUTHOR OF "IN THE REPUBLIC OF LETTERS," ETC.

SECOND EDITION REVISED

METHUEN & CO.
36 ESSEX STREET, W.C.
LONDON
1901

EDINBURGH
COLSTON AND COY. LIMITED
PRINTERS

CONTENTS

PORTRAITS OF TENNYSON.

THE earliest portrait of Tennyson was painted by Samuel Laurence in 1838. Five were painted by G. F. Watts (who also painted a portrait of Mrs Tennyson), *a profile* in 1856, *a three-quarters* in 1858, another in 1859, *a full face* in 1865 (in the National Portrait Gallery), *a three-quarters* in 1891 (in Trinity College, Cambridge). To these may be added a portrait by Herkomer in 1878. Woolner, the sculptor, executed *a portrait medallion* in 1850, *a profile bust* in 1856 (in Trinity College, Cambridge, *replica* in Westminster Abbey), *a three-quarters* in 1867, and another *bust* in 1873. Of photographs of Tennyson among the best and best known are those taken by Mrs J. M. Cameron.

A TENNYSON PRIMER.

CHAPTER I.

ALFRED TENNYSON, the acknowledged representative of his age in poetry, was born on August 6, 1809, at Somersby Rectory, in the village of Somersby, in Lincolnshire. His parents were of gentle blood: his father, the Rev. George Clayton Tennyson, rector of Somersby and vicar of Great Grimsby, a man of exceptional culture, Parentage versatile powers, imaginative temper, and **and** strongly marked character; his mother, a Childhood. daughter of the Rev. Stephen Fytche, vicar of Louth. Frederick and Charles*(afterwards Charles Tennyson-Turner), who preceded Alfred in a family of twelve, both became distinguished as poets in after life. From his earliest years Alfred was devoted to poetry, and seemed destined for a poetical career. His first recorded verse was the cry that broke from him, when a child of five, as the wind hurried him down the garden walk :

>   " I hear a voice that's speaking in the wind."

While still very young, some verses written upon his slate—the subject, the flowers in the rectory garden—modelled upon Thomson, the only poet he had then read, were rewarded by a " Yes, you can write," from his brother; a little later the death of his grand-

* The eldest brother, George, born 1806, died in infancy.

A

mother was the theme of a poem which drew from
his grandfather half a sovereign, and the prophecy,
soon to be falsified, " That is the first money, my boy,
that you've made by poetry, and, take my word for
it, it will be the last."

Perhaps the lines in the *Poems by Two Brothers*, beginning, " There on the bier she sleeps," are an improved version of this early attempt.* In his twelfth
year he was busy on an epic in imitation of Scott,
which ran to some thousand lines, and in his fifteenth
he essayed a drama. Of these poems it is interesting to note that, in his father's judgment, they gave
promise of a famous future. " If Alfred die," said
Mr. Tennyson, " one of our greatest poets will have
gone."

For three years Alfred attended the grammar school
at Louth,† which was followed by home tuition. The
changes hardly broke the tranquil, dreamy life spent
by the boy, chiefly alone—for he was naturally of re-
tiring disposition—or in long rambles with his favourite brother Charles. The news of Byron's death, in
1824, was the first wave of emotion from the outside
world that touched him. " I thought," he said,
" that everything was over and finished for every one
—that nothing else mattered. I remember I walked
out alone and carved ' Byron is dead !' into the sand-
stone." Two years later Alfred and Charles joined
in a poetical venture, and put forth a small volume ;
but rather, it appears, in search of pocket-money
than fame. A Louth bookseller, Jackson by name,
was induced to give twenty pounds for the copyright of
their *juvenilia*. The *Poems by Two Brothers* (1826),

---

* Signed, however, " C. T." in the 1893 edition.
† 1816-1820.

containing one hundred and two short poems, was published, and the money spent on a tour round the churches of Lincolnshire.

The scenery of Lincolnshire*is faithfully sketched as background to all the early poetry of Tennyson which is not purely derivative ; the rich meadow and gradual slope, the " ridged wolds," the picturesque wandering lanes, as well as the " glooming flats" and less attractive features of the fen country, appear in it, even the

> ". . . woods that belt the gray hillside,
> The seven elms, the poplars four
> That stand beside my father's door."
>
> —*Ode to Memory.*

In 1828 Charles and Alfred went up to Trinity College, Cambridge, whither Frederick had preceded them. Alfred's rooms were in Corpus Buildings, overlooking the main quadrangle of King's College, and within hearing of its chapel organ. The change from the quiet, rural **At** life of his childhood to that of the univer- **Cambridge.** sity, where many of the lasting friendships of his life were made, was fraught with important influences upon Tennyson's career. He became the central figure of a group of brilliant young men, not a few of whom bore names afterwards distinguished : Richard Monckton Milnes (afterwards Lord Houghton), James Spedding (the " J. S." of the poem, " You ask me why, tho' ill at ease"), J. M. Kemble (the " J. M. K." of the sonnet, " My heart and hope is with thee"), Richard Chenevix Trench (afterwards Archbishop of Dublin), W. H. Brookfield (to whom the sonnet, " Brooks, for they

* The Tennysons frequently visited the Lincolnshire coast.

called you so that knew you best," was addressed), Henry Alford (afterwards Dean of Canterbury), Edmund Lushington, Charles Merivale (afterwards Dean of Ely), and Arthur Hallam, the eldest son of Henry Hallam, the historian.* Between Arthur Hallam and Alfred Tennyson grew up a friendship so close and deep as rightly to be named ideal—a friendship which, though cut short by Hallam's death in less than five years (*In Memoriam*, xxii.), must be reckoned one of the great determining forces of the poet's life. Hallam, Tennyson's junior by two years, was at this time the more widely read and accomplished scholar, and gave equal promise of future name and fame. His engagement, in the year in which he left Cambridge, to Emily Tennyson, Alfred's sister, promised to add another bond to that of friendship (*In Memoriam*, lxxxiv.), a promise sadly unfulfilled.†

Before going up to the University, Tennyson had been at work upon a poem entitled *The Lover's Tale*. After a few years' interval the first and second parts appeared in print in 1833 (the same year as Browning's *Pauline*), "when," wrote the author (in the preface to the edition of 1879), "feeling the imperfection of the poem, I withdrew it from the press." Copies were, however, in circulation, and the work was reprinted without his consent and without the improvements which were in contemplation. In self-defence a corrected and improved version, with the addition of a third part, *The Golden Supper*, a work of the author's mature life, was published in 1879. *The Lover's Tale* contains one line—

" A center'd glory-circled memory"—

* Thackeray, afterwards a warm friend, was also a contemporary of the Tennysons at Trinity College.

† She married Captain R. Jesse, R.N.

of which Tennyson had already made use in his now famous university prize poem, a fact which may be noted as an example of his almost parsimonious habit of treasuring a good line like a jewel until he could find for it a suitable setting.   Three lines, also from the same poem, appear again in the *Ode to Memory*.*

In 1829, Milnes, Hallam, and Alfred Tennyson were all competitors for the Vice-Chancellor's medal in English verse—the subject " Timbuctoo."   Tennyson was a candidate at his father's request, and the verses sent in were remodelled to some extent from an unfinished earlier poem on the Battle of Armageddon.   To him the medal was awarded, despite the fact that it was supposed to be *de rigueur* that the compositions should be in the heroic couplet, and Tennyson had chosen for his metre blank verse.   Promise of great poetry to come was found in *Timbuctoo* by several acute readers, and it is creditable to the discernment of the examiners that they were able to appreciate its merit.   Both here and in *The Lover's Tale* the influence of Shelley is clearly evidenced, but the ring and movement of the blank verse which we now recognise as Tennysonian unmistakably display themselves.

During the autumn of 1830 Hallam and Tennyson visited Spain—a visit commemorated in *The Valley of Cauteretz*—to carry money and letters of encouragement to the revolutionists, with some of whose leaders they had interviews.†   The enthusiasm of the youth-

---

* " Sure she was nigher to heaven's spheres,
Listening the lordly music flowing from
Th' illimitable years."
—*Ode to Memory*.

† " A wild time we had of it," Hallam said.   " I played my part

ful poets had been kindled by the struggle for freedom in the Spanish war of independence, much as the spirits of Wordsworth and Coleridge had been aroused by the hopes of the French Revolution.   But, like Wordsworth, Tennyson came to a different and perhaps wiser mind when his knowledge of revolutionary men and methods was nearer and more personal.   In this year of the visit to the Pyrenees was published Alfred's first independent volume of verse, *Poems, Chiefly Lyrical.*   The original design had been to include poems by Hallam in the volume, but owing to the disapproval expressed by Hallam's father the idea of a poetic partnership was given up, and the book appeared as we have it.   In this year also appeared a volume of poems, *Sonnets and Fugitive Pieces*, by Charles Tennyson, the brother with whom Alfred had joined in the production of the *Poems by Two Brothers.* Wordsworth, writing from Cambridge about this time, remarked : " We have also a respectable show of blossom in poetry—two brothers of the name of Tennyson ; one in particular not a little promising."

The death of his father in March, 1831, brought Tennyson's University career to a close without a degree, nor does it seem that he had any regard for the traditions of Cambridge or breathed its atmosphere with any keen enjoyment.*   He had taken little part

as conspirator in a small way, and made friends with two or three gallant men, who have since been trying their luck with Valdes."

   * The following sonnet, written in pencil, appears on the fly-leaf of the 1833 volume in the Dyce collection of the South Kensington Museum :

　　" Therefore your halls, your ancient colleges,
　　　Your portals statued with old kings and queens,
　　　Your gardens, myriad-volumed libraries,
　　　Wax-lighted chapels, and rich carven screens,

in the life a university offers, and was never a candidate for academic distinctions. To a chosen few, a coterie known as "the Apostles" (*In Memoriam*, lxxxvii.), he was accustomed to read his verses as they were composed, but it was understood that no criticism would be acceptable. From the first the natural sensitiveness of the poet, which increased in later life to an almost morbid degree, made him extremely averse to a word of dispraise. The same sensitiveness debarred him from playing any active part in the world of men, and at no period was his circle of acquaintanceship large. But while impatient of adverse criticism, there was never author who turned it to better account when it came ; and the day of its coming was not long delayed. The first rude breath of censure blew from the critical journals, *Blackwood* and the *Quarterly*, soon after the appearance of *Poems, Chiefly Lyrical*, and the *Poems* of 1832. These reviews dealt in the trenchant style of the time with the affectations and weaknesses apparent to every cultivated reader in the work of the new poet. He was described as "the pet of a cockney

Your doctors, and your proctors, and your deans,
    Shall not avail you, when the day-beam sports
New risen o'er awakened Albion—no !
    Nor yet your solemn organ-pipes that blow
Melodious thunders thro' your vacant courts
    At morn and eve—because your manner sorts
Not with this age wherefrom you stand apart,
    Because the lips of little children preach
Against you, you that do profess to teach,
    And teach us nothing, feeding not the heart."

The following note is appended : " I have a great affection for my old university, and can only regret that this spirit of under-graduate irritability against the Cambridge of that day ever found its way into print." This sonnet is reprinted in the life of the poet by his son.

coterie," a remark at the time not very wide of the truth. Though unsympathetic, therefore, his early critics were no less valuable friends to Tennyson than his band of faithful admirers. His education as an artist was far from complete, his instrument not yet in tune, and it is with the manner rather than the matter of the reviews that any reasonable quarrel can be raised. While Tennyson replied to the *Blackwood* article bitterly enough in the verses, afterwards suppressed, describing Wilson as " rusty, fusty Christopher," he was careful to adopt his suggestions almost without exception ; and though the *Quarterly* review was resented, it was honoured scrupulously in the same way. This was to exhibit the temper of the child, but to act like a man. The voices, moreover, were very far from being all against Tennyson. Coleridge praised the poems, while he expressed the opinion that the new poet was not yet master of the metrical craft, and confessed to his own difficulty in scanning some of the verses. The *Westminster Review* of January, 1831, had been full of eulogy ; Hallam himself, in the *Englishman's Magazine* of August, had warmly praised the genius of his friend in a glowing article, and Leigh Hunt, in the *Tatler* of the same year (February and March), in reviewing Alfred's poems, together with the volume of sonnets by Charles, while he praised both, had predicted the laurel of the future for Alfred.

In the year that Arthur Hallam took his degree (1832) he was a guest at Somersby. "Fifty years hence people will make pilgrimages to this place," he said. About this time his engagement to Emily Tennyson was made public, and he went up to London to begin his career at the bar, the profession he had chosen as the best avenue to the public life to which he looked. Until compelled, the following year, to seek health abroad, Hallam was domiciled at 67 Wimpole Street — "the dark house in the long, unlovely street." "You will always find me at sixes and sevens," he was accustomed to say as a mnemonic for his friends. In September of 1833 the end came.

> ——" In Vienna's fatal walls
> God's finger toucht him, and he slept."

He was buried at Clevedon, not far from where the Severn meets the sea and " in the hearing of the wave."

After Arthur Hallam's death Tennyson went to reside in London. So poignant a sorrow as the early loss of his best-loved friend hung like a heavy cloud over his life. It was the poet's "dark hour," how dark we learn from *The Two Voices*.* No volume was published between the *Poems* of In London. 1832 and the revised and enlarged edition, in two volumes, of 1842. Occasional verses had appeared in 1831 in the *Gem*, and in the following year in the *English Magazine*, the *Yorkshire Literary Annual*, and *Friendship's Offering;* and others followed.

During these silent years in London Tennyson became one of Carlyle's most frequent visitors—none more congenial—" a true human soul or some authentic approximation thereto, to whom your own soul can say, Brother !" The poet of these London days was described in Carlyle's picturesque style thus : " A great shock of rough, dusty-dark hair; bright, laughing, hazel eyes; massive aquiline face, most massive, yet most delicate ; of sallow brown complexion, almost Indian-looking; clothes cynically loose,

* Originally entitled *Thoughts of a Suicide.*

B

free and easy ; smokes infinite tobacco. His voice is
musically metallic—fit for loud laughter and piercing
wail, and all that may lie between ; speech and speculation free and plenteous ; I do not meet in these late
decades such company over a pipe."   In 1838 he appeared as a member of the Anonymous Club, of
which Carlyle, Mill, Thackeray, Landor, Macready,
Sterling, Cunningham, and other men of letters were
members.   Some of his poems were handed about in
manuscript and read by friends.   Some were even
in print, for Tennyson had prepared for his private
use in 1842 a volume entitled *Morte d'Arthur,
Dora and other Idylls*, containing eight blank verse
poems.   The details of this period of Tennyson's
life are but scanty, and there is little for a biographer to relate.   We know that he became strongly
attached to Rogers, the veteran poet, and at his house
met, among men of note, Gladstone, Leigh Hunt, and
Tom Moore.   The following note occurs in the diary
of Henry Crabb Robinson :

" 31 Jan., 1845.   I dined this day with Rogers.   We
had an interesting party of eight—Moxon, the publisher ; Kenny, the dramatic poet ; Spedding, Lushington, and Alfred Tennyson, three young men of
eminent talent, belonging to literary young England
—the latter, Tennyson, being by far the most eminent
of the young poets.   He is an admirer of Goethe, and
I had a long *tête-à-tête* with him about the great poet."

It is certain that Carlyle's influence was a potent
factor in the enlargement and development of his intellectual sympathies ; and to it, as well as to Hallam's
death, is due the graver, more philosophical note
soon to be heard in Tennyson's poetry.   While he
still continued to pay studious attention to the ex-

ternal form of his verse, he essayed higher subjects and grappled with the deeper problems. In these days he met and talked far into the night, smoking "infinite tobacco," with his chosen friends, or read far and wide, and brooded over the poems that were to set the seal upon his reputation in the 1842 volumes ; in Carlyle's words, " carrying a bit of chaos about him which he was manufacturing into kosmos." With the publication of the volumes just mentioned Tennyson's place in English literature was beyond question assured. The author of *Locksley Hall, Ulysses*, the *Vision of Sin*, and the *Morte d'Arthur* was universally acknowledged the first poet of the day. " He is decidedly," wrote, in 1845, Wordsworth, whom he had met for the first time two years earlier, " the first of our living poets." That year saw the fourth edition of the two volumes, and Moxon, his publisher, confessed that Tennyson was the only poet by the publication of whose work he was not a loser.

In 1837 the Tennyson family had left Somersby for Beech Hill House, near Hill Beech, situated on the border of Epping Forest, and near Waltham Abbey, whose bells are addressed in the fine greeting to the New Year, now familiar to all English ears :

" Ring out, wild bells, to the wild sky !"

In 1840 came another change to Tunbridge Wells, and in the next year still another to Boxley, near Maidstone. Here Alfred's youngest sister, Cecilia, was married to Edmund Law Lushington, professor of Greek in the University of Glasgow, the wedding which is the subject of the closing section of *In Memoriam*. In 1845,* through the influence of Milnes,

* In 1844 Edgar Allen Poe, carried away by the artistic beauty of

Tennyson's name was placed by Sir Robert Peel, who had never previously heard of the poet, upon the Civil List for a pension of two hundred pounds a year, and his pecuniary anxieties, for some time pressing, were at an end. Though approved of by the majority, by some the pension was considered premature, and Bulwer Lytton, in his satire, *The New Timon*, made a sharp attack upon Tennyson, both as poet and pensioner. He was there spoken of as " School-Miss Alfred," and his poetry described as

> . . . " a jingling medley of purloined conceits
> Out-babying Wordsworth, and out-glittering Keats."

A note to the passage stated that Tennyson had been " quartered on the public purse in the prime of life, without either wife or family." The reply was not delayed, and a set of verses in *Punch*, signed " Alcibiades," proved that stinging satire was quite within Tennyson's reach also, had he cared to enter that field.* An *Afterthought*, now included in his works

form in Tennyson's poems, wrote enthusiastically : " I am not sure that Tennyson is not the greatest of poets."

> * " We know him out of Shakespeare's art,
>   And those fine curses which he spoke—
>   The old Timon with his noble heart,
>   That strongly loathing, greatly broke.
>
> " So died the Old, here comes the New ;
>   Regard him—a familiar face ;
>   I thought we knew him. What, it's you,
>   The padded man that wears the stays—
>
> " Who killed the girls and thrilled the boys
>   With dandy pathos when you wrote—
>   O Lion ! you that made a noise,
>   And shook a mane *en papillotes*.
>   *   *   *   *   *

under the title of *Literary Squabbles*, appeared the following week over the same signature, and more justly represents Tennyson's true attitude towards such controversies. The passage of detraction in the *New Timon* was subsequently excised ; and the *amende honorable* was acknowledged by the dedication, in 1876, of the drama of *Harold* to the novelist's son. Among other attacks may be noted the *Bon Gaultier Ballads* (the work of Theodore Martin and W. E. Aytoun), 1845, which contained some clever parodies of the 1842 poems.* About this time Howitt wrote of Tennyson : " It is very possible you may come across

> " But men of long-enduring hopes,
>   And careless what the hour may bring,
> Can pardon little would-be Popes,
>   And Brummels when they try to sting.

> " An artist, sir, should rest in art,
>   And waive a little of his claim ;
> To have the great poetic heart
>   Is more than all poetic fame.
>   *   *   *   *   *
> " A Timon you ! Nay, nay, for shame,
>   It looks too arrogant a jest—
> That fierce old man—to take his name,
>   You bandbox ! off, and let him rest."

* The following stanza from *The Laureate*, parodying *The Merman*, will serve as an example :

> " Who would not be
>   The Laureate bold,
>   With his butt of sherry
>   To keep him merry,
> And nothing to do but to pocket his gold.
> 'Tis I would be the Laureate bold."

This was written on the death of Southey (1843), and was intended as an ironical demand for the appointment of Tennyson.

him in a country inn, with a foot on each hob of the fireplace, a volume of Greek in one hand, his meerschaum in the other, so far advanced towards the seventh heaven that he would not thank you to call him back into this nether world."

Although Tennyson's reputation was now firmly established, there wanted not on the part of the best critics a certain reticence as to the quality of his attainment. In 1846, Wordsworth, in conversation with Thomas Cooper, spoke some weighty words which probably represented the more reserved and less enthusiastic verdict of the time, the opinion of those who felt that so far the new poet had given signs indeed of very unusual power, but had trifled with his art rather than given himself seriously to its greater aims· "There is little," said Wordsworth, "that can be called high poetry. Mr. Tennyson affords, indeed, the richest promise. He will do great things yet, and ought to have done greater things by this time." Erelong he was to show the best he had to give. In 1848 a new issue of *The Princess* (published the previous year) "produced among the fogs and smuts of Lincoln's Inn," appeared, a poem, the plan of which had been talked over as early as 1839, and was thought by the author to contain some of his best blank verse.* But the central year of the century was Tennyson's *Annus Mirabilis*, the year which saw the publication of his greatest poem, his marriage, and his appointment as Poet Laureate.

In 1850 Tennyson left Cheltenham, where he had chiefly resided from 1844. The years that lay between these two dates were mainly occupied in the composition of the great elegy which enshrines the memory of Arthur Hallam. *In Memoriam* appeared in 1850, at first

* *E.g.*, the passage beginning "As one that climbs a peak," etc.

anonymously. On June 13 of the same year, the author
was married at Shiplake Church, Oxfordshire, to Emily
Sellwood, a niece of Sir John Franklin, the
Arctic explorer.* Wordsworth had died   **Marriage**
earlier in the year, and in November Al-   **and Poet**
fred Tennyson was appointed his succes-   **Laureateship.**
sor as Poet Laureate,† and the seal of
national recognition placed upon his already great
fame. For two years after his marriage, on his return from a wedding journey in Italy,‡ the poet lived
at Twickenham, famous on account of Pope's residence there, and now (as Mr. G. J. Cayley, in a blank
verse letter, wrote to the Laureate) "twice classic."

From this year until that of his death Tennyson's
career was a summer of unbroken splendour, clouded
only by the death of his brother Charles, in 1879, and
his son Lionel, in 1885. Unlike most poets, he lived
a long life through in the sunshine of critical as well
as popular favour, honoured by all and reverenced by

* Her younger sister was the wife of Charles Tennyson-Turner.
† The post was offered to and declined by Rogers.
‡ See *The Daisy*.
His verses *To the Queen*, written after his appointment to the
Laureateship, have been so altered and amended that scarcely a line
of the original remains as at first. The original MS. contained
these two verses, afterwards omitted :

> " Nor should I dare to flatter state,
>   Nor such a lay would you receive
>   Were I to shape it, who believe
> Your nature true as you are great.
>
>   *   *   *   *   *
>
> " She brought a vast design to pass
>   When Europe and the scatter'd ends
>   Of our fierce world did meet as friends
> And brethren in her halls of glass."

The reference here is to the Crystal Palace of 1851.

many as among the very greatest of English poets. No such supreme lot has perhaps ever fallen to a poet of any race or country in the history of the world.

Tennyson's almost immediate and unanimous acceptance as a poet—a circumstance in itself usually far from prophetic of enduring fame—may be set down as due in part to the versatility of his poetic manner, and in part to the absence of serious rivals. He was fortunate in the possession of many brilliant gifts; he was perhaps even more fortunate in his birth time, and in the length of days granted him, with faculties unimpaired, and with ample space wherein to stablish his monument and enjoy his fame. Of the great poets of the century, but few reached even middle life ; for Keats and Shelley and Byron the light was early quenched ; Wordsworth and Southey and Coleridge had overlived their poetic prime, and the fruit of public acceptance was once more ripe for plucking. And Tennyson, in whose brain the man of the world was not unrepresented, took the nearest way to fame in that he made appeal, in almost every volume of verse published in his earlier years, to the people as well as to the critics. He was the man of the hour, and, with no very bold or illuminating opinions to offer, gave expressions in his poetry to the prevailing feelings, the prevailing thought of the time. The admiration of the few and the critical was excited by the perfection of his art, the admiration of the many and unsophisticated readers of poetry by the simple and graceful treatment of themes generally themselves simple, frequently English. The few were delighted to find their own thoughts in the delicate and exquisite version of a scholar of perfect taste ; the many could not deny that here were poems which never ran on to undue lengths, easily understood, even more easily enjoyed, and praised by all poetical authorities.

The first year of Tennyson's married life was partly spent in Italy, the route chosen being through the Riviera to Florence. Save for a few stanzas in *The Keepsake*, a farewell sonnet to Macready, read by John Forster at the banquet **Married Life,** given the actor on the eve of his depart- **Travels, and** ure, and the dedication " to the Queen"* **Political Poems.** of the seventh edition of the *Poems*, there was nothing of importance published during the year. But in 1852 the political horizon became clouded and threatening, and Tennyson, in company with most of his countrymen, viewed with extreme distrust the events taking place in France. The period of excitement that followed the *coup d'état* of December, the abolition of the constitution of the French Republic by Louis Napoleon, gave birth to three patriotic lyrics, published under the pseudonym of " Merlin" in the *Examiner*. It was not until 1872 that Tennyson acknowledged the authorship of these lyrics by the publication in the library edition of his works of the stirring lines entitled *The Third of February*, which, with the poems, *Britons, Guard your Own* and *Hands all Round*, had given full expression to the national feeling in England towards the French emperor and those weak-kneed English peers who,

---

* Tennyson was presented to the Queen at Buckingham Palace, on his appointment to be Poet Laureate, March 6, 1851. It is said he was dressed in Rogers' court dress, worn on a former occasion by Wordsworth.

to purchase peace at any price, would have "salved the tyrant o'er."

In September 1852 the Duke of Wellington died, and upon the day of his funeral appeared in the *Times* the first version of Tennyson's funeral ode, a poem which, if studied in its various editions, will give considerable insight into the author's careful methods of work. There was little enthusiasm over the ode in its early form, and it was severely criticised in the Press. Tennyson was much gratified by Henry Taylor's approval—"It has a greatness worthy of its theme, and an absolute simplicity and truth, with all the poetic passion of your nature moving beneath"— and replying, wrote : "Thanks ! thanks ! In the all but universal depreciation of my ode by the Press, the prompt and hearty approval of it by a man as true as the Duke himself is doubly grateful." The second edition, published in 1853, was greatly altered and extended, and further improvements were introduced before its reappearance in the *Maud* volume of 1856. The following lines in the first were omitted in all the subsequent editions :

> " Perchance our greatness will increase ;
>   Perchance a darkening future yields
> Some reverse from worse to worse,
>   The blood of men in quiet fields,
>   And sprinkled on the sheaves of peace."

In this year the poet's eldest son, Hallam, was born at Twickenham, and in the following year the family removed to Farringford, in Freshwater. The lanes and breezy downs, the meadow and wood and views of sea of the Farringford district form the background of his later poetic descriptions, as the flats and level wastes and marshes of Lincolnshire had done in the earlier. In his poetic invitation to the Rev. F. D. Maurice, on the occasion of his expulsion from King's College, London, Tennyson accurately describes the surroundings of his home in the Isle of Wight :

> " Where, far from noise and smoke of town,
>   I watch the twilight falling brown
>   All round a careless-order'd garden
>   Close to the ridge of a noble down.
>   *   *   *   *   *
> " For groves of pine on either hand,
>   To break the blast of winter, stand ;
>   And further on, the hoary Channel
>   Tumbles a billow on chalk and sand."

Here, where Lionel, his second son, was born in 1854, Tennyson lived until 1870. In 1853 appeared the eighth edition of the *Poems* and the fifth edition of the *Princess*, which, like the *Ode on the Death of the Duke of Wellington*, had undergone many alterations and editions. In 1853 he was asked whether he would permit his name to be put forward for the Lord Rectorship of the University of Edinburgh, but declined. In 1854 * appeared in the *Examiner* (December 9) the first draught of *The Charge of the Light Brigade*, a poem of which three versions are extant. The final version appeared as a separate publication, with the following note by the author :

"Having heard that the brave soldiers before Sebastopol, whom I am proud to call my countrymen, have a liking for my ballad on the Charge of the Light Brigade at Balaclava, I have ordered a thousand copies of it to be printed for them. No writing of

---

* In this year Dr. E. K. Kane, the Arctic explorer, named a columnar rock in Greenland, "Tennyson's Pillar."

mine can add to the glory they have acquired in the
Crimea ; but if what I have heard be true, they will
not be displeased to receive these copies of the ballad
from me, and to know that those who sit at home
love and honour them.

"August 8, 1855.   ALFRED TENNYSON."

"The people's voice" was never more distinctly
heard than in the poetry of Tennyson written in
times of grave national anxiety. His sympathy with
popular feeling, as here, aroused by the war in the
Crimea, was closer and deeper, aristocratic poet
though he was, than that of any poet of the democracy that England has yet seen.

In May, 1855, the year of the publication of *Maud*,
the honorary degree of D.C.L. was conferred on the
Poet Laureate by the University of Oxford. Of all
Maud and The Idylls of the King. Tennyson's poems, *Maud* was received
with the least favour ; it was severely criti-
cised in *Blackwood* (September), and the
National Review (October), and a hot controversy ensued over its merits and de-
merits. An "*Anti Maud*, by a Poet of the
People," appeared and ran into a second edition.
The germ of *Maud*, "a drama of the soul," is to be
found in the lines, "O, that 'twere possible," contributed
in 1837 to the *Tribute*, and it is on record that its
genesis may be traced to a remark of Sir John Simeon *
(Tennyson's friend and neighbour), to the effect that
the lines suggested a story which ought to be told. The
poem was mainly composed in Sir John Simeon's garden
at Swainston. Though the author's favourite poem,
Maud has never taken firm hold of the popular imagi-

* *In the Garden at Swainston* enshrines his memory with that
of Hallam and Lushington.

nation, and only a few of the more eminent critics have spoken enthusiastically in its favour.   Chief among the charges made against it is that of obscurity, a charge which can, however, with difficulty be maintained.   The best-known vindication of *Maud*, a reply to the animadversions of the critics, was published by Dr. Mann (1856), and is of special interest as approved by Tennyson himself.   In a letter to the author, Tennyson wrote: "No one with this essay before him can in future pretend to misunderstand my dramatic poem, *Maud;* your commentary is as true as it is full."   Rightly understood, *Maud* will be taken as a proof of the real range and fertility of Tennyson's lyric power.   More truly dramatic than any of his poems composed in the traditional form of the drama, it serves to display the character of his genius, which was capable of the development of intense individual *moods* such as he could realise in his own person, and their presentation in the emphatic form of subtly modulated lyric verse.   In a monodrama whose action unfolds itself in a series of lyric poems, his intense individualism was a source of strength, just as it was a source of indisputable weakness when he essayed a great dramatic theme in *Queen Mary* and *Harold*.

Maud was the poem which the author most frequently chose to read aloud.*   Perhaps the most interesting occasion upon which it was so read was in the September of 1855; Robert Browning and his wife were present, and Dante Gabriel Rossetti.   Rossetti made a pen-and-ink sketch of the poet as he declaimed his verses, which is still preserved.   Tennyson is sketched seated on the sofa, in a loose coat. His left hand grasps his foot in a curious fashion,

---

* He styled it "a little Hamlet, the history of a morbid poetic soul."

and the right holds the book. Of Tennyson's reading, several descriptions have been given. It seems to have been a kind of chant, guided by the music of the verse rather than by the sense of the words, and in this way a striking contrast to Browning's, whose stress of voice was not intended to be musical, but indicative of the meaning. The contrast is significant as interpreting in the case of each poet his conception of the aim of his own art. " I rather need to know what he is reading," said Sir Henry Taylor of Tennyson, "for otherwise I find sense to be lost in sound from time to time."

Two American men of letters have left interesting records of their personal impressions of Tennyson during 1857. Bayard Taylor was the poet's guest at Farringford, and walked with him over the cliffs to the Needles. " I was struck," he wrote, " by the variety of his knowledge. Not a little flower on the downs escaped his notice, and the geology of the coast, both terrestrial and submarine, was perfectly familiar to him. I thought of a remark I once heard from a distinguished English author (Thackeray), that Tennyson was the wisest man he knew." Of the outward man he spoke as " Tall and broad-shouldered as a son of Anak, with hair, beard, and eyes of Southern darkness." * Hawthorne found the poet "as un-English as possible," though not American in appearance. " I cannot well describe the difference, but there was something more mellow in him, softer, sweeter, broader, more simple than we are apt to be." †

It may be noted here that Whittier, a warm ad-

* *At Home and Abroad*, by Bayard Taylor (London, 1860).
† July 30, 1857.

mirer of Tennyson's poetry, wrote to him in 1885 to ask for some memorial verses for the cenotaph of Gordon—a request which produced the well-known stanza beginning :

> " Warrior of God, man's friend"—

Some years later he wrote to Walt Whitman an acknowledgment of the gift of that poet's photograph :

" DEAR WALT WHITMAN : I thank you for your kind thought of me. I value the photograph much, and I wish that I could see not only this sun picture, excellent as I am told it is, but also the living original. May he still live and flourish for many years to be. The coming year (1888) should give new life to every American who has breathed a breath of that soul which inspired the great founders of the American Constitution, whose work you are to celebrate. Truly the mother country, pondering on this, may feel that how much soever the daughter owes to her, she, the mother, has nevertheless something to learn from the daughter. Especially I would note the care taken to guard a noble Constitution from rash and unwise innovators."

This year (1857) saw in print,* though it never was published, the first of the series of poems dealing with the Arthurian cycle of legends which we now possess under the single title *Idylls of the King*. For long Tennyson's mind had been occupied upon the material for poetic treatment lying unused in the ancient British romances. In every volume published by him appear traces of their influence upon his

---

* *Enid and Nimue ; or, The True and the False.*

imagination. *The Lady of Shalott, Sir Galahad,* and *Morte d'Arthur* were pieces of exquisite jewel work such as a consummate artist alone could have achieved, but they were little more than beautiful fragments, and the subject demanded a larger treatment. The poet, too, had now other ideals in poetry than those which had floated before his youthful mind. Not yet had his work given proof of the architectonic power of the masters, and he had earned the right to enter the lists with them for the highest prize. It had been left for a nineteenth - century poet to attempt the authentic English epic, the great national poem unifying the deeds of the great national hero of Britain's legendary age. The development of Tennyson's poem was very gradual. In 1859 appeared *Enid, Vivien, Elaine,* and *Guinevere* in a volume of which ten thousand copies were sold within a few weeks. At long intervals from this year until 1885, the date of *Balin and Balan,* was built up, book by book, the poem of Arthur and the Round Table. An expectant but critical audience received the first volume with mingled feelings of admiration and disappointment. Longfellow wrote in his diary : " Finished the four idyls. The first and third (*Enid* and *Elaine*) could have only come from a great poet. The second and fourth (*Vivien* and *Guinevere*) do not seem to me so good." Carlyle was more outspoken in his dissatisfaction. In a letter to Emerson he wrote : " We read at first Tennyson's *Idylls* with profound recognition of the finely elaborated execution, and also of the inward perfection of vacancy, and, to say truth, with considerable impatience at being treated so very like infants, though the lollipops were so superlative. We gladly changed for one of Emerson's *English*

Traits." Fitzgerald, one of Tennyson's oldest friends, shared the disappointment, but for different reasons from Carlyle's. Tennyson's poetic progress had been in his judgment a deterioration. The early poems, Fitzgerald's first love, had been added to indeed, but not outshone. Of *In Memoriam*, though he spoke admiringly, he confessed that for him it had "the sense of being evolved by a poetic machine of the highest order," and of *The Princess* he wrote to Frederick Tennyson : " I am considered a great heretic for abusing it ; it seems to me a wretched waste of power at a time when a man ought to be doing his best ; and I almost feel hopeless about Alfred now—I mean about his doing what he was born to do." When the *Idylls* appeared he said : " I wish I had secured more leaves from that old 'Butcher's Book' torn up in old Spedding's rooms in 1842, when the press went to work with, I think, the last of old Alfred's best." Without literally endorsing Fitzgerald's mournful verdict, the majority of the good critics sorrowed over Tennyson's desertion of the field in which his early laurels had been reaped for the excursion into epic territory, and the regret was even more unanimous and widespread when he essayed drama. His reputation indisputably suffered during these epic and dramatic periods, and was not altogether restored even by the publication in 1880 of *Ballads and Other Poems* in his seventieth year, described by Theodore Watts as "the most richly various volume of English poetry that has appeared in this century."

A personal note in connexion with a passage in *The Holy Grail* may here find a place :

" Let visions of the night or of the day
 Come as they will ; and many a time they come.

C

> Until this earth he walks on seems not earth,
> This light that strikes his eyeball is not light,
> This air that strikes his forehead is not air
> But vision—yea, his very hand and foot—
> In moments when he feels he cannot die,
> And knows himself no vision to himself,
> Nor the high God a vision, nor that One
> Who rose again."*

Here, and, as will be presently noted, elsewhere in his poetry Tennyson describes a mental state which was one frequently present in his own experience. He describes it as follows (May 7, 1874) : "I have never had any revelations through anæsthetics, but a kind of waking trance (this for lack of a better name) I have frequently had quite up from my boyhood, when I have been all alone. This has often come to me through repeating my own name to myself silently, till, all at once, as it were, out of the intensity of the consciousness of my individuality, the individuality itself seemed to resolve and fade away into boundless being, and this not a confused state, but the clearest of the clearest, the surest of the surest, utterly beyond words, where death was an almost laughable impossibility. The loss of personality (if so it were) seeming no extinction, but the only true life."

In *The Ancient Sage* we have an exact reproduction of this description in verse :

> " For more than once when I
> Sat all alone, revolving in myself
> The word that is the symbol of myself,
> The mortal limit of the Self was loosed,
> And past into the Nameless, as a cloud
> Melts into Heaven.   I touch'd my limbs, the limbs
> Were strange, not mine—and yet no shade of doubt,
> But utter clearness, and thro' loss of self

* "These three lines," said Tennyson, "are the (spiritually) central lines in the *Idylls.*"

> The gain of such large life as match'd with ours
> Were sun to spark—unshadowable in words,
> Themselves but shadows of a shadow-world."

A similar account of trance-like state is quoted by Mr. Knowles from a conversation of Tennyson's : * "Sometimes as I sit here alone in this great room I get carried away out of sense and body and rapt into mere existence, till the accidental touch or movement of one of my own fingers is like a great shock and blow, and brings the body back with a terrible start." With these experiences we may compare that delineated in the ninety-fifth section of *In Memoriam*.

> " So word by word, and line by line
>   The dead man touch'd me from the past,
>   And all at once it seem'd at last
> The living soul was flash'd on mine,
>
> " And mine in his was wound and whirl'd
>   About empyreal heights of thought,
>   And came on that which is, and caught
> The deep pulsations of the world."

In 1859 Tennyson's strong patriotic sentiment once more found expression in verse, this time inspired by the volunteer movement, the outcome of a period of political unrest and the feeling of the necessity of provision for national defence. The *Times* of March 9 printed *The War* (best known as *Riflemen, Form !*), a poem known to be by the Laureate, though unacknowledged by him. Tennyson's interest in the volunteer force was keen and sustained. In 1867 he wrote to the late Colonel Richards : "I most heartily congratulate you on your having been able to do so much for your country ; and I hope that you will not cease

* *Aspects of Tennyson, Nineteenth Century* (January, 1893).

from your labours until it is the law of the land that every man child in it shall be trained to the use of arms."

After the first volume of the *Idylls of the King*, Tennyson took another new departure in *Sea Dreams*, which, with *Enoch Arden* and *Aylmer's Field*, is an essay, not altogether successful, in decorative treatment of subjects taken from modern English life. His extraordinary versatility—at once a strength and a weakness—appears in the comparison of these poems with *Tithonus*, contributed at Thackeray's request to *Cornhill*, the magazine of which he was at the time editor, and written in the same year as *Sea Dreams*. In the former we have a faultless rendering of one of the most beautiful of the classic myths, deepened and widened in its spiritual and moral significance, subdued in tone yet full of exquisite colour—in short, a poem in which Tennyson's genius displays itself in its most commanding presence ; in the other, as in *Enoch Arden*, the embroidered splendours of the form only serve to belittle or remove into the region of fantastic unreality the substance of the poem.

In 1859, accompanied by his friend, Professor Palgrave, Tennyson visited Portugal, and in 1861 revisited the Pyrenees, whither in 1830, with Arthur Hallam, he had made the enthusiastic revolutionary excursion of his youth. It was on this occasion that the lines *In the Valley of Cauteretz*,* commemorating that early journey, were composed. In 1864 Garibaldi was a visitor at Farringford. As a memorial of his visit, and at Mrs. Tennyson's request, he planted in the grounds, already beautiful with ilex

* See *Remains of Arthur Hugh Clough*, vol. i., pp. 264–69.

and cedar, a *Wellingtonia gigantea*. In the *Demeter* volume, Tennyson, in a poem to W. G. Palgrave (*To Ulysses*), makes a graceful reference to the visit and the memorial act :

> " Or watch the waving pine which here
>   The warrior of Caprera set,
>   A name that earth will not forget
> Till Earth has rolled her latest year."

Except for such visits, occasional journeys abroad, and the publication of his poems, the Laureate's long life, like that of most men of letters, was a life of uneventful years.   In 1869 the even tenour of the home at Farringford was exchanged during the summer and autumn months for Aldworth, a house built for the poet from designs by Mr. J. T. Knowles on the borders of Sussex, near the village of Haslemere. Partly to provide a secluded retreat where, in his increasing horror of hero-worshippers, he might have a certain refuge, and partly for the sake of Mrs. Tennyson's health, the change was made.   As the years wore on Tennyson bore with decreasing patience the penalty of fame, and his dislike of publicity * may have had something to do with his refusal of a baronetcy twice offered him, in 1873, and again in 1874.

The Laureate's contribution about this time to the "Eyre Defence Fund" occasioned much popular indignation.   Eyre had entered Louth Grammar School shortly after the Tennysons left for Cambridge, and had in later life come prominently before the public eye by his prompt and decisive suppression of an insurrection among the natives in Jamaica, where he was stationed.   A charge of wanton cruelty was preferred against Eyre by a large and influential body of

* He occasionally visited the Metaphysical Society.

religious sentimentalists ; and the action of Carlyle, Kingsley, Ruskin, and Tennyson in subscribing to a fund for his defence produced an almost fierce resentment. The Laureate's letter on the occasion is of more than passing interest: " I sent my small subscription as a tribute to the nobleness of the man, and as a protest against the spirit in which a servant of the State, who has saved to us one of the islands of the Empire and many English lives, seems to be hunted down. . . . In the mean time, the outbreak of our Indian Mutiny remains as a warning to all but madmen against want of vigour and swift decisiveness."*

Of the lesser poems written by Tennyson during his epic and dramatic periods, by far the most remarkable is *Lucretius.* I am not sure that the poet's highest reach is not attained in this, the most splendid of his masterly studies of classical subjects. No other poem displays his best qualities in such powerful combination, in such flawless perfection. Admirably balanced, magnificent in its metrical movement, and in its final version closed by perhaps the most dramatic touch in all Tennyson's poetry, it marks in my judgment the high-water mark of his achievement. Among his other poems there may be found some to equal, none, I think, to surpass it.

In 1868 Henry Wadsworth Longfellow visited Tennyson at Farringford, whither the most distinguished visitors to England now made a pilgrimage. An account of an expedition to the newly built and inaccessible Aldworth, made about this time by a party of guests, is given by Lord Houghton, one of their number :

* *Life of E. J. Eyre, late Governor of Jamaica,* by Hamilton Hume.

"Our expedition to Tennyson's was a moral success, but a physical failure ; for we had so bad a pair of posters that we regularly knocked up seven miles from the house, and should have had to walk there in the moonlight, if we had not met with a London cab. The bard was very agreeable, and his wife and son delightful. He has built himself a very handsome and commodious house in a most inaccessible site, with every comfort he can require, and every discomfort to all who approach him. What can be more poetical ?"

That in his poetry he had built himself an imperishable monument was never, it seems, a settled conviction in Tennyson's mind. He was often visited by doubts regarding the enduring quality of his poetical achievement. Looking on one occasion at Aldworth, in company with its architect, Mr. Knowles, he said, "That house will last longer than I shall. It will last five hundred years." Ambitious to try his hand in the highest department of literature, and uncertain how the work already done might fare at the hands of time, Tennyson, led by the irony of fate, gave up some of the best years of his life to the composition of dramatic poetry, to which his genius cannot be said to have inclined him, and in which he certainly attained no crown of lavish praise. Fine as are occasional passages and dramatic as are many of the scenes in *Queen Mary*, *Harold*, and *Becket*, these plays are essentially poems upon which a dramatic form has been impressed, but impressed unconvincingly. Neither in action nor in presentation of character are we persuaded that they are dramatically conceived.

Queen Mary, the play in which the author thought

his character drawing at its best, was produced by Mr. Irving at the Lyceum in April 1876.* In spite of the excellence of the stage management, the representation was a failure. *Harold*, in some respects a play of better construction for stage purposes, although absolutely inferior as poetry, followed, but in published form only, and has never been acted.

But in the very hour of his failure as a dramatist Tennyson was engaged upon poems which were to prove how great an error he made in deserting the field best suited to his genius, and how much greater was the error of the critics who saw visible decline writ large upon his later work. " Eh ! he has got the grip of it," cried Carlyle when the ballad of *The Revenge* was read to him ; and many another friend, dissatisfied with the epic and the dramas, rejoiced over the marvellous virility of the verse collected in the volume entitled *Ballads and Other Poems* of 1880. This book was the first sign of the gorgeous Indian summer which was to diffuse its golden splendours over the remainder of Tennyson's career, and to end only with his life. For his genius there lay in wait no "winter of pale misfeature."

In April, 1879, Charles Tennyson Turner† died. At Grasby, where he had been rector, he left behind him many affectionate memories, and to the world of letters a reputation not indeed of such far-shining brilliance as his brother, but of tender and enduring ray. A collected edition of his poems, with Alfred's prefatory memorial lines " At Midnight," was published in the year following that of his death. Frederick, the eldest of this poetic brotherhood, still lives,

* Tennyson thought Irving's *Philip* comparable to Salvini's *Othello*.

† The name " Turner " was taken under the will of a relation.

the author of many poems which, bearing any name but that of Tennyson, might have made the name illustrious.

In *The Falcon*, 1879, called by Fanny Kemble "an exquisite little poem in action," the Laureate again essayed success as a dramatist, this time with a vastly less ambitious play ; a mere graceful poetic setting of a plot from Boccaccio, the ninth novel of the fifth day of his *Decameron*. *The Falcon*, too, like its predecessors, failed, and it was not until the production of a short tragedy of undoubted merit, *The Cup*, that success rewarded Tennyson's persevering efforts in the dramatic form. This play owed its public favour in some degree to the actors and to the management under which it was produced in a style of profuse magnificence.

In 1880 Tennyson was invited to become a candidate for the Lord Rectorship of the University of Glasgow, but declined the honour of a nomination on hearing that he was to be the candidate of the Conservative Party, in the following terms : " I only consented to stand for your Lord Rectorship when informed by the letter of introduction which your agreeable deputation brought, that my nomination was 'supported by a large majority, if not the totality of the students of Glasgow.' It now seems necessary that I should, by standing at your invitation, appear, what I have steadfastly refused to be—a party candidate for the Conservative Club. . . . You are probably aware that some years ago the Glasgow Liberals asked me to be their candidate, and that I, in like manner, declined ; yet I would gladly accept a nomination, after what has occurred on this occasion, if at any time a body of students, bearing no political party name, should wish to nominate me, or if both Liberals and Conservatives should ever happen to agree in foregoing the excitement of a political contest, and in desiring a Lord Rector who would not appear for installation, and who would, in fact, be a mere *roi fainéant*, with nothing but the literary merits you are good enough to appreciate."

The note struck by Tennyson in the *Ballads and Other Poems* was a fuller, richer, deeper note than had yet been heard in his poetry. The voice that spoke in it was a manlier voice. The dreamy melody of the verse of his youth had given place to a more strenuous music and themes of graver human interest. Had his career closed before 1880, it might fairly have been said of him that he had given the best he had to give, that nothing more was to be expected. There is not, I think, in the history of literature so signal an example of poetic power steadily advancing in strength and compass through so long a life, and until its very close. Or if there be, to find a parallel we shall need to journey far : Tennyson is only matched by Sophocles.

In 1882, under the direction of Mrs. Bernard Beere, *The Promise of May*, Tennyson's fifth drama—a prose one this time—was produced at the Globe Theatre, and proved a luckless failure. It was popularly though wrongly supposed* that, in the character of 'Edgar,' Tennyson intended to pourtray the ordinary agnostic, and the portrait was regarded as unnecessarily insulting. Much excitement was caused on the fourth night of the representation by an interruption from

---

* In a letter to Mr. Hall Caine, Tennyson wrote : " I meant Edgar to be a shallow enough theorist. I never could have thought that he would have been taken for an ' ordinary freethinker.' "

the Marquis of Queensberry, who rose in the theatre and exclaimed, "I am an agnostic, and I protest against Mr. Tennyson's gross caricature of our creed."

The transient decline in popularity produced by this play and by the general ill success of Tennyson's dramas, was increased when, on his return from a yachting cruise to Copenhagen with Mr. Gladstone, he accepted a peerage. The Poet-Peer's attendance at the debates in the House of Lords was very rare ; on one occasion he took part in a division, voting for a measure in extension of the franchise ; on another he paired in favour of the "Deceased Wife's Sister" bill.

The Laureate's sixth drama, *Becket*, was published in 1884. It is pleasing to record the graceful act of courtesy done his old friend, Mr. Aubrey de Vere, in connexion with its composition. "He would not write it," says Mr. de Vere in a private letter, "till he ascertained from me (my *Thomas of Canterbury* had been published a few years earlier) that, so far from being annoyed at his writing on the same great man, I should much rejoice at it."

Of the remaining years of Tennyson's life there is little for the unofficial biographer to record save the publication of successive volumes of a veteran poet's verse, which never lost its charm, while it grew in power and drew at last to an almost tri-umphant close. It is good to think that Tennyson, like Shakespere, in his latest work delivered a message of hope to the human race, a message even prophetic in its tone of deep and solemn assurance. The *Tiresias* volume (1885), fitly dedicated to Robert Browning, contained among

Closing Years.

many noble and striking poems one in particular, *The Ancient Sage*, which, to me at least, seems to sum up all that is noblest and best in the life-teaching of Tennyson.

It is of interest to note that in this year he expressed his opinion in very definite language of the proposal to disestablish the English State Church. "I believe," he wrote, "that the disestablishment and disendowment of the Church would prelude the downfall of much that is greatest and best in England."* Tennyson was given to expressing his opinions strongly and with no uncertain note. When the news of the persecution of the Russian Jews reached England in 1891, "I can only say," he wrote, "that Russia has disgraced her church and her nationality. I once met the Czar. He seemed a kind and good-natured man. I can scarcely believe that he is fully aware of the barbarities perpetrated with his apparent sanction."

In 1886 Lionel Tennyson died on his voyage home from fever contracted in India, where he had been as a member of the Viceroy's staff. His death was the one great trial of the poet's declining years, and is the main theme of the pathetic poem dedicating the *Demeter* volume (1889) to the Marquis of Dufferin and Ava.

> " For he—your India was his Fate,
>   And drew him over sea to you—
>   He fain had ranged her thro' and thro'
> To serve her myriads and the State.
>
>   *   *   *   *   *   *
>
> " But while my life's late eve endures,
>   Nor settles into hueless grey,
>   My memories of his briefer day
> Will mix with love for you and yours."

* Letter to Mr. Bosworth Smith.

Among the visitors to Farringford and Haslemere during the last years of Tennyson's life were his old friends, the Duke of Argyll, Professor Jowett, and Mr. Theodore Watts, and from across the Atlantic journeyed a welcome guest in Oliver Wendell Holmes. Just before his own death in December, 1889, Browning wrote his last letter to Tennyson on the occasion of the Laureate's eightieth birthday :

" MY DEAR TENNYSON : To-morrow is your birthday, indeed a memorable one. Let me say I associate myself with the universal pride of our country in your glory, and in its hope that for many and many a year we may have your very self among us—secure that your poetry will be a wonder and delight to all those appointed to come after. And for my own part, let me further say, I have loved you dearly. May God bless you and yours."

The closing years of Tennyson's life found him beloved, honoured, venerated by an inner circle of close friends, amongst whose names appear almost all those of his distinguished contemporaries, and by an ever-widening circle of readers in the English-speaking countries, for whom he stood as the truest interpreter of the thought and sentiment of his age. His poems were read with equal pleasure in the scholar's study, in the poor man's cottage, and in the palaces of kings. Tennyson was no less at home in the society of the artizan or labourer than in that of men of rank or scholarship, and the natural directness and simple humanity which distinguished his character are perhaps nowhere better displayed than in his relations with the Queen, between whom and the poet there existed for many years a close bond of sympathy and affection, without a trace of patronage on the one side or of mere conventional loyalty on the other. The Queen's womanliness, the poet's manliness, shine through all the records of their conversation and correspondence.

Versatile and graceful to the last, even in fields remote from that of his power, he published in 1892 his last drama, *The Foresters*, a romantic pastoral play, which achieved a brilliant success when produced by Mr. Daly in New York, with Miss Ada Rehan as Maid Marian. Sherwood Forest, Robin Hood, Maid Marian, and the life under the greenwood tree must have conveyed something of the charm of English country life in the olden time to American audiences, whose ancestors' life indeed it was.

But the harp from whose magic strings flowed the ever-varying, ever-melodious music that had seemed in English ears the sweetest of its time, was soon to be silent. In the autumn of 1892, but a few weeks before the publication of *The Death of Œnone and Akbar's Dream*, rumours were heard of the poet's illness, and on October 6, before dawn, but in a room flooded with the quiet moonlight, the end came. He was buried among his peers and beside his friend, Robert Browning, in Poets' Corner, Westminster Abbey.

CHAPTER II.

In the spring of 1827, Charles and Alfred Tennyson were partners in a literary venture. The preface to the volume, which had for motto the line from Martial,

" Hæc nos novimus esse nihil,"

stated that the "poems were written from the ages of fifteen to eighteen, not conjointly, but individually." In Messrs. Macmillan's "Poems edition of 1893 the preface by Hallam, by Two Lord Tennyson, contains the further in- Brothers," formation obtained from his father that he 1827. (Alfred) was between fifteen and seventeen when the poems were written, his brother Charles between fifteen and eighteen, and that four poems now signed "F. T." were by Frederick Tennyson, the eldest brother. In this latter edition the initials, supplied by Frederick Tennyson, of the supposed authors, either "A. T." or "C. T.," are appended to each of the poems, but we are warned that there is no certainty as to the authorship in individual cases.*
Without the help of the initials, however, and despite the fact that the music now familiar as Tennysonian is nowhere to be heard in the book, there is little difficulty in determining the work of each author.

* Some additional poems are for the first time printed in this edition. They belonged to the original MS. of 1827, but were omitted for some forgotten reason.

After one perusal I was struck by the fact that the more ambitious poems are the work of one hand, and that hand is proved to be Alfred's by the occasional phrases to be met with which appear again in his later poetry—as, for example, in this volume, in the poem entitled *Egypt*, occur these lines:

> " The first glitter of his rising beam
> Falls on *the broad-based pyramids* sublime;"

and in *A Fragment*, published by Alfred in the *Gem* in 1830, these occur :

> " Yet endure unscathed
> Of changeful cycles, *the great Pyramids*
> *Broad-based* amid the fleeting sands."

And here in *Oriana* the lines,

> " Winds were blowing, waters flowing,
> We heard the steeds to battle going,
> Oriana ;
> Aloud the hollow bugle blowing,
> Oriana,"

echo a similar movement in the *Vale of Bones :*

> " When on to battle proudly going,
> Your plumage to the wild winds blowing,
> Your tartans far behind ye flowing."

I have noticed a number of these similarities and resemblances, and think it would be no difficult task to pick out with tolerable certainty the poems by Alfred from among the one hundred and two poems of which the volume is composed. The vein of feeling in Charles's poems is more tranquil, more domestic, and the themes chosen far less difficult. Alfred is the bolder adventurer, and ranges further in his search for subjects. His work seems to express a more deliberate determination to be poetic, and effort is more distinctly characteristic of his contributions to the book than those of Charles, which may be unhesitatingly described as by comparison spontaneous and natural. It may at once be said that there is no mark of distinction, no promise of future greatness in these poems. They are rather, indeed, remarkable for the absence of the puerility one might naturally expect to be somewhere betrayed in a series of such youthful efforts, than by any positive qualities. Many of the poems written by Alfred Tennyson in later years, such as, for example, *The Skipping-Rope* or *The English War Song* (of 1830), reach a lower deep of inanity than any printed in this first volume. For the rest an acquaintance with the poetry of the world such as few schoolboys can boast is plentifully exhibited in the mottoes prefixed to most of the verses. The Latin poets, Lucretius, Virgil, Horace, are laid under contribution ; Milton, Gray, Byron, Scott, and Moore among English poets ; and occasional prose authors are represented—in short, a goodly company—among which, of course, the English writers, and Byron in particular, predominate. The boys, and it is significant when we attempt to fix for ourselves the place which the future will assign to Alfred Tennyson—the boys were cradled into poetry by the best poets of the world. The determination to be poets preceded any true poetic faculty, and in Alfred's case we must regard that determination, leading as it did to lifelong, indefatigable labour in the effort to obtain an artist's command over his medium, an artist's mastery in technique, as in large measure the power which, joined with the true poetic vision of later years, made him the poet he eventually became.

D

The versification and metrical movement of this early verse are, of course, entirely derivative ; Byron's *Hebrew Melodies* and Moore's *Irish Melodies* supply much of the inspiration. The boys had indeed, as Coleridge said of Alfred, " begun to write poetry without very well understanding what metre was," and this volume is composed of a series of imitative metrical essays. Imitative they are, however, in a catholic spirit, no one model being exclusively followed.

The only notice of the book in which the brothers " crossed the Rubicon" together, as they expressed it in the preface, appeared in The *Literary Chronicle and Weekly Review* (May 19, 1827). " This little volume," remarked the writer, " exhibits a pleasing union of kindred tastes, and contains several little pieces of considerable merit."

In the first year of his Cambridge residence Tennyson was a candidate for the Chancellor's Medal in English Verse—the subject Timbuctoo. Among his

Timbuctoo, and the "Poems" of 1830. rivals were Monckton Milnes and Arthur Hallam. Hallam's poem, composed in the *terza rima* of Dante, may be read in the volume of his *Remains in Verse and Prose*, published in 1834. Tennyson's poem is now accessible in Messrs. Macmillan's edition of *Poems by Two Brothers*, to which it forms a natural conclusion. The exercises were submitted to the University Examiners in April, and upon June 12, 1829, the following announcement appeared in the *Cambridge Chronicle and Journal:* " On Saturday last the Chancellor's Gold Medal for the best English poem by a resident undergraduate was adjudged to Alfred Tennyson, of Trinity College." This is the first public mention of the name of Alfred Tennyson in connexion with poetry. In the *Athenæum* of July 22, a very flattering notice of the prize poem appeared. "We have accustomed ourselves," wrote the reviewer (perhaps John Sterling or Frederick Maurice, at that time the joint editors), "to think, perhaps without any very good reason, that poetry was likely to perish among us for a considerable period after the great generation of poets which is now passing away. The age seems determined to contradict us, and that in the most decided manner ; for it has put forth poetry by a young man, and that where we should least expect it—namely, in a prize poem. These productions have often been ingenious and elegant, but we have never before seen one of them which indicated really first-rate poetical genius, and which would have done honour to any man that ever wrote. Such, we do not hesitate to affirm, is the little work before us ; and the examiners seem to have felt it like ourselves, for they have assigned the prize to its author, though the measure in which he writes was never before, we believe, thus selected for honour." The measure here referred to was blank verse, a bold experiment on Tennyson's part, the traditions being all in favour of the heroic couplet. I have little doubt, however, that, so far from attenuating his chance of success by his choice of metre, Tennyson really increased it ; the novelty of the measure calling attention to and emphasizing the novelty of method and manner conspicuous in the poem. Without echoing the high praise of the *Athenæum* reviewer, it is not too much to say that *Timbuctoo* is a very remarkable prize exercise, vague indeed in its general conception and purpose, but indisputably original; the first English poem to mark the direction in which the richly decorative art of Keats was to find its development. Written very shortly after the *Poems by Two Brothers*, it is a surprising advance in poetic technique. The obviously imitative measures of his boyhood poems are forgotten, and Tennyson has found himself. The music is the familiar music that we associate with his name—

> " Where are ye,
> Thrones of the Western wave, fair Islands green?
> Where are your moonlight halls, your cedarn glooms,
> The blossoming abysses of your hills?
> Your flowering capes, and your gold-sanded bays,
> Blown round with happy airs of odorous winds?"

The inspiration here, as indeed throughout, is essentially Keats; read *Hyperion* and you have traced this manner to its fount. The influence of Wordsworth, traceable in some of his later poems, is not yet visible, nor was there anything either of Wordsworth, the revealer, or Wordsworth, the unconscious artist, grand in the bare simplicity of his style, in Tennyson at any period of his poetic history. They may be taken as representatives of methods in poetry mutually exclusive. If Wordsworth was a great poet, he was a great poet by reason of his revelation, by reason of the truth and the beauty of his thought when it crystallised in a perfect and inevitable because a quietly natural form of expression. If Tennyson was a great poet, it was because, like Pope, he could set forth a philosophy and adorn a pathetic tale in a more graceful and more appropriate key of words than any man of his time; and, what Pope could not do, give lyric expression to intense individual moods with almost the passionate power of Burns, and an intellectual precision not at all times attained by Shelley. Essentially a lyrist, and original only in his presentation of his own moods or states of feeling, Tennyson, when he travelled beyond the range of his own experience, was a scholarly and accomplished versifier, a later Pope, who from among the ideas current at the time selected the best, and gave them out again in his own elegant and exquisite version. *Difficile est proprie communia dicere.*

The rich and dreamy melodies, the alternate languor and swiftness of emotion, and the subtleties of its delineation, displayed in *Poems, Chiefly Lyrical,* at once exercised a fascination over the sensitive temperaments of the young men who were readers of poetry in 1830. Verse like this, from the first poem in the volume, *Claribel,* was a source of new and delightful sensations :

> " At eve the beetle boometh
>   Athwart the thicket lone :
> At noon the wild bee hummeth
>   About the moss'd headstone ;
> At midnight the moon cometh,
>   And looketh down alone.
> Her song the lintwhite swelleth,
> The clear-voiced mavis dwelleth,
>   The callow throstle lispeth,
> The slumbrous wave outwelleth,
>   The babbling runnel crispeth,
> The hollow grot replieth
>   Where Claribel low lieth."*

* In Henry Alford's journal there are some interesting references to the brothers Tennyson. Referring to Alfred's " Poems" of 1830, and Charles's *Sonnets and Fugitive Pieces,* published the same year, he wrote :

" Oct. 12, 1830. Looked over both the Tennysons' Poems at

It was a new departure in English poetry ; there had been nothing like it before ; and although the intellectual equipment of the author, so far as revealed in the poetry, was really of the slightest, and although some of the poems were hardly worthy of a place in any printed book, curiosity and admiration were aroused, and an interest excited in the personality of the new poet.   The best and most characteristic poems in this volume were *Claribel, Mariana, Isabel, Adeline, Oriana,** *The Dying Swan, A Character, The Poet, The Poet's Mind,* and *Circumstance.*   There were fifty-three poems in all, of which almost half (twenty-five) were afterwards suppressed, a few being restored to places in the collected editions of later life.   The following is a list of the suppressed poems : *Elegiacs ; The How and the Why ; Supposed Confessions of a Second-rate Sensitive Mind not in Unity with Itself ; The Burial of Love ; To Juliet ; Songs* (three) ; *Hero to Leander ; The Mystic ; The Grasshopper ; Love, Pride, and Forgetfulness ; Chorus in an Unpublished Drama,* written very early ; *Lost Hope ; The Tears of Heaven ; Love and Sorrow ; To a Lady Sleeping ; Sonnets ; Love ; The Kraken ; English War Song ; National Song ; Dualisms ; We are Free,* οἱ ῥέοντες.   Tennyson's judgments on his own poems, unlike those of Wordsworth, were almost unerring, and, as a consequence, the incessant revision to which his work was subjected rarely failed to be happily effective.   How finely some of his poems were retouched may here be illustrated by per-

night ; exquisite fellows.   I know no two books of poetry which have given me so much pure pleasure as their works ; " and again later :

"Met Tennant, Hallam, Merivale, and the three Tennysons at Alfred Tennyson's rooms.   The latter read some very exquisite poetry of his, entitled *Anacaona* and *The Hesperides.*

    * Compare with this *Helen of Kirkconnel.*

haps the palmary example. In its first version, the
closing line of *Lucretius* read :

" What matters ? All is over : Fare thee well"

—a line weak in itself, and weaker as the conclusion of
so matchless and dramatic a reproduction of the classic story. In its later form the last words of Lucretius catch up in questioning echo his wife's despairing
cry " as having failed in duty to him," and once again
the unsolved problem of his philosophic life shapes itself anew, the ruling passion strong even in violent
and untimely death

" Thy duty ? What is duty ? Fare thee well !"

The *Poems* of 1830 were praised by Hallam and
Leigh Hunt, but severely handled by Christopher
North in *Blackwood*. So far there had been no unanim-
ity among the critics as to the rank to be assigned
the representative of the new school of
poetry. At the same time, it was evident The " Poems"
that the younger generation was in his of 1832.
favour, and in 1832 Tennyson put forth
another volume of lyrics in which the distinctive characteristics of his style were still more strongly marked.
Hallam's criticism—" the author imitates nobody"—
made in his review of the 1830 *Poems* in the *Englishman's Magazine*, was even more strictly true of this
second volume. Subtly indefinite as many of the
pieces were, the very absence of definite meaning lent
them the magic of suggestiveness which captivated
many minds. "I am not sure," wrote Edgar Allan
Poe, " that Tennyson is not the greatest of poets. . . .
There are passages in his works which rivet a conviction I had long entertained, that the indefinite is an
element in the true ποιησις. Why do some persons

fatigue themselves in endeavours to unravel such phantasy pieces as *The Lady of Shalott?* As well unweave the *ventum textilem.* If the author did not deliberately propose to himself a suggestive indefiniteness of meaning, with the view of bringing about a definiteness of vague and therefore of spiritual *effect*—this, at least, arose from the silent analytical promptings of that poetic genius which, in its supreme development, embodies all orders of intellectual capacity."* In that musical dream, *The Lady of Shalott,*† in the subtile mod-

* New York *Democratic Review*, December, 1844.

† The original version of this poem differs from the final in sixty or seventy lines. The following was the concluding stanza in the early edition :

> " They crossed themselves, their stars they blest,
>   Knight, minstrel, abbot, squire, and guest ;
>   There lay a parchment on her breast,
>   That puzzled more than all the rest
>   The well-fed wits at Camelot.
> ' The web was woven curiously,
>   The charm is broken utterly ;
>   Draw near and fear not, this is I,
>   The Lady of Shalott.' "

How Tennyson could polish a pebble until it became a gem is nowhere better illustrated than by a comparison of this with the following stanza :

> " Who is this ? and what is here ?
>   And in the lighted palace near
>   Died the sound of royal cheer ;
>   And they cross'd themselves for fear,
>   All the knights at Camelot :
>   But Lancelot mused a little space ;
>   He said, ' She has a lovely face ;
>   God in his mercy lend her grace,
>   The Lady of Shalott.' "

Shalott is a form of Astolat. The poem was suggested by an Italian romance—*Donna di Scalotta*, but modified in the later version to a closer resemblance with the story of Elaine.

ulation, the harmonies and cadences of *The Lotos-Eaters*,* in the finely drawn portraits of *The Dream of Fair Women*, and especially in the highly wrought beauty and deep moral significance of the allegory presented in *The Palace of Art*,†indisputable evidences of original genius were displayed. It was impossible to receive this body of poetry in contemptuous silence ; it was difficult to withhold from it a meed of respect. But the casquet which held these jewels contained some spurious and many faulty brilliants. And in the *Quarterly* of July, 1833, a full and cruel but, in many respects, admirable review of Tennyson's poetry proceeded with caustic irony "to point out," as the writer said, "the peculiar brilliancy of some of the gems that irradiate his poetical crown." The indignation of Tennyson-worshippers against the author of this critique has never slept, but in my judgment it may be justly claimed not only as the most effective, but in the poet's own interest the most valuable review ever written. The supreme excellence of Tennyson's poetry resides, if anywhere, in its flawless perfection of finish. Had Tennyson not been a great, almost a faultless artist, he would have been a poet of inconsiderable rank. He became such an artist by assiduous culture of rare native talent, and the criticism of the *Quarterly* showed the young author the indispensable necessity of the sternest artistic governance, the strictest self - discipline. Lockhart (doubtless the author) was a severe critic, but his severity bore fruit where extravagant praise or indulgent partiality would have proved less than barren.

* Founded on a passage in *Odyssey*. (Bk. ix. 82 seq.)
† "As *The Palace of Art* represents the pride of voluptuous enjoyment in its noblest form, the *St. Simeon Stylites* represents the pride of asceticism at its basest.

Some of the pieces which drew forth his sarcastic com-
ments were omitted from future editions, and almost all
were altered or rewritten in respect of the censured
passages.*   The following poems were dropped in the
next collected edition.   Five *Sonnets* (" Mine be the
strength of spirit fierce and free ;" " O Beauty, passing beauty ! sweetest sweet !" "Blow ye the trumpet,
gather from afar ;" " How long, O God, shall men be
ridden down ;" " As when with downcast eyes we
muse and brood") ; *Lines* " To ——†;" *The Hesperides ;
Rosalind ; Songs—Who can Say ; O Darling Room ; Lines*
"To Christopher North ;" *Kate.*   In the first edition of
The Palace of Art, many passages appeared which were
struck out of all subsequent editions, and four stanzas
descriptive of two statues in the palace were appended
to the poem with a note, together with the following
fine verses descriptive of a tower for astronomical observation :

> " Hither, when all the deep unsounded skies
>   Were shuddering with silent stars, she clomb,
>   And, as with optic glasses, her keen eyes
>   Pierced through the mystic dome.
>
> " Regions of lucid matter taking forms,
>   Brushes of fire, hazy gleams,
>   Clusters and beds of worlds, and bee-like swarms
>   Of suns and starry streams.
>
> " She saw the snowy poles of moonless Mars,
>   That marvellous round of milky light
>   Below Orion, and those double stars
>   Whereof the one more bright
>
> " Is circled by the other."

"In this poem," wrote Lockhart, "we first observed
a stroke of art which we think very ingenious.   No

---

* Compare the first with the later editions of *The Miller's
Daughter.*

† "Clear-headed friend," etc., J. W. Blakesley, Dean of
Lincoln.

one who has ever written verses but must have felt the
pain of erasing some happy line, some striking phrase,
which, however excellent in itself, did not exactly suit
the place for which it was destined. How curiously
does an author mould and remould the plastic verse
in order to fit in the favourite thought ; and when he
finds that he cannot introduce it, as Corporal Trim
says, *anyhow*, with what reluctance does he at last re-
ject the intractable but still cherished offspring of his
brain ! Mr. Tennyson manages this delicate matter in
a new and better way. He says with great candour and
simplicity, ' If this poem were not already too long, *I
should have added the following stanzas,*' and then *he adds
them ;* or, ' I intended to have added something on
statuary, but I found it very difficult ; but I have finished the statues of Elijah and Olympias ; judge
whether I have succeeded ; ' and then *we have those two
statues*. This is certainly the most ingenious device
that has ever come under our observation for recon-
ciling the rigour of criticism with the indulgence of
parental partiality."   Another comment of Lockhart's
may be quoted. The early version of the *Dream of
Fair Women* contained these lines in the description of
Iphigenia's sacrifice :

> '' One drew a sharp knife through my slender throat ;
>   Slowly, and nothing more."

" What touching simplicity," remarked the reviewer,
" what pathetic resignation—he cut my throat—
' *nothing more !* ' One might indeed ask what *more*
she would have ?"*

* The lines now stand as follows—

> '' The bright death quiver'd at the victim's throat ;
>   Touch'd ; and I knew no more."

In April, 1833, Coleridge, than whom no subtler
musician in words has ever written verse, wrote of these
early poems as follows : " I have not read through all
Mr. Tennyson's poems, which have been sent to me,
but I think there are some things of a good deal of
beauty in that I have seen.   The misfortune is that he
has begun to write verses without very well understanding what metre is.   Even if you write in a known
and approved metre, the odds are, if you are not a
metrist yourself, that you will not write harmonious
verses ; but to deal in new metres without considering
what metre means and requires is preposterous.
What I would, with many wishes of success, prescribe
to Tennyson—indeed without it he can never be a
poet in art—is to write for the next two or three years
in none but one or two well-known and strictly defined
metres, such as the heroic couplet, the octave stanza,
or the octosyllabic measure of the *Allegro* and *Pense-
roso*.   He would probably thus get imbued with a
sensation, if not a sense, of metre without knowing it,
just as Eton boys get to write good Latin verses by
conning Ovid and Tibullus.   As it is, I can scarcely
scan his verses."*   How is this criticism of Coleridge's
to be interpreted ?   To censure the author of *The
Lotos-Eaters*, *The Palace of Art*, and *Œnone* as deficient
in a knowledge of what metre was excites surprise,
and were any other than Coleridge the critic, would
excite derision no less.   Yet Coleridge is in a sense
right.   Tennyson, more especially in his earlier poems,
was a melodist rather than a metrist.   He aimed at
musical effects, at sound-effects only perfectible for
the human ear through some more plastic medium

* *Table-Talk of S. T. Coleridge*, vol. ii., p. 164.

than language. The human voice may be regarded as
a perfect instrument of limited range, but as the
organ of articulate speech it is at once ennobled and
degraded—ennobled as the servant of the rational
soul, degraded as a musical instrument. Language-
less emotion it may adequately render, as the harp or
violin render it ; intellectual precision, only attainable in some articulate tongue, is incompatible with
the freedom of its chords, essential for the production
of the purely musical effects attainable through other
mediums.*

For ten years after the publication of the 1832 poems
Tennyson published no volume of verse. When at
length he broke silence, it was to take assured rank
among English poets. " If anything were to happen
to Tennyson," said Elizabeth Barrett, " the
world should go into mourning." The first **Poems of**
of the two volumes published in 1842 was **1842. In**
mainly composed of poems which had al- **Two Vol-**
ready appeared in the previous collected **umes.**
editions of 1830 and 1832, the second of poems, with
one or two exceptions, entirely new. Of the reprinted
pieces some were practically re-written and many were

---

* Edgar Allan Poe, writing in the New York *Democratic Review*
(December, 1844), notices in Tennyson the absence of strict regard
to metre. " His shorter pieces abound in minute rhythmical lapses
—sufficient to assure me that, in common with all poets, living or
dead, he has neglected to make precise investigation of the principles of metre ; but, on the other hand, so perfect is his rhythmical instinct in general, that he seems *to see with his ear*." It were
more correct, I believe, to say that he attempts to reproduce a
melody correctly heard by the ear, but disorganized when set to
words—that is, only imperfectly reproduced; hence the rhythmical
lapses; hence, too, the inapplicability of ordinary metrical principles.

amended. The attempt to chronicle the alterations made by Tennyson in his poetry, even after it was made public, would in itself require a volume. It will suffice to remark that up to the last the successive editions invariably contained changes, many, indeed, slight or verbal, but no less indicative of the scrupulous and incessant attention bestowed upon his work. Take as one example these lines, the opening of *Œnone* in the 1832 volume :

> " There is a dale in Ida, lovelier
> Than any in Ionia, beautiful
> With emerald slopes of sunny sward, that lean
> Above the loud glen river, which hath worn
> A path thro' steep-down* granite walls below
> Mantled with flowering tendril twine."

This might have been written by any one, but in 1842 it had been through the refiner's hands again, and emerged pure Tennysonian :

> " There is a vale in Ida, lovelier
> Than all the valleys of Ionian hills.
> The swimming vapour slopes athwart the glen,
> Puts forth an arm, and creeps from pine to pine,
> And loiters, slowly drawn. On either hand
> The lawns and meadow-ledges midway down
> Hang rich in flowers, and far below them roars
> The long brook falling thro' the clov'n ravine
> In cataract after cataract to the sea."

When Monckton Milnes, on behalf of Tennyson's friends, represented to Sir Robert Peel, then Prime Minister, that the poet's name be placed upon the civil list for a pension, he sent him a copy of these

---

* Tennyson's authorities are always classic :

> " Wash me in *steep-down* gulfs of liquid fire."
> *—Othello.*

poems, marking *Ulysses* and *Locksley Hall.* * Of all his poems probably the latter has gained the widest appreciation. Its colour and picturesqueness, the freshness of its treatment of a simple and familiar theme, and the lively movement of its trochaic measure won for it instant popularity. In a copy of the first edition, originally possessed by Mr. R. W. Proctor, the following verses appear in manuscript after the nineteenth couplet :

" In the hall there hangs a painting, Amy's arms are round my
    neck,
Happy children in a sunbeam, sitting on the ribs of wreck.

" In my life there is a picture : she that clasped my neck is flown,
I am left within the shadow, sitting on the wreck alone."

These lines serve to connect this poem with the *Locksley Hall* of *Sixty Years After*, as they appear in the later poem after the sixth couplet. Several of the readings of the first edition have been changed, *e.g.:*

" Let *the peoples* spin forever down the ringing grooves of change "

and

"'Tis the place, and *round the gables*, as of old, the curlews call."

Among the new poems of this collection the *Morte d'Arthur*, the English idylls, *Dora*, and *The Gardener's Daughter*,† *The Two Voices, Ulysses,*‡ and *St. Simeon Stylites*, are the most remarkable, and call for special notice as marking an advance in the scope and ethical

* " *The May Queen* is all Lincolnshire inland, as *Locksley Hall* its sea-board."

† A note to *Dora* in the 1842 edition stated " The idyll of *Dora* was partly suggested by one of Miss Mitford's pastorals ; and the ballad of *Lady Clare* by the novel of *Inheritance*. The reference here is to the story *Dora Cresswell* in *Our Village*." *The Inheritance* is by Susan Ferrier, of Edinburgh.

‡ Founded on 26 canto of Dante's *Inferno.*

significance of the poet's art.   When these poems were
published Tennyson had passed the first two stages
of his poetical career—the derivative period, during
which he was in turn influenced by preceding writers,
and imitated their several manners, and the period
of musical effects, in which the formal part of poetry, its
sensuous beauty, had occupied his ear and mind.   Experience of real life—the death of his beloved friend,
Arthur Hallam—awoke in him the fuller pulse of manhood.   The ebb and flow of human passion, the deeper
currents in the lives of men, were now the springs of a
less sensuous, more intellectual music.   In youth, it was
the loveliness and the charm of the world that took
by storm his imagination ; in age, its majesty, its un-
riddled mysteries, and far-reaching issues are the burden of his song.   In *Ulysses* the many voices of the
ocean summon the wanderer from inglorious rest, and
once again he calls together his friends for a voyage
of heroic enterprise ; in *The Two Voices,* the old yet
ever new debate on the value and the issues of our
mortal life is evolved with a wonderful skill and a
critical exactness which brings to mind the art of
Dryden, that master logician in verse ; in *St. Simeon
Stylites*, the companion picture to *Ulysses,* the fruitless-
ness of the creed that in its passion for another world
neglects the present is vividly pictured, and we have
in it the most dramatically conceived and executed
poem he had yet written.   Tennyson's mind, as I have
elsewhere attempted to show, was in fuller sympathy with the ethics and ideals of Greek philosophy
than with the self-effacing spirit of the Middle Ages.
In this poem we have his criticism in dramatic form
of the extreme asceticism, the " other-worldliness" of
mediæval Christianity, but it is a criticism full of

* The measure had been employed by Ben Jonson.

sympathy. That he should have entered into its spirit, and exhibited the finer shades of feeling in a spiritual mood so foreign to his own gives to the poem an element of very special interest. It may be said that in *The Idylls of the King*—in some respects his most characteristic work—the mental attitude is distinctly Christian. But I should prefer to describe the symbolism of the idylls as neo-Platonic. The allegory of " the soul at war with sense," though embodied in a chivalric romance, is pervaded by conceptions which have their root in the poetic mysticism of Plato's many-sided mind. The philosophic creed of Browning and the devout faith of Mr. Aubrey de Vere, if their poetry be contrasted with Tennyson's, have their roots deep struck in the soil of pure Christianity,* and borrow from the philosophers subsidiary conceptions only ; with Tennyson, though his creed was indeed Christian, it was grafted on the tree of high pagan speculation.

In these 1842 volumes Tennyson speaks out of his heart and mind. He remained till the last a delicate manipulator of musical phrases, but the substance, or what Aristotle would call " the soul of the poem," is no longer second to the diction, the body in which it resides.

Dora and *The Gardener's Daughter*, like *The Miller's Daughter* of the previous volume, are vignettes of real country life, idyllic scenes, " tasting of Flora and the country green." It is the richness of colour, the lush luxuriance of beauty, not tropical, but through generations ordered by skilful hands—such colour and luxuriance as English landscape alone can show—that

* Note the spirit of sympathy with mediæval Christianity present in their poetry.

E

are lovingly dwelt upon in Tennyson's descriptive poetry. He was a patriot who loved his native country best—her citizens, her government, her traditions, and not less the flowers in her fields, the skies above them, and the sea that keeps her inviolate. It is instructive, however disillusionising, to note the extraordinary "interval" in the fine judgment of such an artist, which permitted these lines (afterwards suppressed), entitled *The Skipping-Rope*,* a place beside the truly great poems of 1842 :

> " Sure never yet was antelope
>   Could skip so lightly by.
> Stand off, or else my skipping-rope
>   Will hit you in the eye.
> How lightly whirls the skipping-rope ;
>   How fairy-like you fly !
> Go, get you gone, you muse and mope—·
>   I hate that silly sigh.
> Nay, dearest, teach me how to hope.
>   Or tell me how to die.
> There, take it, take my skipping-rope,
>   And hang yourself thereby."

The future may discover in this some oracular meaning, but surely Fitzgerald was justified when he said : " Alfred, whatever he may think, cannot trifle. His smile is rather a grim one."†

* Last printed in 6th edition of *Poems*, 1850.
† Fitzgerald's *Letters*, p. 95.

CHAPTER III.

SINCE Shakespeare's day woman had not occupied in English poetry so large and gracious a space as in the character-studies of Tennyson's early volumes. The ideals of chivalry were come again, but enriched and refined.

In *The Princess*, published in 1847, the now widely-known poet became the poetic interpreter and critic of that movement of thought and feeling which concerned itself with the position of woman in the social organisation. In a fantastic and half serious, half sportive allegory, "moving as in a strange diagonal," he outlined and reduced to form the many elements in the problem, and by his statement, no less than by his solution of the questions involved, gave definite and concrete shape to the vague aspirations and somewhat nebulous ideas present in the intellectual atmosphere.

The Princess. 1847.

Criticise it as you will, and the early reviewers were not tardy in expressing disapproval, *The Princess* is a poem full of Tennyson's own peculiar charm. "A medley," as it was called, incongruous and unreal, if it betrays the poet's faults and weaknesses, it cannot be denied to possess many of his most winning and most characteristic excellences. Like most of his longer poems, it was built up to its present shape through successive editions. The second edition, published after a year's interval, contained few changes, and was dedicated to Henry Lushington,* an ardent admirer, with whom the author was on a visit in September, 1847, and whose friendship was one of the most prized in his life. With the third edition (1850) began the series of extensive emendations, omissions, and additions, which were continued in the fourth and fifth editions of 1851 and 1853. The hint for the story is by some believed to have been given in Johnson's *Rasselas*. "The princess thought, that of all sublunary things, knowledge was the best; she desired, first, to learn all sciences, and then proposed to found a college of learned women, in which she would preside, that, by conversing with the old and educating the young, she might divide her time between the acquisition and communication of wisdom, and raise up for the next age models of prudence and patterns of piety." It has been suggested by others that the inspiration came from Defoe or Margaret Cavendish's *Female Academy*. By others, again, the clue to the genesis of *The Princess* is found in the lines :

> "This *were* a medley ! we should have him back
> Who told the ' Winter's Tale' to do it for us,"

and the central idea in the plot of *Love's Labour's Lost*, which turns upon a three years' enforced seclusion in study and apart from women:

> "Our court shall be a little Academe,
> Still and contemplative in living art."

The question is not a grave one and need not be

* " If all Mr. Tennyson's writings had by some strange accident been destroyed, Henry Lushington's wonderful memory could, I believe, have reproduced the whole." — *Memoir of Henry Lushington*, by G. S. Venables. The poet called him " his most suggestive critic."

definitely answered. The scene of the Prologue is laid in the south of England, and the surroundings may be those of Sir John Simeon's garden at Swainston The host, in whose grounds the opening festival is held, is probably the poet's friend under the disguise of Sir Walter Vivian. Some lines (afterwards omitted) in the Epilogue, which was almost entirely rewritten for the third edition, give an account of the original design, and its subsequent development:

> " Here closed our compound story, which at first
>   Had only meant to banter little maids
>   With mock heroics and with parody ;
>   But slipt in some strange way, crost with burlesque,
>   From mock to earnest, even into tones
>   Of tragic, and with less and less of jest
>   To such a serious end."

Besides remodelling the Prologue and Epilogue, and in many respects shaping the poem to a later design, Tennyson added to the third edition the exquisite songs, which alone secure for the work in which they are set an immortality of remembrance. It already contained that wonderful isometric lyric, *Tears, Idle Tears*, which I am inclined to regard as the most characteristic of his genius of any poem ever written by the author, and that for two reasons. It is his most successful expression of the emotion of vague regret, of dumb inarticulate pain of heart, a province of universal human feeling, which Tennyson alone among poets* has found a voice to render, and thus made peculiarly his own.

Here, as in the lines :

* If he have a rival in this province it is Goethe.

> " Break, break, break
>   On thy cold gray stones, O Sea !"*

he has sounded the hidden and mysterious places of
the soul, whence at times wells up a nameless and a
causeless sorrow, and to its incommunicable speech the
chords of his music vibrate.   And of the music the
form, too, is all his own.   That the measure is the
measure of *Hamlet* and the *Paradise Lost* is difficult to
realise.   The subtle sweetness of the modulation is
typical of Tennyson's handling of our great national
metre, and is displayed here in its fullest perfection.
He discovered in it a lyric quality hitherto unsus-
pected, and if it be objected that the division into
stanzas and the recurrence of the phrase "*days that
are no more*" serves to compensate for the absence of
rhyme, it is only necessary to turn to the " small
sweet idyll," " Come down, O maid, from yonder
mountain height,"†where without stanza or definite
rhyme the effect of lyric movement is perfectly attained.   In the concluding lines of the last-named
poem there is much onomatopœic beauty : ‡

> " Myriads of rivulets hurrying through the lawn,
>   The moan of doves in immemorial elms,
>   And murmuring of innumerable bees."

† Written during an Alpine tour in 1846.
‡ " Onomatopœic effects are common in Tennyson, as in such
a passage as this :

> " *Plunged : and the flood drew ; yet I caught her ; then*
>   Oaring one arm, and bearing in my left
>   The weight of all the hopes of half the world,
>   *Strove to buffet to land in vain.*"
>
> —*The Princess.*

"Who after three such lines," wrote Charles Kingsley, "will talk of English as a harsh and clumsy language, and seek in the effeminate and monotonous Italian for expressive melody of sound ? Who cannot hear in them the rapid rippling of the water, the stately calmness of the wood-dove's note, and in the repetition of short syllables and soft liquids in the last line : *

> "The murmuring of innumerable bees"?

I may here note, in passing, possible suggestions for one or two of the songs. For the third † Moore's lyric, *How Sweet the Answer Echo Makes,* and for the fifth the tenth section of Canto I. of Scott's *Lay,* and the Anglo-Saxon fragment, *Gudrun.*

To the fourth edition of *The Princess* were added the passages relating to the "weird seizures" of the Prince, and a few minor alterations were introduced into the text ; the fifth contained for the first time the

Or here, where the sound of the violin is imitated in the "n"s and "u''s.

> "All night have the roses heard
> *The flute, violin, bassoon :*
> All night has the casement jessamine stirred
> *To the dancers dancing in tune."*
>
> *—Maud.*

* Of this Idyll Symonds writes in his *Studies of the Greek Poets :* "It transfers with perfect taste the Greek idyllic feeling to Swiss scenery ; it is a fine instance of new wine being successfully poured into old bottles, for nothing could be fresher, and not even the Thalysia is sweeter." But Mr. Symonds is wrong when he speaks of it (Appendix) as containing "*no reiterated sounds.*" Let any one read the first half-dozen lines and judge for himself. The place of rhymed endings is taken by interlaced repetitions of the same words and phrases. The rhyming may not be regular, but the poem is full of rhymes.

† Suggested by the echoes at Killarney.

fifteen lines in the Prologue, beginning "O miracle of women." Among the many omissions which were made between the successive issues one possesses an interest which make it perhaps worthy of record. It occurs in the speech of the Princess in answer to Lady Blanche.

> " But Ida with a voice, that like a bell
> Toll'd by an earthquake in a trembling tower,
> Rang ruin, answered full of grief and scorn
> *What ! in our time of glory when the cause*
> *Now stands up, first, a trophied pillar—now*
> *So clipt, so stinted in our triumph—barred*
> *Ev'n from our free heart-thanks, and every way*
> *Thwarted and vext, and lastly catechised*
> *By our own creature ! one that made our laws !*
> *Our great she-Solon ! her that built the nest*
> *To hatch the cuckoo ! whom we called our friend !*
> *But we will crush the lie that glances at us*
> *As cloaking in the larger charities*
> *Some baby predilection : all amazed !*
> *We must amaze this legislator more.'*

[Here follow eight retained lines.]

> " *Go help the half-brained dwarf Society,*
> *To find low motives unto noble deeds,*
> *To fix all doubt upon the darker side ;*
> *Go, fitter there for narrowest neighbourhoods,*
> *Old talker, haunt where gossip breeds and seethes,*
> *And festers in provincial sloth ! and you,*
> *That think we sought to practise on a life*
> *Risk'd for our own and trusted to our hands.*
> *What say you, sir? you hear us ; deem ye not*
> *'Tis all too like that even now we scheme,*
> *In one broad death confounding friend and foe,*
> *To drug them all ? revolve it ; you are man,*
> *And therefore no doubt wise.*"

Both the poem and the character of the Princess

have gained much by the rejection of these weak and tasteless lines.

The pause that occurs at the close of the fourth canto when Lilia sings :

> " Thy voice is heard thro' rolling drums,"

marks the " change in the music," the transition from gay to grave, the point at which the " enchanted reverie" passes into the serious allegory.   It will be noticed that the songs at once reflect and focus the significant or uppermost sentiment of the cantos they separate and unite, and may be read as a clue to the poet's philosophy of the relations between the sexes. Around the child gather all the elements in the social problem, and in so far as Tennyson offers any solution of that problem it is by emphasising the laws of nature which determine in their inexorable fashion the place of the man and the place of the woman in any social system that is to endure.   To say that

> " Woman is not undevelopt man
> But diverse ; could we make her as the man,
> Sweet Love were slain ;"

to say that they must

> " Sit side by side, full-summ'd in all their powers,
> Dispensing harvest, sowing the To-be"—

this is but to give poetic expression to very evident things, but it is also to give expression to the only " thinkable" philosophy of the matter.   Tennyson has added nothing to our knowledge, but he has beautifully summed for us, as an artist should, the teaching of nature, our mother.

In many respects the distinctive elements in Tennyson's poetic genius—certainly those of his youthful genius—the branches of his art in which he excelled are most prominently exhibited and may be most advantageously studied in this poem.   The idyll was a form borrowed indeed from the Greek, but, suited as it was to his powers, the form which he made especially his own.   And *The Princess* is an idyll or series of idyllic pictures where the sweetness of his versification, his subtle skill in word-painting, and his keen and yet gracious vein of pleasantry meet under the felicitous auspices of a subject eminently appropriate to their display.

The Laureate's model in blank verse was Milton, and his verse displays the artist's reverence for a greater artist. Compared with Milton's, his blank verse is distinguished by the much larger proportion it contains of words of pure English stock, by the comparative frequency with which the pause comes at the end of the line and by his preference for the internal pause after the fourth syllable to that after the sixth, which was Milton's favourite.   The splendour of the great wheeling circles of Milton's verse, its organ-like harmony, the billowy mounting volume of its music, is in large measure due to its periodic structure.   Milton constructed his verse in paragraphs, caring more for the effect of the whole than of its constituent parts, and so arranging the pause and cadence of his single lines that the ear remains attent until the final strain is reached, in which the suggested harmonies are all resolved, each paragraph

> " swelling loudly
> Up to its climax, and then dying proudly."

With Tennyson the single line is more frequently sufficient for itself, the periodic system less conspicu-

ous. The traditional licences, elision such as is exhibited here :

> " *O swallow, swallow, if I could follow and light*
> Upon her lattice, I would pipe and trill"—

an occasional initial trochee, or in the second or fourth
foot, in room of the iambus, and feminine endings, are
to be found in Tennyson, as in most other writers, but
he is more uniformly careful to avoid abruptness or
harshness ; so much so, that his verse exhibits a more
evenly polished surface than that of any other English
poet. Among musical devices, alliteration ranks as
his first favourite, and is used throughout his poetry
with unusually fine effect and with less insistence than
by Mr. Swinburne, whose monotony in this respect is
not infrequently exasperating. Tennyson's alliteration, skilfully introduced in its unapparent form
when the similarity of sound occurs in the body rather
than in the initial letters of words, as, for example :

> " A *l*ife that *lead*s me*lod*ious *d*ays,"

accounts for much of his melodic beauty. His poverty in rhymes, a point in which he offers a striking
contrast to Browning, who is royal in affluence, is
particularly noticeable in his longest rhymed poem,
In Memoriam ; * a poverty compensated by studied
and ingenious arrangement of alliterative phrases, as
once more, for example :

> " *W*i*ld b*ird who*s*e *warb*le *l*iqui*d s*weet."

Instances may be found, I believe, in every section of
this poem. A critical and scientific workman in his

* See *Tennyson and " In Memoriam,"* by J. Jacobs (David
Nutt, London.)

measures, Tennyson might have been trusted to write upon any subject at any length without fear of descent into the slipshod or turgid movement of Wordsworth's lengthy disquisitions.

The word-painting of *The Princess*, no less than its versification, will reward a careful study. It seems that the author was in the habit of noting a scene or aspect of nature in a few brief phrases, as a painter might with a dash or two of colour suggest a scheme for future elaboration. Here is the result where the memory of an approaching storm, seen from the brow of Snowdon, supplied the original suggestion :

> " As one that climbs a peak to gaze
> O'er land and main, and sees a great black cloud
> Drag inward from the deeps, a wall of night,
> Blot out the slope of sea from verge to shore,
> And suck the blinding splendour from the sand,
> And quenching lake by lake and tarn by tarn
> Expunge the world."

I am unacquainted with any poem exhibiting a more luxuriant richness of colour or more vivid and delicate picturesqueness of imagery. Illustration is needless, but take this :

> " Many a little hand
> Glanced like a touch of sunshine on the rocks,
> Many a light foot shone like a jewel set
> In the dark crag."

In its entirety, *The Princess*, though not his most ambitious work, displays, as I have already indicated, the qualities of Tennyson's genius which the future will speak of as " Tennysonian," as exclusively his own, the qualities which of all English poets he possessed and cultivated in the fullest measure. It is the highest conceivable reach in decorative art, nor can lyrical sweetness be further sweetened. Half classic, half mediæval in feeling, wholly modern in subject and treatment, it represents the character of the author's mind. His culture enabled him to embellish and enrich with a wealth of suggestion and illustration so fresh a theme as the emancipation of woman, in a style of captivating, dream-like phantasy, and, as in *The Idylls of the King*, the strongest elements in his nature, mysticism and romance, are subtly woven through the whole.

The following letter, the most important and interesting ever written by Tennyson in connexion with his poetry, was addressed to Mr. S. E. Dawson, author of *A Study of " The Princess."* It naturally claims a place here :

"ALDWORTH, HASLEMERE, SURREY,
November 21, 1882.

"DEAR SIR : I thank you for your able and thoughtful essay on *The Princess.* You have seen, among other things, that if women ever were to play such freaks, the tragic and the burlesque might go hand in hand. I may tell you that the songs were not an afterthought. Before the first edition came out I deliberated with myself whether I should put songs in between the separate divisions of the poem ; again, I thought, the poem will explain itself ; but the public did not see that the child, as you say, was the heroine of the piece, and at last I conquered my laziness and inserted them. You would be still more certain that the child was the true heroine, if instead of the first song as it now stands,

" ' As thro' the land at eve we went,'

I had printed the first song which I wrote, *The Losing*

of the Child. The child is sitting on the bank of the river, and playing with flowers ; a flood comes down ; a dam has been broken through ; the child is borne down by the flood ; the whole village distracted ; after a time the flood has subsided ; the child is thrown safe and sound again upon the bank, and all the women are in raptures. I quite forget the words of the ballad, but I think I may have it somewhere.

"Your explanatory notes are very much to the purpose, and I do not object to your finding parallelisms. They must always recur. A man (a Chinese scholar) some time ago wrote to me, saying that in an unknown, untranslated Chinese poem there were two whole lines of mine almost word for word. Why not ? Are not human eyes all over the world looking at the same objects, and must there not consequently be coincidences of thought and impressions and expressions ? It is scarcely possible for any one to say or write anything in this late time of the world to which in the rest of the literature of the world a parallel could not somewhere be found. But when you say that this passage or that was suggested by Wordsworth or Shelley or another, I demur, and, more, I wholly disagree. There was a period in my life when, as an artist—Turner, for instance—takes rough sketches of language, etc., in order to work them eventually into some great picture ; so I was in the habit of chronicling, in four or five words or more, whatever might strike me as picturesque in nature. I never put these down, and many and many a line has gone away on the north wind, but some remain—*e.g.* :

" ' A full sea glazed with muffled moonlight.'

"Suggestion : The sea one night at Torquay, when

Torquay was the most lovely sea village in England, though now a smoky town ; the sky was covered with thin vapour, and the moon was behind it.

> " ' A great black cloud
> Drags inward from the deep.'

" Suggestion : A coming storm seen from the top of Snowdon.   In the *Idylls of the King* :

> " ' With all
> Its stormy crests that smoke against the skies.'

" Suggestion : A storm that came upon us in the middle of the North Sea.

> " ' As the water-lily starts and slides.'

" Suggestion : Water-lilies in my own pond, seen in a gusty day with my own eyes.   They did start and slide in the sudden puffs of wind till caught and stayed by the tether of their own stalks—quite as true as Wordsworth's simile, and more in detail.

> " ' A wild wind shook—
> Follow, follow, thou shalt win.'

" Suggestion : I was walking in the New Forest.   A wind did arise, and :

> " ' Shake the songs, the whispers and the shrieks
> Of the wild wood together.'

" The wind, I believe, was a west wind, but because I wished the Prince to go south, I turned the wind to the south, and naturally the wind said, ' Follow.'

" I believe the resemblance which you note is just a chance one.   Shelley's lines are not familiar to me, though, of course, if they occur in *The Prometheus* I must have read them.

" I could multiply instances, but I will not bore you ; and far indeed am I from asserting that books, as well as nature, are not and ought not to be suggestive to the poet. I am sure that I myself and many others find a peculiar charm in those passages of such great masters as Virgil or Milton where they adopt the creation of a bygone poet, and reclothe it, more or less, according to their own fancy.

"But there is, I fear, a prosaic set growing up among us, editors of booklets, bookworms, index-hunters, or men of great memories and no imagination, who impute themselves to the poet, and so believe that he, too, has no imagination, but is forever poking his nose between the pages of some old volume in order to see what he can appropriate. They will not allow one to say, 'Ring the bells' without finding that we have taken it from Sir P. Sydney, or even to use such a simple expression as the ocean 'roars' without finding out the precise verse in Homer or Horace from which we have plagiarised it. (Fact!)

"I have known an old fishwife who had lost two sons at sea clench her fist at the advancing tide on a stormy day and cry out: 'Ay, roar; do! How I hates to see thee show thy white teeth!' Now, if I had adopted her exclamation, and put it into the mouth of some old woman in one of my poems, I dare say the critic would have thought it original enough, but would most likely have advised me to go to nature for my old woman, and not to my imagination; and, indeed, it is a strong figure. Here is another little anecdote about suggestion. When I was about twenty or twenty-one I went on a tour to the Pyrenees. Lying among these mountains before a waterfall that comes down one thousand or twelve hundred feet, I sketched it (according to my custom then) in these words:

" 'Slow-dropping veils of thinnest lawn.'

When I printed this a critic informed me that ' lawn'
was the material used in theatres to imitate a waterfall, and graciously added : ' Mr. T. should not go to
the boards of a theatre, but to nature herself, for his
suggestions.' And I had gone to nature herself. I
think it is a moot point whether, if I had known how
that effect was produced on the stage, I should have
ventured to publish the line. I beg you to believe
me, etc.,   A. TENNYSON."

" P. S.—By the by, you are wrong about ' the trem-
ulous isles of light ;' they are isles of light, spots of
sunshine coming through the eaves, and seeming to
slide from one to the other, as the procession of girls
' move under the shade.' And surely the ' beard-blown
goat ' involves a sense of the wind blowing the beard
on the height of the ruined pillar."

F

CHAPTER IV.

ARTHUR HENRY HALLAM, Tennyson's college friend and constant companion, died in September, 1833. From their first meeting until the companionship was broken by death not quite five years elapsed,* and almost seventeen years passed away before **InMemoriam.** the elegy which has become the imperish-
1850. able monument of their friendship was given to the world.† The poems composing it were written at intervals during Tennyson's life in London, and the whole was complete or almost complete long prior to its publication. "A. T. has near a volume of poems—elegiac—in memory of Arthur Hallam," wrote Fitzgerald in January, 1845 ; "don't you think the world wants other notes than elegiac now? *Lycidas* is the utmost length an elegiac should reach. But Spedding praises ; and I suppose the elegiacs will see daylight, public daylight, one day." When the elegiacs did see daylight, five years later, they were published anonymously, but Tennyson's name upon the title-page was not necessary to proclaim him the author.

* *In Memoriam*, xxii.

† An interesting circumstance connects Hallam with another great English elegy, *Adonais*. It was first printed in Pisa, under the direction of Byron, and a copy of the pamphlet was brought by Hallam from Italy. The poem appeared for the first time in an English edition, accessible to English readers, in *The Transactions* of the Cambridge Union, 1834.

The attention of a reader of *In Memoriam* is at the outset naturally directed to the form of the stanza, which is unvaried throughout. The arrangement of the transposed quatrain has much to do with the effect produced by the poem as a whole and in its several parts ; it strikes the key-note of the elegiac mood, and thus preserves throughout sections that deal with very varying subject-matter the unity of sentiment which binds them together ; and when the poet is dealing with the philosophical problems that naturally suggest themselves in such a poem, the thought flows with less interruption into the mould of this than it could conceivably have done into any other rhymed form among English measures. I have no doubt that the possibilities in the stanza for reflective elegiac poetry were suggested to Tennyson by the short elegy composed in the same metre by Ben Jonson.* Might one not accept this, for example, as part of the later poem ?

> " Who, as an offering at your shrine,
>   Have sung this hymn, and here entreat
>   One spark of your diviner heat
> To light upon a love of mine."

The same measure was employed by Lord Herbert, of Cherbury,† in a short love poem of small merit but more interest, as containing verses such as these, which so nearly recall the later music :

> " O no, belov'd ! I am most sure
>   Those virtuous habits we acquire,
>   As being with the soul entire,
> Must with it evermore endure.

* Ben Jonson's *Underwoods*. The suggestion was probably unconscious.

† Born 1581. Died 1648. Elder brother of George Herbert.

" Else should our souls in vain elect ;
    And vainer yet were heaven's laws,
    When to an everlasting cause
  They gave a perishing effect.

" These eyes again thine eyes shall see,
    And hands again these hands infold ;
    And all chaste pleasures can be told,
  Shall with us everlasting be."*

I am not sure that Tennyson has anywhere invented
a new poetic form ; but here, as throughout his poetry,
he proves his possession of that singular penetration
of judgment which made choice with perfect instinct
of the formal mould best suited to his theme.   As will
be seen, I incline to regard the pre-eminent quality in
his genius as keen-sighted judgment rather than power
of initiative or originating way of thought.   The original thinker is original in the disengagement of his mental processes from the grooves in which the thoughts
of ordinary men run, and in his presentation of the
facts with which all are familiar in new and unexpected relationships.   Tennyson—and no better example of my meaning need be adduced than this poem
—is a great and deservedly popular poet because his
way of thought is that of the cultivated minds of his
time ; and his large and indisputable influence in the
shaping of the ideas of that time is in great degree
due to the ripeness of the popular mind to receive
those ideas, and to the fact that his precision and
beauty of expression made clear to his readers what
they had already themselves obscurely felt and
thought.   Does any one ask : "Is this not to be a great
poet, a poet of the first order?"   I would answer, "It

* From *An Ode upon the Question moved, Whether Love should
continue forever ?*

is to be a great poet, but not a poet of the first order, for it recalls the greatness of Pope and of Gray, it suggests no companionship with Dante, with Milton, or with Wordsworth." It may, perhaps, again be asked : "Is not Virgil a poet of the first order, and is not Tennyson comparable to Virgil ?" To me it seems that fortunate as Tennyson was in the hour of his birth, he lacked a supreme poetic lot such as fell to Virgil—still, in Bacon's words, "The chastest poet and the royalest that to the memory of man is known"—to be the acknowledged poetic representative of Rome's imperial race, to have for theme, majestic and incomparable, the foundation and the glories of Rome itself.

Published when the century had reached its middle year, *In Memoriam* best reflects of any poem written during the century the current moods of its thought and feeling. Here are put into verse the problems of the head and heart that were uppermost in men's minds in the days in which he wrote, so that the poet, while he speaks of his personal sorrow, is really a man of his time, speaking for his contemporaries. For this reason *In Memoriam* is an elegy in a class by itself, nor can it, to any purpose, be compared with poems like *Lycidas* or *Adonais*. Each of these is a dirge, in which the person of the lost friend is never lost sight of, whereas the later elegy is a series of lyrics, many of which are general reflections in the presence of death the thought-compeller, rather than songs of mourning for a definite grief.* And, moreover, be-

* " It is rather the cry of the whole human race than mine. In the poem altogether private grief swells out into thought of and hope for the whole world. It begins with a funeral and ends with a marriage, begins with death and ends in promise of a new life—a sort of Divine Comedy, cheerful at the close. It is a very im-

cause it mirrors the life of the mind and heart in the valley of the shadow, its appeal is to emotions that are universal and thoughts that visit the homes of all the world. While, then, an expression of personal loss, and modern in its theological and philosophical features, *In Memoriam* is most purely human*in its interest of all elegiac poems that ever were written. Like Gray's elegy, in this predominance of the human element over the personal it takes a place in the hearts of its readers that the marvellous art and witchery of colour in *Lycidas* and *Adonais* can never give them.

In the history of theology *In Memoriam* marks the beginnings of that school of thought represented within the Church by Frederick Denison Maurice—the Broad Church movement, as it is called, which was itself the outcome of the more liberal and deeper view of life, its meaning and its issues, presented in the Transcendental philosophy. But while the influences of Kant and the later German thinkers, radiated in England by Coleridge and Carlyle, are abundantly apparent in Tennyson's philosophy, fairly summed in this poem, we must be careful to abstain from any effort to find in the poetic statement of his thought any definite scheme or system. If I were asked to give some succinct statement of Tennyson's philosophy, I should say that he emphasises in every line of his reflective poetry the creed of the higher emotions. Born as he was into a critical epoch, he

personal poem, as well as personal. There is more about myself in *Ulysses*, which was written under the sense of loss and all that had gone by, but that still life must be fought out to the end. It was more written with the feeling of his loss upon me than many poems in *In Memoriam.*"—"*Remarks of Tennyson,*" quoted by the editor in the *Nineteenth Century*, January, 1893.

  * It was sometimes called by the author *The Way of the Soul.*

could not but feel the uncertainties that mar, the doubt that threatens the most firmly built and most zealously guarded dogmas. Yet Tennyson's strength as a thinker seems to me to have lain in the sceptical attitude of his mind, not indeed towards the older forms of faith, but towards the newer creeds of science, which in the first flush of their youth claimed an easy victory, ere the ground upon which the battle was to be fought lay clearly mapped or determined before men's eyes. In his refusal to accept the negatives of science —a refusal more than justified even before his own death—in his conviction that the uncertainties of the new teaching were more uncertain, the doubts as to the reality of its solutions of the old problems to be doubted more gravely than those attaching to revelation, in this the penetration of his judgment was eminently proved. It is this grasp of real amid innumerable false issues, this intellectual sanity, which dignifies Tennyson as a thinker no less than a poet. If he lacked the power of imaginative synthesis, which in a brain like Plato's marshals the facts of the world under the unity of a self-consistent system, his analytic faculty probed deep and far.

I have said that briefly summed Tennyson's creed may be described as the creed of the higher emotions. The powerlessness of the human mind face to face with the tremendous problems of " why? whence? whither?" its inherent incapacity to solve these questions, was forced upon him, as it was forced upon his contemporaries, Clough and Arnold. But while with them in this, he did not share their spiritual dejection or sad stoic acquiescence in an unavoidable lot. Falling back upon a testimony higher than any that could be submitted to a critical scientific examination, he

took up his position in the ancient and impregnable
fortress of the soul that refuses to doubt its Divine
origin, its home in God.

> " If e'er, when faith had fallen asleep,
>   I heard a voice, ' Believe no more,'
>   And heard an ever-breaking shore
>   That tumbled in the Godless deep;
>
> " A warmth within the breast would melt
>   The freezing reason's colder part,
>   And like a man in wrath the heart
>   Stood up and answer'd, ' I have felt.' "*

This creed, based upon the higher emotions, or, as
we may perhaps call it, the evidence of the best and
noblest moments of the spirit's inner life, is the spiritual message borne to his youthful friend by the *Ancient Sage:*

> " For nothing worthy proving can be proven,
>   Nor yet disproven ; wherefore thou be wise,
>   Cleave ever to the sunnier side of doubt,
>   And cling to faith beyond the forms of faith."

The history of the soul in grief, such a grief, with
its accompanying cloud of torturing doubts, as Death,
the parter of friends, alone can bring, is in this poem
delineated with a fidelity we dare not challenge. Its
passage from affection for an earthly to devotion towards a heavenly friend, from vague doubt to hopeful trust, from " wild unrest " to peace, is strikingly
matched in the history of the soul in Carlyle's *Sartor
Resartus.* From "the everlasting no" until the
" centre of indifference" is passed the shadow lies
deep upon the path, and then slowly "a full new life"

* * In Memoriam, *cxxiv.

is breathed, drawn in part from the subtle helpfulness of Nature in her time of spring,* until "the everlasting yea" is realised. *In Memoriam* has been compared with the sonnet-sequence of Shakespeare, and the comparison is not without interest. Many of Tennyson's phrases were borrowed from these sonnets; in both series of poems the deepest feelings and convictions of the heart and mind are reflected, and in both the labour of the artist strangely mingles a pleasure with its pain.

While it outlines no system of thought, no philosophy of consolation, *In Memoriam* is pre-eminently a poem strong in soothing influences, in assuaging remedies for the pain of loss. It can hardly be said that Tennyson fortifies the mind and heart as Browning or as Wordsworth fortifies them. He supports and consoles, indeed, in that the reader is taken into his confidence, and learns what were the supports and consolations of the poet in his dark hour. Thus by sympathy with the sorrow he is drawn insensibly to sympathy with hope renewed and faith regained. In the presentment of his own experience, in that series of delicate sketches of the healing influences of time and nature allied against victorious despair Tennyson speaks to every mourner an unforgettable word.

Here, perhaps, may be fitly noticed the art displayed by Tennyson in making Nature sympathise with his varying moods. He finds in her an echo of his own secret feeling, and her sights and sounds minister to his heart.

> " Calm is the morn without a sound,
>   Calm as to suit a calmer grief,
>   And only thro' the faded leaf
> The chestnut pattering to the ground."

* *In Memoriam*, lxxxvi.

The lucid beauty and completeness of the scenes depicted in his earlier poems, in themselves delightful, prepare in each case the mind for the mood or sentiment that prevails throughout the story. In *The Lotos-Eaters*, for example, or in such idyllic scenes as are drawn in poems like *The Miller's Daughter*, Nature is in perfect harmony with the prevailing emotion, at once intensifying and interpreting it. Much of the charm resident in Tennyson's setting of tales, themselves destitute of any special interest, may be directly traced to the exquisite appropriateness of the background chosen and the no less exquisite skill in its pourtrayal.

A careful study of *In Memoriam* reveals more of design than is at first apparent in the arrangement of the lyrics.* Probably because it was long mature, before it was given to the world, the changes in later editions, if we except verbal alterations, are fewer than is the case with most of Tennyson's longer poems.† Two sections only were added : xxxix. (" Old warder of these buried bones") in the pocket volume edition, and lix. ("O Sorrow, wilt thou live with me ?") in the fourth edition of 1851. The design, therefore, was complete from the first, and the sequence of sections has not been interfered with. It seems clear that Nos. i.–lvi. (now lvii. by reason of the interpolated "yew tree" section) were complete in themselves and were written, most of them, in the first year. No.

---

* Tennyson is quoted by Mr. Knowles (*Nineteenth Century*, January, 1893) as saying that there are "nine natural groups" of stanzas in the poem. These are : 1–8 ; 9–20 ; 20–27 ; 28–49 ; 50–58 ; 59–72 ; 72–98 ; 99–103 ; 104–131.

† Few for Tennyson ; about fifty verbal and other changes were made since its publication.

lvi. (lvii.) has a marked conclusion, and lvii. (lviii.) is
introductory to a supplement. That supplement began with " He past, a soul of nobler tone," to which
he afterwards prefixed lix. It is to be observed that
he himself makes lix. begin the sixth of his nine
groups. These five groups might be called Death,
Burial, the Past, Christmas Hopes, the Future. The
lapse of time is clearly marked ; the three Christmas
seasons following the death of Hallam, in September,
1833, are each the subject of a section or sections,*
and the whole is therefore a mental history of the
years of the poet's life immediately following 1833.
The Epilogue is a marriage greeting to Cecilia Tennyson, who, in October, 1842, was married to Edmund
Law Lushington.

One more word may be added. I note in this poem
a purity of colour in its pictorial passages, a quieter
music than is elsewhere to be found in Tennyson's
poetry. To one who takes up a volume of his verse
after a volume by, let us say, a contemporary—Matthew Arnold—the colour seems glaring, and at times
the music almost importunate. Arnold's ideal in the
poetic art was a chastened simplicity, a reliance for
effect in a poem, to use his own phrase concerning
Wordsworth, solely on the weight and force of that
which with entire fidelity it utters. Tennyson's decorative art, his love of colour for its own sake, of music
for its own sake, lead him at times into what must
always seem to the highly cultivated sense extravagances of colour, an over-profusion, a lush luxuriance,
and into similar extravagances of sound. To put it
briefly, he rarely trusts his thought, as Wordsworth

* xxviii.–xxx. ; lxxviii ; civ.–cv.

trusted it, to build for itself a natural home of expression. So much an artist was he that Nature could not speak his language, and hence the inevitable word is rarely heard in his poetry. Compare a poem like that entitled *Palladium*, or a poem like that *To Marguerite*, beginning :

> " Yes, in the sea of life enisled"—

compare these with almost any poems by Tennyson, and it will be seen that in the one case the power and charm of the verse belong in the main to the idea, in the other case are almost wholly dependent upon the language in which it is clothed.

Save in *In Memoriam* and in some of the finer passages of the *Idylls*, I do not know that elsewhere in Tennyson's more ambitious poetry is the decorative instinct, the laying of colour for the sake of colour, so restrained, the reliance upon the emotion or the idea so complete, the expression so simply and directly natural, as in the above and in a hundred other poems by Wordsworth or Arnold. If I am right, therefore, a purer ideal of art, a more fastidious taste guides the artist's hand in this than in any other part of his work :

> " Till now the doubtful dusk reveal'd
>   The knoll once more where, couch'd at ease,
>   The white kine glimmer'd, and the trees
> Laid their dark arms about the field ;
>
> " And, suck'd from out the distant gloom,
>   A breeze began to tremble o'er
>   The large leaves of the sycamore,
> And fluctuate all the still perfume,
>
> " And gathering freshlier overhead,
>   Rock'd the full-foliaged elms, and swung
>   The heavy-folded rose, and flung
> The lilies to and fro, and said,

" ' The dawn, the dawn,' and died away ;
   And East and West, without a breath,
   Mixt their dim lights, like life and death,
To broaden into boundless day."

Had he been content at all times to trust his subject
as he has trusted it here, Tennyson would not only
have been a greater poet, he would have been even a
greater artist than he was, for the greatest artists are
those who allow Nature to write in their names, and
are themselves too wise to interfere with or add a
word to the language she speaks.

It seems a far journey from the philosophy of *In
Memoriam* to the philosophy of *Maud*,[*] from the
poetry of a sad resignment to that of revolt ; yet
there is little difficulty in recognizing the same hand
in both, the same worker in different moods. As
has been already observed, the germt from
which *Maud* was developed is the lyric, **Maud and**
"O, that 'twere possible," contributed in **Other Poems.**
1837 to *The Tribute*, a collection of miscel-   **1855.**
laneous unpublished poems by various
authors, published by John Murray, and edited by
Lord Northampton. Among the other contributors
were Wordsworth, Landor, Aubrey de Vere, Henry
Taylor, Southey, Monckton Milnes, and Charles Tennyson. The proceeds from the sale of this publication were intended to relieve the necessities of the
Rev. Edward Smedley, a clergyman in ill health and
threatened with loss of eyesight. Smedley died before the book appeared, and the proceeds were given
to his family. In reply to Milnes' application to him
for a contribution, Tennyson wrote : " Three summers
back, provoked by the incivility of editors, I swore an
oath that I would never again have to do with their

* " The antiphonal voice to *In Memoriam*."—J. R. LOWELL.

vapid books, and I broke it in the sweet face of
Heaven when I wrote for Lady What's-her-name
Wortley.   But then her sister wrote to Brookfield, and
said she (Lady W.) was beautiful ; so I could not help
it.   But whether the Marquis be beautiful or not, I
don't much mind ; if he be, let him give God thanks,
and make no boast.   To write for people with prefixes
to their names is to milk he-goats ; there is neither
honour nor profit."   This characteristic effusion
evoked an indignant remonstrance from Milnes, to
whom Tennyson again wrote : "What has so jaun-
diced your good-natured eyes as to mistake harmless
banter for insolent irony ?" and promised his help.
The promise was fulfilled by the contribution above
mentioned.   These stanzas developed into the lyrical
drama, to which Tennyson's own remark may be
applied—" Poetry is like shot silk with many glancing
colours.   Every reader must find his own interpretation according to his ability and according to his
sympathy with the poet."   The edition of 1855 gave
the poem as continuous ; the edition of the following
year contained some new passages.   In subsequent
issues the poem was divided into two, and eventually
into three parts, and styled " a monodrama."

Maud was greeted with an almost unanimous chorus
of disapproval.   Readers, critical and uncritical alike,
complained that it was unreal, fantastic, had " the
serious defect of leaving one in a painful state of confusion as to the limits of the sane and the insane ; "*
the chief charge of all being that it was an inde-
fensible defence of war.   As a psychological study of
a difficult subject, it was natural that *Maud* should be

* To this it might be replied that the same charge may be brought
against *Hamlet*, and that in nature no defining line can be drawn.

misunderstood and unappreciated. The critical judgments are not now arrayed against the author's favourite work as they were at first, but it still remains and will remain the least favoured by his readers. In many respects it must, I think, be regarded as the most dramatic of Tennyson's poems, dramatic as the presentation not of the characters of a group of individuals and their mutual interaction, but as reflecting the varying moods of a single person of eager temper wrought upon by violent passions in a period itself full of exciting actions, of nerve-stirring emotions and of arousing ideas.* *Maud* is a lyrical monodrama, and into the lyrics which compose it Tennyson poured much of his strongest feeling, many of the thoughts which came from the closest corner of his brain. It is a sincere, a characteristic utterance, a real transcript of the poet's mind ; hence his love for it,† hence, too, its interest to students of his poetry. Whatever regard Tennyson in his poetry paid to the conventions —and as an artist he was to some extent their prisoner —he is here moving with a freer, more natural step, speaking to please himself, and himself alone. The subject, too, is a favourite one. *Maud* may fairly be

---

* Mr. Knowles quotes Tennyson as saying : " It should be called *Maud, or The Madness.* It is slightly akin to *Hamlet.* No other poem (a monotone with plenty of change and no weariness) has been made into a drama where successive phases of passion in one person take the place of successive persons. The whole of the stanzas where he is mad in Bedlam, from " Dead, long dead " to " Deeper, ever so little deeper," were written in twenty minutes, and some mad doctor wrote to me that nothing since Shakespeare has been so good for madness as this."—*Nineteenth Century,* January, 1893.

† " I've always said that *Maud* and *Guinevere* were the finest things I've written."

compared with the two *Locksley Halls*,* the poems of his youth and age that came most directly from the heart, taking them as a single work for the purpose of the comparison.   In both the undercurrent of his nature becomes for the time the uppercurrent.   Each is the story of a lost love ; in both there are noble aspirations, disappointed hopes, a touch of scorn, the outcome of such unfulfilled longing.   The hero of each suffers the same sharp reverse, both would mix with action to keep at bay the tiger despair, both are critics of life, who find it an unweeded garden ; in both the vein of bitterness gives place to more self-honouring resolve.

" Follow light and do the right, for man can half control his doom,
  Till you find the deathless angel seated in the vacant tomb,"

is a counsel at one with the resolve of the hero of *Maud*,

" It is better to fight for the good than to rail at the ill.
  I have felt with my native land, I am one with my kind,
  I embrace the purpose of God and the doom assigned."

For the rest, *Maud* passes now and then from the sphere of poetry into that of rhetoric, but in the best of the lyrics there is much of Tennyson's best, the imperishable beauty that belongs to the musical expression of sincere emotion.   For a defence of the battle-ardour of *Maud*, we may read the *Epilogue* to *The Charge of the Heavy Brigade*.   But a defence is unnecessary.   Only the purblind moralist who knows nothing of life can fail to recognise that terrible as are its accompaniments of suffering and horror, by war are evoked the noblest elements of human character as well as its most debasing ; that in the furnace of its fires men are tried as gold in the refining pot, and

* "There is not a touch of biography in it," said the author.

that not seldom has it discovered beauties and hero-
isms, an unselfishness and devotion, the existence of
which in self-seeking times of peace the most subtle
observer could not even have suspected.

Maud is not a world-poem ; it is not even a poem of
great imaginative range or far-reaching power, but it
finds the vulnerable points in modern civilisation, and
has its place with those true works of art which will
not leave us at rest with ourselves until we know our
minds and sound the real depth of our feelings.

In addition to *Maud*, this volume of 154 pages con-
tained *The Charge of the Light Brigade, Will, The Daisy,
Ode on the Death of the Duke of Wellington, Lines to the
Rev. F. D. Maurice,** *The Brook*, and the *Letters*.

Of the remaining poems few words are called
for here. *The Brook* takes its rightful place among
the English idylls, a vignette of English country
life, peaceful and sweet. *The Daisy* is a record
of the poet's wedding journey, brought in after
years to mind by a faded flower. The lines *To
Frederick Denison Maurice*,† " the truest Christian he
ever knew," recall a controversy of the past and picture the surroundings of the poet's home in the Isle of
Wight. The *Ode on the Death of the Duke of Wellington*
and *The Charge of the Light Brigade*, Tennyson's two
most famous patriotic poems, need no comment. The
early printed versions of each underwent even more
than the customary revision, the labour of the file, and

---

* Maurice had dedicated his *Theological Essays* to Tennyson.

† Even this short poem was considerably altered in later versions. Lushington, comparing it with *The Daisy*, remarked of
the latter : " How the simple change in the last line from a dactyl
to an amphibrachys changes a mere experiment into a discovery
in metre."

in their present form are very different from the originals.

As a whole, the volume may be noted as containing some interesting experiments in metre. *Maud*, the *Ode on the Death of the Duke*, *The Daisy*, the lines *To Maurice*, *Will*, all exhibit Tennyson moving in hitherto untrodden metrical paths. I do not know that any English poet has employed and achieved success in so many and various measures.

CHAPTER V.

AMONG the books published by William Caxton at the first printing-press set up in England, at Westminster, was Sir Thomas Malory's *Morte d'Arthur* in the year 1485. Malory was a compiler of genius, with a real skill in language and a real feeling for the spirit of the old legends which he attempts to unify. He so alters, arranges, and combines the stories, so nobly conceives the cycle of the Arthurian chivalric romances, that at his hands the whole is clothed, and indeed for the first time, with almost epic interest, the interest of simple yet heroic actions on an ample field, unified by their relation to a great central figure. Into the neglected treasury of chivalric legend—neglected from the time that the Renaissance revived men's sympathies with classic ideals and the myths of older days—into this treasury of chivalric legend, neglected and even scorned by so great and true a poet as Chaucer, Malory stepped boldly, and committing a splendid theft from contemporary or older writers on the Continent, made himself the undisputed possessor in English prose of the story of King Arthur and his knights. In his version the story is at once more human, more tragic, more convincing, and more natural than in that of any of the earlier compilers ; and for this reason it is that the more recent poets, and Tennyson among them, follow Malory, except in some instances, in preference to any of his

Idylls of the King. 1859-85.

predecessors in other languages who handled the same subject. And the name of his predecessors is legion and of many nationalities, divided from each other by long centuries.

The origin of the Arthur story is lost in the mists of remote Celtic tradition. There are traces of a hero named Arthur even before the time in which we hear of him as a king who lived and reigned in the sixth century, and of whom the tale was told that he united all the petty princedoms under his sovereign rule, and as the champion of his people and of the Christian faith long resisted the invading bands of the Saxon heathen. But the earliest references to Arthur in the lays of the Welsh bards celebrate him as a valiant hero only, and it is not until we come to the accounts of Nennius,* and especially to those of Geoffrey of Monmouth, that the romantic and marvellous elements enter, that we hear of him as *rex quondam rexque futurus*, and that the legends begin to take the shape and display the character with which we are now familiar. To the influence of Geoffrey of Monmouth's version,† compiled according to his own words from " a certain very ancient book in the British tongue," may be traced the inexhaustible harvest of chivalric romances which grew up around the person of the mythic

---

* Popularly supposed to have been a writer of the seventh century, but really much later—probably the twelfth.

† Geoffrey of Monmouth was consecrated Bishop of St. Asaph in 1152. Before that date he composed the *Chronicon sive Historia Britonum*, a work which the author professes to have translated from a chronicle entitled *Brut of Brenhined*, a history of the kings of Britain, found in Brittany, and given him by Walter Calenius, Archdeacon of Oxford.

British prince. How far Geoffrey may have been the conduit pipe through which real historical facts were conveyed is, indeed, difficult to determine, but that the greater part of his work is fiction, partly, perhaps, even fiction of his own invention, is more than probable. With him the legends entered upon the period of their Christian and chivalric treatment in the metrical romances of the twelfth and thirteenth centuries, both in French and (later) in English. In these romances Arthur becomes the ideal knight, the founder of the noble brotherhood of the Round Table. A king of mysterious lineage and endowed with supernatural gifts, he keeps his court at Caerleon, and thence his chosen knights go forth on knightly quests, to succour the distressed and helpless, to protect women, and do service in their honour, and to venture themselves in every heroic contest which may issue in glory and the triumph of justice and virtue. The whole atmosphere of these romances is charged with enchantment and mysticism, the imagination ranges freely, and the bare outlines of the original history are by this time completely lost in the colour and variety of the new poetic setting. It will be seen, then, that the Arthurian cycle had its origin in remote antiquity, its germ in ancient Celtic tradition; that, after it had already undergone many and important variations, and received accretions from various sources, it passed, mainly through the version of Geoffrey of Monmouth, into the hands of the French trouvères* and German minnesingers, and returned again to England to find its way into ballad litera-

* The greatest by far was Chrétien de Troies of the twelfth century.

ture, and eventually into the *Morte d'Arthur* of Malory, Tennyson's main source for the *Idylls*.

There is yet another source to which Tennyson is indebted.* In 1849, Lady Charlotte Guest translated into English a Welsh collection, entitled the *Mabinogion*, containing tales not to be found in Malory, but of about the same date, the fourteenth and fifteenth centuries. Although these stories were in all probability also originally translated from the French, they display a character of their own which distinguishes them from the stories of the *Morte d'Arthur*. Matthew Arnold and other critics have found in these chivalric versions of the Arthurian legend traces of a greater antiquity. " These are no mediæval personages," Arnold writes in his *Celtic Literature;* " they belong to an older pagan mythological world. The first thing that strikes one in reading the *Mabinogion* is how evidently the mediæval story-teller is pillaging an antiquity of which he does not fully possess the secret ; he is like a peasant building his hut on the site of Halicarnassus or Ephesus : he builds, but what he builds is full of materials of which he knows not the history, or knows by glimmering tradition merely ; stones ' not of this building,' but of an older architecture, greater, cunninger, more majestical." The English literary history of the Arthurian legends from Malory to Tennyson is rather a curious history of projects than of achievements. The great dramatic period of our literature produced one play only on an Arthurian subject, *The Misfortunes of Arthur*, presented at Gray's Inn before the Queen in 1587, the author, Thomas Hughes. References to the legends occur in a few passages in Shakespeare, but

* For the story of *Enid*.

his only connexion with them—a bond of the slightest
—is to be found in the fact that the plots of *King Lear*
and of *Cymbeline* were originally taken from the
chronicle of Geoffrey of Monmouth, though Shakespeare himself derived them from Holinshed. With
Spenser, gleams of the Arthurian romance shine
through the texture of his strangely-woven song,
where Aristotelian scheme, classic myth, and Italian
verse-form are the conspicuous elements; but Spenser was not destined to unify the Arthurian legends.
A greater than Spenser came near doing so.

In his youth, Milton tells us, "I betook me among
those lofty fables and romances which recount in
solemn cantos the deeds of knighthood, founded by
our victorious kings, and from thence had in renown
over all Christendom." He had for long in contemplation an epic poem whose subject should be
taken from ancient British history,* but a higher
argument claimed him, and the Arthuriad remained
unwritten. Dryden, too, contemplated an epic poem
on a national theme, but hesitated, doubtful whether
to choose as subject Arthur conquering the Saxons,
or Edward the Black Prince, in his Spanish wars.
The times, however, were not ripe for such an effort.
As Scott writes:

> " Dryden in immortal strain
> Had raised the Table Round again,
> But that a ribald king and court
> Bade him toil on to make them sport."

The worthy knight, Sir Richard Blackmore, was
the first to achieve the distinction of a completed

---

* See his Latin poems, *Mansus* and *Epitaphium Damonis;* also
Paradise Lost, Bk. ix. 20, for the reasons for a different choice.

Arthurian epic. "In leisure hours he dealt in epic song," and produced several poems of epic proportions, if not of epic dignity, among them *Prince Arthur* and *King Arthur;* but Blackmore failed to make good his claim to be England's national poet, and it was not until after the dawn of the Neo-Romantic epoch, of which Chatterton was the true harbinger, that the long-delayed poetic justice was done to the ancient British legends. The life of these legends was renewed in poetry and art by the Romantic revival. Scott in his *Bridal of Triermain* treated an episode from the romances. Heber, Wordsworth, Lytton, and others found in them stimulus for the imagination, and there were few among the poets who were Tennyson's contemporaries for whom the spell of the old enchantment was not too strong to be resisted.

Subjects drawn from the Arthurian story appear in several of Tennyson's early poems: in the 1832 volume *The Lady of Shalott, Sir Galahad* and *Sir Lancelot and Queen Guinevere* in 1842. *The Palace of Art* contains a reference to Arthur — "mythic Uther's deeply wounded son;" and elsewhere may be found traces of the effect made by the beauty of these tales of old-world chivalry upon his mind. That the ambition to weave the Arthurian legends into a poetic whole was early cherished by him is evidenced in *The Epic*, which, published among the *Poems* of 1842, introduced the fragment, *Morte d'Arthur*, where the intention* to give a permanent poetic form to the Arthurian history is indicated :—

* Or its tentative accomplishment.

"'You know,' said Frank, 'he burnt
His epic, his *King Arthur*, some twelve books.'" *

In this fragment a new note is struck, the pre-Raph aelite mediæval style of *The Lady of Shalott* and *Sir Galahad* has given place to a manner worthy of epic material. The *Morte d'Arthur*, then, opens the long period of his life during which Tennyson was more or less occupied with his epic scheme.† This is the poem referred to by Landor, who wrote in 1837 : " A Mr. Moreton, a young man of rare judgment, read to me a manuscript by Mr. Tennyson, very different in style from his printed poems. The subject is the death of Arthur. It is more Homeric than any poem of our time, and rivals some of the noblest parts of the *Odyssea*."

For more than a decade we hear no more of the design, but in 1857 was published a small volume, already mentioned, *Enid and Nimue ; or, The True and the False*, which had a very brief spell of public life, being immediately withdrawn from publication. In June of the next year, 1858, Clough, " heard Tennyson read a third Arthur poem—the detection of Guinevere, and the last interview with Arthur." This, entitled *Guinevere*, together with three other poems, *Enid*,‡ *Vivien*, and

---

* Mrs Ritchie quotes Tennyson as saying : 'When I was twenty-four, I meant to write a whole great poem on it (the Arthurian story), and began it in the *Morte d'Arthur*. I said I should do it in twenty years, but the reviews stopped me. By Arthur I always meant the soul, and by the Round Table the passions and capacities of a man. There is no grander subject in the world than King Arthur."

† A long visit to Caerleon on Usk prepared the way for the descriptions of scenery in the *Idylls*.

‡ Afterwards entitled *Geraint and Enid, Merlin and Vivien, Lancelot and Elaine, Arthur and Guinevere*.

Elaine, appeared in 1859 as *Idylls of the King*, the first
occasion upon which the name was employed.   Three
years later the dedication to the memory of the Prince
Consort was prefixed to the poems, which remained
unaltered, save for a few unimportant verbal changes.
After another interval of seven years, in 1869, four
new poems were added—*The Coming of Arthur, The
Holy Grail, Pelleas and Ettarre*, and *The Passing of
Arthur*.*   The last named was an extended version
of the *Morte d'Arthur* of 1842.   In 1871 *The Last
Tournament* appeared in the *Contemporary Review*,
and in 1872 *Gareth aud Lynette*.†   After yet another
long interval, *Balin and Balan*, which serves as an
introduction to *Merlin and Vivien*, was published
in 1885, and in 1888 *Geraint and Enid* was divided
into two parts, the first being named *The Marriage
of Geraint*, and the second retaining the former
title.

Such is the external history of the *Idylls of the
King*.   The history of the author's purpose and its
gradual development, as indicated in the additions
and alterations, made from time to time in the text of
successive editions, can here be but briefly sketched.
Through fully half a century, as I have shown, the
Arthurian story had possession of Tennyson's mind.
Throughout that period it seems as if he were slowly
feeling his way towards the best solution of the difficult problem—how to create a living interest in the
old-world legend, how to re-tell these tales of centuries ago, that they might touch the modern mind,

* " *The Coming and the Passing of Arthur*," said Tennyson,
"are simpler and more severe in style, as dealing with the
awfulness of Birth and Death."

† The lines " To the Queen " were added in this year.

affect with real power the men who live the altered life of to-day.

Although the subject was in many respects suitable for a great English poem, and offered practically an open field which any poet might make his own possession, were his genius equal to the task, the choice of method was a difficult one. The Arthurian romances embody the ideals of chivalry, but they were never true to the real life of any age, and some indeed have thought that no treatment, however skilful, could give them more than a poetic-antiquarian interest :

> " No part have these wan legends in the sun,
> Whose glory lightens Greece and gleams on Rome.
> Their elders live ; but these—their day is done ;
> Their records written on the winds, in foam
> Fly down the wind, and darkness takes them home.
> What Homer saw, what Virgil dreamed, was truth
> And died not, being divine ; but whence, in sooth,
> Might shades that never lived win deathless youth ?"

It was too late by many centuries to build out of these misty legends the heroic epic, whose readers should find in Arthur a real king, and follow with believing, beating heart the record of his knightly deeds. Whatever else may be said of Tennyson, we must willingly grant the wisdom of his choice of the only way in which the material could be handled with any measure of success in these later days. An allegorical treatment of the romance of Arthur was the sole possible treatment for a poet of the nineteenth century. Nor did the romances present any features incompatible with such treatment ; they lent themselves readily to it. Already around the person of Arthur had collected many myths of symbolic import, through which inner meanings ran, and the whole story had been treated by Malory in the spirit of one who, while he tells a particular tale, relates a chapter of universal human history.

The idea of an allegorical treatment of the Arthurian story was, I think, present with Tennyson from the first, but his conception of the whole scheme was in the beginning far from definite, and the presence of the symbolism is hardly felt in the four *Idylls* of 1859. He was not sure how far the allegory might be justly carried. By Arthur, as he tells us, he always meant the Soul, but it was not until 1869, when he published *Pelleas and Ettarre* and *The Holy Grail*, that the allegoric purpose is clearly present. In the address to the Queen, which concludes the whole, and was published in 1872, he sets forth the aim of his work, and speaks of it as an

> " old imperfect tale,
> *New-old and shadowing Sense at war with Soul*
> Rather than that gray king, whose name, a ghost,
> Streams like a cloud, man-shaped, from mountain-peak,
> And cleaves to cairn and cromlech still ; or him
> Of Geoffrey's book, or him of Malleor's, one
> Touch'd by the adulterous finger of a time
> That hover'd between war and wantonness,
> And crownings and dethronements."

The constant revision to which, almost until the last, the various poems were subjected was designed to emphasise their true character, and to bind them into a closer unity. After the publication of *Balin and Balan*, in 1885, Tennyson wrote but one other poem, a lyric, on an Arthurian subject. In *Merlin and the Gleam* the poet seems to allegorise his own life and teaching, and, in his faith that the ideal is indeed the *vera lux* that must lead the world, once more

restores the hope that in the failure of the Table
Round had seemed almost wholly quenched.

I have said that Tennyson's treatment of the Arthurian romances was the only possible one—a frank
literary and symbolic handling of the legendary cycle ;
it remains to ask, Was it successful? I shall not stay
to discuss the wisdom of the choice of title, nor to
enter upon the barren logomachy, so long waged by
the critics, whether or no the poems constitute an
epic. Like all Tennyson's poems, the lyrics excepted,
the *Idylls of the King* have the elements of strength
and of weakness, we may say the elements of the
author's characteristic strength, the elements of his
characteristic weakness. The cardinal defect, inherent in the subject, a lack of unity, was precisely the
defect which the limitations of Tennyson's genius rendered him least able to repair. It would have been
repaired by Milton had he essayed the task ; I believe
no English poet since Milton possessed the architec-
tural faculty, the unifying imagination essential to
complete success. Tennyson's *Idylls* are a series of
pictures—as their name indeed implies ; there is no
link strong enough to bind the constituent parts into
an organic whole. The figure of Arthur is too dim,
too undefined to serve as centre to the movement of
the various poems ; he comes and passes away, but his
influence is slight. Within the work itself, it can
hardly be said that there is " a beginning, a middle
point, and an end," as Aristotle justly demanded in an
epic. We are conscious that many more such poems
might have been added, that some might have been
omitted without serious disturbance to the poem as a
whole. To say so is to say what cannot be asserted
of an organic growth, to which nothing can be added

and from which nothing can be taken away.   Yet in the room of *unity* we have *symmetry*, a delicate balance and proportion, artistic and admirable, with which we may well be content.

Turning from the poem as it might have been to a consideration of it as given to us, the most serious defect arises out of the unfortunate contrast between the cold, colourless, faultless Arthur and the human-hearted though sinning Lancelot.   It is not enough to say that, viewed in its spiritual meanings, the comparison must be in favour of the blameless king.   The story affects us before the symbolism is apparent, and our sympathies are enlisted on the side of flesh and blood, and cannot again be alienated.   Our instincts teach us that Lancelot is the nobler type of manhood. The story, if the poem is to be perfect, must be complete and interesting in itself.   But the necessities of the symbolism clash at times and cannot be harmonised with the tale, and when " we come suddenly upon the moral, it gives us a shock of unpleasant surprise, a kind of grit, as when one's teeth close on a bit of gravel in a dish of strawberries and cream."   This and the inevitable sense of depression which the failure of its ideals, the final ruin of Arthur's once noble court, leaves within the mind, are faults without remedy. But the compensations are not a few—such, indeed, as Tennyson rarely failed to supply in any work.   In the *Holy Grail**and in *Guinevere*, as in *Elaine* and indeed in almost all the poems, there are as noble passages as any to be found in the whole range of English poetry. The felicitous rendering, too, of natural scenery, and its equally felicitous use for purposes of illustration, are as conspicuous as ever.   Take the often-quoted lines that follow :

* " I have expressed there my strong feeling as to the Reality of the Unseen."

" So dark a fore-thought roll'd about his brain,
  As on a dull day in an Ocean cave
  The blind wave feeling round his long sea-hall
  In silence."*

The greatest artist in colour among modern poets is present in the *Idylls* from the first line to the last.

Of the allegory itself, no strict interpretation is possible, nor is it desirable. But it may be outlined as the history of the soul of man in its warfare upon earth.† In Arthur, who builds and reigns in Camelot, we have symbolised the soul and the city that the genius of man has erected for himself—the whole ordered social fabric, the human institutions built up to serve his needs. In *Guinevere* the beauty of the world of sense is typified, the beauty which the soul would fain make its own, finding in it a winning, inexhaustible charm. But in the world of sense, with all its charm, there resides a principle which is antagonistic to the spirit ; while it attracts it also repels, and the problem which man has to face lies here. He is a citizen of two worlds, a spiritual and a material, and while this life lasts a perfect reconciliation is impossible. Arthur comes and establishes his kingdom upon earth, and for a time all goes well. The ideals of the soul are slowly but surely organizing a human after the pattern of a divine society. But the difficulties are many, human weaknesses and frailties hinder the evolution of a perfect reign of love and law, the hostile forces are ceaselessly at work. In *Gareth and Lynette*, in *Balin and Balan*, in *Geraint and Enid* the warfare is

---

* Written in one of the Ballybunion caves, Ireland.

† " The whole is the dream of man coming into practical life and ruined by one sin. Birth is a mystery and death is a mystery, and in the midst lies the table-land of life, and its struggle and performance."—*Conversation of Tennyson quoted by Mrs. Ritchie.*

maintained between the spiritual and material influences in the heart of man, and the spiritual are still
undefeated.   But more powerful forces of evil enter.
These in *Merlin and Vivien* and in *Pelleas and Ettarre*
are triumphant, and the shadow of its approaching
dissolution begins to lower over the once splendid
court.   In *The Holy Grail* is symbolised the quest for
the true spiritual principles, the true religion which
throughout the centuries has inspired the noblest
souls.   But many of the seekers for the Grail are led
astray by wandering fires, and only those in whose
hearts burns the flame of pure devotion attain to a
sight of it.   Lancelot is the type of perfect manhood,
in whom the love of earthly beauty has not until too
late been subdued by a vision of what is still more
lovely.   With the sin of Lancelot and Guinevere the
end draws near ; the winter of failure, the final darkness approaches, and the Round Table, "which was an
image of the mighty world," is dissolved.   But though
dissolved, the ideal at which it aimed shines as it ever
shone ; no failure can dim the brightness of its chal-
lenging fires.   Arthur, the king that was, the king
that will be, is not dead ; and in *Merlin and the Gleam*,
though not a part of the poem, the allegory finds its
true conclusion.   The poet's last word is one of encouragement :

> " After it, follow it,
> Follow The Gleam."

The *Idylls of the King*, when criticism has spoken its
last word, may fairly be called a noble poem ; perhaps
the noblest poem since the *Faerie Queen*, in the order
to which it belongs.   For those, indeed, who value
breadth and scope of conception in art above all
beauty of expression, all exquisiteness of detail ; who
demand authentic warrant in the idea for each word of

the language that conveys it ; who refuse to diction, be it verse or prose, the right to shine in itself, believing that in its highest reach it challenges no attention, but, itself unseen, is but the perfect mirror of the thought or feeling it presents—for those, in a word, who set the whole above the parts that compose it, the *Idylls* can never rank with the supreme poetry of the world. But it will be conceded by the future, as it has already been conceded in the present, that few of the qualities of enduring poetry are here unrepresented. Steeped in the golden splendours of an heroic past the legends keep their intrinsic power to charm, while, in their modern form, the magic and melody and mystery in which they seem to float diffused, the mediæval glamour of a world of old romance that pervades the whole, the deep spiritual significance of the allegory—with these the poet weaves for many readers the spells of an enchanted land. Let us not, therefore, speak of the grandeur of the *Idylls of the King* ; let us rather speak of their splendour, their luxuriance of colour, their exquisite grace of word and phrase, their pictorial magnificence, the undying charm of their high and truthful eloquence. Beautiful, indeed, they are, yet with limitations ; χαλεπὰ τὰ κάλλιστα—perfection is a difficult mark to hit.

"Tennyson's plays," said George Eliot, speaking of *Queen Mary* and *Harold*, "run Shakespere's close." When one hears criticism of this kind from a writer of genius, one is inclined to say, Let us henceforth forever dispense with criti- **Enoch** cism. Such criticism is pestilential, it goes **Arden,* etc.** far to destroy all standards of excellence **1864.** in literature, all sense of distinctions ; it

* The title of the volume was originally *Idylls of the Hearth*, but it was altered while in the press. It was dedicated to Mrs. Tennyson.

H

goes far to create a positive distaste for even the best literature. "*Enoch Arden*," said Mr. Dawson, an ardent admirer of Tennyson, "is his noblest and best" poem. "I find in it almost every quality of the poet, true sympathy and all the rest. *There is not a fine word in it.*" We are growing more and more accustomed to outrageous insanities in criticism; we seem to find in violence of expression some drug or charm to compensate us for the absence of reality. Like the novelist, the critic rides "the many-headed beast" with whip and spur, and the hour of inexorable justice is delayed a week or a day. That a critic should say of *Enoch Arden*, therefore, that "there is not a fine word in it," may not surprise us; though the truth is just the opposite of this, that it is a poem in which a simple subject is adorned with all "the fine words," all the wealth of language at the poet's command. It is, as Mr. Bagehot long ago said, a perfect instance of ornate or decorative as opposed to pure art.

> "While Enoch was abroad on wrathful seas,
> Or often journeying landward ; for in truth
> Enoch's white horse, and Enoch's ocean-spoil
> In ocean-smelling osier, and his face,
> Rough-reddened with a thousand winter gales,
> Not only to the market-cross were known,
> But in the leafy lanes behind the down,
> Far as the portal-warding lion-whelp,
> And peacock yew-tree of the lonely Hall,
> Whose Friday fare was Enoch's ministering."

"So much," as Mr. Bagehot said, "has not often been made of selling fish." We are presented with a portrait of an unreal sailor, painted in unreal colours, upon an unreal canvas, "a sailor crowded all over with ornament and illustration." The key to this poem is to be found in a letter of Fitzgerald's, written just before its composition—"Alfred wants a story to treat, *being full of poetry with nothing to put it in.*"— The subject when found was all but lost beneath the magnificence of its "poetic" treatment. *Enoch Arden* is the best example that can be selected from the author's works of that weakness in his artistic nature which seemingly made it impossible for him to trust his subject, to permit it to speak for itself. But the grand distinction of the greatest artists is this, that their action predominates over their expression, that they regard the whole more than the parts, the idea, therefore, above the language; and their aim is accomplished not in the luxuriance of their imagery, the wealth of their colour, or the multiplicity of their illustration, but, as I have elsewhere phrased it, when they leave upon the reader's mind one pure, simple, affecting outline, one undying image of perfect feature. In this poem of Tennyson, as in many other of his poems—here, I think, pre-eminently—he errs by overlaying a simple and pathetic tale by splendour of language altogether alien to it, by whose instrumentality it is removed out of the real world of things as they are into an altogether unreal world of things as they are not. The action is not permitted to control the expression, but is really subordinated to it; is made the occasion of a magnificent display of verbal and pictorial wealth. When one thinks of *Enoch Arden*, one thinks first of that matchless description of the island in the tropics upon which the shipwrecked sailor is thrown: a description, as I say, matchless, but quite unessential to the story, quite out of keeping with the feelings of the shipwrecked sailor, a purple patch which distracts the mind from the main business of the piece, which is to tell a simple, pathetic tale of simple fisher-folk.

It is a noteworthy fact that this poem is among the most popular, if not the most popular, of Tennyson's works ; it certainly has been more frequently chosen for translation into other languages than any other of his poems—a proof, if any were required, how few are the lovers of pure, of restrained, of classic art even among the readers of poetry. The popularity of *Enoch Arden* is comparable with the popularity of the *May Queen*, a poem so full of false sentiment and false pathos as to be painful to a reader who can feel how Wordsworth would have permitted such a tale to write itself, and in its sheer simplicity subdue heart and mind. How impossible, too, for an artist in the great style, like Milton, to indulge in these puling sentimentalities ! But it was with poems such as these that Tennyson made his irresistible appeal to the wide circle of his uncritical admirers, an appeal which may be compared with that made by the later pictures of his contemporary, Millais.

A noticeable contrast to *Enoch Arden* is the first of the dialect poems, the *Northern Farmer*, published in the same volume. This is a study of real life ; here the patient, observing eye has been at work, here the artist for once conceals his art, and speaks the real language of men. The poems in dialect are more dramatic, because infinitely more true to life, than any work can ever be of the order to which *Enoch Arden* belongs. They are remarkable, too, as revealing an unexpected humorist in the aristocratic poet, a sympathetic humorist, who was at home in the rural cottage as much as in the courts of princes. *The Northern Farmer* was another proof of the extra-

ordinary versatility of Tennyson's genius, and in some respects the most striking poem in this volume. *Aylmer's Field*, of which the story was told to the author by his friend Woolner, the artist, is redeemed from slightness by the intensity and fervour of its rhetoric, culminating in the funeral sermon. In *Sea Dreams* the decorative method employed in *Enoch Arden* is again conspicuous, but the theme is trivial and the treatment almost languid. But in *Tithonus**
the old mastery, the old, inimitable skill is once more apparent. It is in the classical studies that Tennyson's art seems faultless. With all their exquisite beauty of form there is a dignity, a reserve apparent which adds immeasurably to their charm. *Ulysses*, *Tithonus*, *Lucretius*, and *Demeter* are something more than delicately woven dreams, phantasies in colour and sound. Akin to *The Lady of Shalott*, they yet possess something higher ; here is the Greek sharpness of outline, with the Greek simplicity of motive ; here is a chiselled perfection of phrase. The classical studies are, in my judgment, the poems of the author which give us by far the highest sense of his power, whether intellectual or poetic.

Of the remaining poems in this volume, *The Grandmother* may be noted as a favourite with the poet himself, and *The Flower* as a not unnatural protest against the fickle admirers and critics who found nothing in the poet's work to reverence until it became the object of imitation, and then, again, when " most could raise the flower, since all had got the seed," found it of trivial value. The other pieces were *The Voyage*, *The Ringlet* (afterwards omitted), *The Sailor Boy*,

* First appeared in the second number of the first volume of *Cornhill* (1860).

previously published—in a *Miscellany*, " *The Victoria Regia*"—in 1861, *The Islet*, and *The Attempts at Classic Metres in Quantity*, which had appeared in the *Cornhill* for December, 1863.   In these last Tennyson's delicate perception of form enabled him to reproduce for English readers the musical aroma of some of the most complex classical metres, never before so exquisitely rendered.   To them we may here add the Sapphic stanza, written for Professor Jebb's Primer of Greek Literature, in which, as he tells us, the genuine Greek cadence is preserved :

> " Faded every violet, all the roses ;
>   Gone the glorious promise, and the victim,
>   Broken in this anger of Aphrodite,
>   Yields to the victor."

It may be said of this volume that it was a series of experiments, most of which were comparative failures.   In the domestic idyll Tennyson was not working the true vein of his genius. *Enoch Arden, Aylmer's Field*, and *Sea Dreams* were subjects which Wordsworth might have treated, but the very simplicity of the themes here chosen jars with the jewelled phrasing, the ornate manner of Tennyson's setting.   The artist is too conspicuously present in his creations.

CHAPTER VI.

VERSATILITY and growth in power were the signal features of Tennyson's art and artistic life. That the author of *The Miller's Daughter* should become the author of *The Revenge*, that in the brain of the poet of *Claribel* there was hidden the poet of **The Dramas.** *Lucretius*, that *Queen Mary* and *Harold* and *Becket* belong to the same life-history as *The Lotus-Eaters*, *The Talking Oak*, and *Locksley Hall* —this is a source of natural admiration and wonder. And how plainly in his work appear the qualities and defects which mark the achievement of a scholar and recluse! That it is so may perhaps best be realised if one thinks of the events of the age in which his life was cast, and how little his poetry reflects or moralises them. Born while the shadow of Napoleon's destiny overhung Europe, in the year of Talavera, which drove Soult from Portugal, his early life was passed during the troublous close of the reign of George III. He was busy with *Claribel* and *Madeline* and *Mariana* in the year of the second French Revolution, and with *Eleänore*, *The Miller's Daughter* and *Œnone*, when the great Reform Bill was introduced by Lord Grey and a civil war almost precipitated in England. Tennyson saw the abolition of slavery, the Chartist Agitation, the rise of the Second Empire in France, the Tractarian Movement, the Indian Mutiny, the Franco-Prussian War, and many another event which profoundly stirred the hearts of men, his contemporaries. He saw the application of steam to marine and land locomotion, and all the wonders of the new reign of Science. Yet in an age so full of change, so constructive of the future, he held his own course in almost exclusive devotion to his art and to the thoughts which live and move in the deeper currents of human life and feeling, having their home not amid the passing events of the hour, but in the underworld of the soul's unquenchable desire and unearthly ideals.

There is a passage in the *Georgics* of Virgil in which the poet chooses for himself not rivalry with the majestic muse of Lucretius, nor for subject the lofty philosophic theme, but the countryside, the woods and streams. Tennyson when he speaks of Milton seems to make a similar choice.

> " Me rather all that bowery loveliness,
> The brooks of Eden mazily murmuring—"

He knew where his own strength lay, and that the future would find in him not an epic nor a dramatic poet, the priest of universal humanity, but a scrupulous artist who, in an age and country which more and more gives itself to the worship of the gods of a material world, preserved in his poetry an aloofness from such idolatry, and attached himself to the highest things of the mind and heart, making his art a mirror of the best of which his times had vision ; an artist who found no less than in the achievements of her children, in the natural beauties of his native country, in the skies and meadows, woods and waters of England, a subject near his own heart, to the interpretion of which he brought the devotion of a lover, and achieved as his reward a lover's triumph, consummate and indisputable. This also is the true point of view for the critics who are lovers of Tennyson, the point of view from which his greatness is most clearly discernible. While we stand at this point we can hardly praise too highly. But to forget that there are other points of view is to forget the true function of criticism, which is to draw distinctions, to insist upon distinctions, and to show wherein they exist. Splendidly versatile as was Tennyson's genius, the critic must say, then, he was not successful as a dramatist : two things stood in the path of his success. The genius of the time was against him ; the seclusion in which he chose to live his life was even more against him. Had any large share of the dramatic faculty fallen to his lot, these hostile influences might in some degree have been overcome ; as it was, the discerning observer marks with surprise not, indeed, his failure, but the measure of his success. I have already indicated that we need not look for our author's strength in breadth and scope of conception, in imaginative synthesis, but in the balance of his judgment, in his analytic subtlety, in his assimilative powers, in the rich accessories of his artistic detail. To the most ordinary observer the plays are evidently full of fine things ; for example, the second scene in the third act of *Queen Mary**is grandly conceived and executed, as is also the concluding scene in the play, but this cannot satisfy us ; fine things do not make, they have never yet made, a drama. We must ask, Are Tennyson's plays dramatically conceived ; that is, do they find their natural home upon the stage ? Is the action an inevitable march ? Is the characterisation vital ? Is the effect one and indivisible ? These questions cannot be answered in the affirmative, and yet in these we have only a few of the essentials

* Produced 1876, at the Lyceum.

of a drama.   The plays of Tennyson in any real
meaning of the word *drama* are failures ; we may
speak of them thus frankly.   His admirers will tell us
it is not so ; they will tell us that Tennyson is a great
dramatist, that, as George Henry Lewes said, "The
critics of to-morrow will unanimously declare Alfred
Tennyson to be a great dramatic genius."   It may be
so, but some of us, when we read the tragedy of *Mary
Tudor*, will do so more frequently in the version of
Sir Aubrey de Vere than in that of the greater poet,
and will content ourselves with saying that, although
Tennyson's dramas are indisputably failures, they are
quite as indisputably charged with high interest, with
evidences of fine literary tact, with intellectual force ;
and, above all, we will connect them with the growing
power on the part of the author of holding his hand
as he acquired a stronger because a severer style.
The years devoted by Tennyson to the composition of his dramatic works left their impress in the
nobler, more virile poetry of his later life.

Harold, Becket, and *Queen Mary** are studies of great
crises in the history of the English race.   Their interest is not merely individual, it is also national.   In
each the conflicting forces of English national life are
represented in the persons of prominent men and
women, outstanding historical figures of the time.
The tragedy in each life is a scene in the great
drama of the development of England.   The tragedy
of Saxon Harold, dead at the feet of Norman William,
marked a crisis which seemed to bode for England a
bitter future, but it proved the beginning of her greatness.   In the tragedy of Becket, the struggle of the
Church, the champion of the people's rights against

* "This trilogy of plays," said the author, "portrays the
making of England."

the Crown, is represented in the person of that great churchman and of his king. Once more, what seemed ominous for the future was proved by the future the opening-day of English freedom. In *Queen Mary* the issue involves both the spiritual and temporal life of England. Shall the nation guide its own destinies, take its own counsel in matters ecclesiastical, as in civil, or do homage to a foreign power and accept the decrees of Rome? Here, again, the cause of liberty rises triumphant from its own ashes, and the darkest hour is seen to be only the hour before the dawn. Throughout these dramas the idea of a Providence in history is the ruling idea in Tennyson's mind, a Providence that shapes the nation's ends, let kings and statesmen rough-hew them how they will.

Harold, called by the author his "Tragedy of Doom," a play which mingles, as De Vere said, an epic spirit with its dramatic form, was dedicated to Lord Lytton, the son of the Lord Lytton who had attacked Tennyson in the satire of *The New Timon*. The old quarrel was thus healed, and in the introductory sonnet to *Harold* the hate-healing influences of time are glanced at, and the blossoming of unexpected good out of the heart of conflict and of evil.

There is much in *Harold*, as there is much in *Queen Mary*, to praise; the movement is more rapid, the action predominates over the dialogue and the analysis of emotions to a greater degree than in the earlier play; but no such interest as attaches to the person of Mary is present in it, and thus *Harold* falls shorter of success. There is little reason to believe that if represented on the stage this play could long hold a place among English dramas whose reappearance is always welcome.

In *Becket*,* as in *Queen Mary*, Tennyson, though he attains no dramatic success, creates striking characters in the persons of the stern Ecclesiastic and the unhappy Rosamond. Few readers can fail to be impressed by these powerful studies—studies of real insight and force. They redeem Tennyson's dramatic work and preserve our interest in it despite all the faults and weaknesses, which, regarding it as a whole, are too palpably betrayed. *Harold* cannot rank with either in poetical strength. The *Falcon*, produced at St. James' Theatre in December, 1879,† is a light, unambitious, fanciful piece, in which the plot, borrowed from the story of Sir Federigo, told by Boccaccio in the ninth novel of the fifth day of the *Decameron*, gains nothing in the new dramatic setting. The humour of the *Falcon* is without point, and the element of romance in the original has melted away in the new version. In *The Cup*, produced at the Lyceum in January, 1881,‡ Tennyson was happier in subject, as well as treatment, and achieved a deserved and unequivocal success. The story, short and tragic, is derived from Plutarch's *De Mulierum Virtutibus*. The interest is centred in few characters, the action proceeds rapidly, and the catastrophe is impressive and pathetic. In this brief drama the author approached very near the production of a play that might have held the stage. He seemed to be progressing in that knowledge of effects and that management of situations without which dramas may be written for the reader, but cannot hold the attention of the spectator. But from unequivocal success

* Produced at the Lyceum by Mr. Irving and Miss Ellen Terry in February, 1893.
† By Messrs. Hare and Kendal.
‡ With Miss Ellen Terry as *Camma*.

Tennyson passed to unequivocal failure once more. *The Promise of May,** written at a friend's request in 1882, was the only prose work published by the representative poet of his time. It was also his only dramatic work in which he touched upon a subject which in so many of his poems he had treated with an intensity of feeling and a delicacy of judgment unsurpassed by any other poet—the problem of the relation between Faith, the daughter of the Heart, and Science; the daughter of the Head. In his dramatic presentation of that problem in its social aspects Tennyson's judgment failed him. Whether intentional or not—and we know on the author's own authority that it was unintentional†—the conclusion inevitably offers itself that out of agnosticism must proceed social ruin, that the loss of religion is the beginning of anarchy. The thesis, in itself perhaps legitimate, is enforced illogically and through an offensive situation. The dramatic instinct is absent from the play as a whole, and we need not wonder that critics, no less than people, felt that it was unworthy of its great author.

It was a happy circumstance that in his last essay in drama Tennyson turned again to a world of old romance. *The Foresters*, an English woodland piece, though slight in texture, possesses the true Tennysonian charm. The plot is that of one of the best-known midland tales, told in the spirited ballad, *A Lytel Geste of Robyn Hood*. The atmosphere is the atmosphere of *As You Like It*. There breathes through it the poet's love of England and English traditions and English folk, and in the forest walks there lurks no concealed problem of modern life. An idyllic

---

* It ran for five weeks at the Globe Theatre.
† See biography above, p. 34.

masque, it recalls to the senses the glad sights and sounds of natural country life, and mingles with them the dream-like enchantment of a legend that recounts a merry, roguish life lived long ago. In this romantic pastoral Tennyson's dramatic essays found a fitting and fortunate conclusion.

There can be no more striking passage in the history of poetry than that which puts on record the fruitage of Tennyson's genius in old age. Few even among thoughtful critics conceived of his **Ballads and** dramatic period as other than a day of de-**Other Poems.** cline, filled with experiments in an uncon-**1880.** genial form by one who had already exhausted his best powers in the work that lay behind him. Nothing more was expected of Tennyson, the book seemed naturally and not unworthily closed, nor was there need to await further development ere assigning to him his place among the poets of his race and country. Yet in the drama he had lost and found himself. Out of the heart of failure there blossomed a marvellous success, the more marvellous, perhaps, because unlooked for. The *Ballads* of 1880 had a vigour, a breadth, a movement surpassing any previous volume. The pulse of action, the spirit of true dramatic art, beat strongly in poems free at last from all traces of daintiness, of superfine graces. The very music breathed a nobler air and moved to manlier measures. The Monologue, a form doubtless suggested by Browning's example, prevails, and is nowhere used even by Browning with greater ease or finer talent for rapid effects. In *The Revenge** and in *The Defence of Lucknow* we have

* The closeness with which Tennyson followed his authority—Raleigh—in his account of the fight between the Revenge and a

ballads comparable with any in English ; in *Columbus*
a stirring force of passion and passion-matching language ; in the dialect poems, *The Northern Cobbler* and
The Village Wife, a powerful realism; in *De Profundis*
a deep-reaching philosophy, for which it will be in
vain to look in the poetry of twenty years previous.
A full and grave maturity shines in the verse of
Tennyson's closing years.

The *Ballads and Other Poems* were inscribed to the
poet's grandson, another Alfred Tennyson, then a
year and a half old:

> " Crazy with laughter and babble and earth's new wine."

In addition to the poems already mentioned, the
volume contained *The First Quarrel, Rizpah, Sir John
Oldcastle, Lord Cobham, The Sisters, In the Children's
Hospital, A Prefatory Sonnet*, contributed to the first
number of *The Nineteenth Century*, edited by Tennyson's friend, Mr. Knowles ; *Sonnets* to W. H. Brookfield and to Victor Hugo, and a sonnet entitled *Montenegro;* translations, *The Battle of Brunanburh* and
Achilles over the Trench, the lines *To the Princess
Frederica of Hanover*, the lines for Sir John Franklin's cenotaph in Westminster, and the lines *To Dante*.
The only other poem not mentioned above which was
printed in this volume was *The Voyage of Maeldune*.
Maildun is the hero of an ancient Celtic romance.*

" navy of Spain " is only matched by that of Wolfe in his famous
verses on *The Burial of Sir John Moore*. Much of Tennyson's
ballad, save for the metrical arrangement, is almost word for
word taken from Raleigh's pamphlet. See *A Report of the Truth
of the Fight about the Iles of Azores this last sommer, betwixt the
Revenge, one of her Majesty's shippes, and an Armada of the King
of Spaine*. (Reprinted by Edward Arber, 1871.)

* See Joyce's *Ancient Celtic Romances*.

The story belongs to the group of tales of sea voyages of which *St. Brendan* is the best known. The marvels seen by Maildun and his men are only partially related in Tennyson's ballad, and the tone of the original is lost, but the fantastic imaginative splendour of the legend could hardly be hidden even in its modern dress.

The *Tiresias* volume was inscribed to Robert Browning, and strikes the personal as its predominant note. In the dedication to Fitzgerald, the translator of *Omar Khayyam*, and in the epilogue which speaks of his death ; in the teaching of the *Ancient Sage*, where in the person of the seer Tennyson sums the beliefs of his own life ; in the prefatory poem to his brother's volume of Sonnets, published after the author's death—in all these we may read the veteran poet's sense of an end not very far off :

Tiresias and Other Poems. 1885.

> " Remembering all the golden hours,
> Now silent, and so many dead."

While they retain the original Tennysonian sweetness of phrase, the poems in this book are fuller of interest, deeper of tone, chaster of expression than those of his youth. *Tiresias* is another piece of classic sculpture for the gallery in which *Lucretius, Ulysses,* and *Tithonus* had already place. *Balin and Balan,* an unexpected addition to the *Idylls,* was written as an introduction to *Merlin and Vivien. The Dead Prophet* is a characteristic, indignant, passionate remonstrance against "the scandal and the cry" which in these latter days are wont to follow upon the biographer's revelations of the private life of public men. Here, there is little doubt, by the *Dead Prophet* is meant

Tennyson's old friend, Carlyle ; and the profanation of his name by curious, scandal-loving readers, no less than the opportunity given them by the biographer, is the subject of the poet's savagest scorn and invective.

To me *The Ancient Sage*＊is the poem of by far the greatest interest in this volume, for can we not say that we have here the authentic, outspoken expression of the poet's creed, the first and last word in his confession of faith ?   I have already spoken of that creed as the creed of the higher emotions. I may say of the faith in his own words, that it is " a faith beyond the forms of faith."   The spiritual energies of his nature flowed into no mould of traditional doctrine, but they were the inspiration of his solemn visions and prophetic hopes.   In the *Two Voices*, the poem of his youth which most closely corresponds to this of his age, the same problems are presented, but presented in a clever, logical texture, whose threads are finely drawn, but whose conclusions leave us cold.   In the later poem, more vigorous and more dramatic in conception, from out a life's experience, from out a poet's heart of fire springs the living word of an intense and secure conviction.   If the future hold for men an increase of knowledge which may warrant an increase of hope, then, indeed, "they will look back on Tennyson as no belated dreamer, but as a leader who, in the darkest hour of the world's thought, would not despair of the destiny of man.   They will look back on him as Romans looked back on that unshaken Roman who purchased at its full price the field of Cannæ, on which at that hour the victorious Hannibal lay encamped with his Carthaginian host." †

＊ " The whole poem," said the author, " is very personal."
† F. W. H. Myers, *Tennyson as Prophet.*

I

The results of Tennyson's studies in the drama may be seen in his heightened power in dealing with such situations as those of *The Wreck, The Flight*, and that most tragic of any in Tennyson's poetry, or, indeed, possible, in *Despair*. The lines *To Virgil* are the expression of a life-long affection for a poet with whom, perhaps, Tennyson had more in common than any other, while the lines entitled *Frater Ave atque Vale* convey to English readers something of the beauty and pathos with which Catullus clothes the emotion of a wistful regret. *The Charge of the Heavy Brigade* falls short of the earlier battle-piece, and is less stirring than the account from which it is taken ; but in *Hands all Round*, originally published in 1852, the patriotic ardour of England's most patriotic poet is bravely and nobly sung. The remaining poems published in this volume are the epitaphs on Gordon, Caxton, and Lord Stratford de Redclyffe, *Freedom, To the Duke of Argyll, Helen's Tower* (written at the request of his friend, Lord Dufferin), *To H. R. H. Princess Beatrice, Early Spring, To-Morrow* (an Irish tale in dialect), *The Spinster's Sweet Arts*, and the lines (subsequently) entitled *Poets and their Bibliographies*. In the last-mentioned verses Tennyson glances at the poetic methods of Virgil and of Horace, methods similar to his own in the ceaseless labour of the file, and resents, with some impatience, the attention of the critics. Doubtless that impatience was in no slight degree due to the parallelisms adduced by them from other writers to many of Tennyson's own thoughts and phrases, and to the implied suggestion that his assimilative powers were conspicuously greater than his inventive. Tennyson was indisputably a great borrower, but he borrowed as only genius bor-

rows, and had he not repudiated with somewhat unnecessary heat and protestation the charge of pla-
giarism, the critic might not have found so keen a
delight in pressing home the charge.

The greater part of the 1886 volume was occupied
by the text of the drama (partly prose), *The Promise of
May*, and, with the exception of the poem which gave
its name to the book, there was little of interest among the new verses. *The Fleet*
and *The Ode on the Opening of the Indian* **Locksley**
and Colonial Exhibition may be passed with- **Hall, Sixty**
out comment. The later *Locksley Hall* is in **Years After,**
etc. 1886.
part a philippic against the moral degrada- **Demeter and**
tion, the moral infirmities of the age, a **Other Poems.**
subject to which the poet returned, but **1889.**
with a larger *motif*, in *Vastness*, published
in *Demeter and Other Poems* in 1889. The
seriousness of their outlook upon life, the intensity
of their feeling, the sincerity and depth of these
poems harmonises with the fuller music, the less
daintily wrought manner of Tennyson's later and
stronger style. The impeachment, passionate though
it be, in the later *Locksley Hall*, of the littleness of
man, is full of stern justice—

> " However we brave it out, we men are a little breed."
>
> (*Maud.*)

In *Vastness* the poet makes the pathetic comparison
between the best and the worst in man, between his
aspirations and his achievements, between the narrow,
circumscribed boundaries of his little life and the infinite ocean that stretches away on all sides of his
island-spot of earth. Vain, paltry, and meaningless,
the history of the human race dwarfed in the immen-

sities of boundless times and spaces becomes no more than

" a trouble of ants in the light of a million million of suns."

Here as elsewhere in Tennyson's poetry the only refuge from permanent intellectual confusion is found in the conviction that the soul and God stand sure, that

" the dead are not dead, but alive."

If the human interest in the youthful poems of Tennyson was slight, the later are almost overcharged with emotion. Colour and melody and fragrance were exchanged for anxious questionings upon the deepest problems of life and death, and in some poems so intensely fraught were they with human feeling, that the passionate expression was almost painfully affecting.

In *Owd Roä*, a rustic study that belongs to the same class as *The Northern Farmer*, in *Forlorn, Happy, The Ring* and *Romney's Remorse*, the passion of sympathy with suffering hearts thrills in the verse till it touches the infinite of pathos, while in *Merlin and The Gleam* and *Crossing the Bar* even the flute-like sweetness of the youthful lyrics is surpassed, and the voice of the poet-seer reaches in these poems an accent of sacred and thrilling impressiveness.

In *Demeter and Persephone* we have a poem equal to anything that the author ever gave us, a poem that with *Lucretius, Ulysses,* and the other classical studies, will keep pace with the years, nor ever suffer wrong at the hands of time.

Akbar's Dream, the veteran poet's last volume, was in the press at the time of his death, and was pub-

lished but a few weeks later. Though it contained
nothing to increase, it sustained to the full
his reputation, and fitly closed the long and
bright career. *The Death of Œnone*, dedi- **The Death of**
cated in a new and difficult verse-form to   **Œnone,**
Dr. Jowett, the Master of Balliol, is a con- **Akbar's**
tinuation and conclusion of the *Œnone* of   **Dream, and**
1832. The blank verse freely and admir-   **other Poems.**
ably handled in this poem, as in *St. Tele-* **1892.**
machus and in *Akbar's Dream*, is the stronger,
less opulent verse of his later life, learnt in his dramatic period—less ornate but no less musical than
that of the *Morte d'Arthur* and *The Princess*.

    St. Telemachus may be taken as a companion study
to *St. Simeon Stylites*, the record of "a deed that woke
the world," marking the contrast between the fruitful
influences of a single good action and the barren vir-
tues of a life of asceticism. In *Akbar's Dream* Tennyson touches yet again upon the old matters of the
meaning and the issues of life, and pleads, as in *The
Ancient Sage*, for a "faith beyond the forms of faith,"
a religion of charity and hope. The *Hymn to the Sun*,
with which it closes, exhibits all the fine qualities of
his poetic workmanship—

" Once again thou flamest heavenward, once again we see thee rise.
Every morning is thy birthday, gladdening human hearts and eyes.
Every morning here we greet it, bowing lowly down before thee,
Thee the Godlike, thee the changeless in thine ever-changing skies.

" Shadow-maker, shadow-slayer, arrowing light from clime to clime,
Hear thy myriad laureates hail thee monarch in their woodland
    rhyme.
Warble bird, and open flower, and men below the dome of azure
Kneel adoring Him the Timeless in the flame that measures
    Time !"

Of the remaining shorter poems in the book, *The Dawn* and *The Making of Man* return to the problem of the moral progress of the race, while in *Faith*, *The Silent Voices*, and *God and the Universe* we have the last words of the poet to his fellows and to his own soul on the threshold of the unknown future—

" ' Spirit, nearing yon dark portal at the limit of thy human state,
   Fear not thou the hidden purpose of that Power which alone is great,
   Nor the myriad world, His shadow, nor the silent Opener of the Gate.' "

CHAPTER VII.

THE death of Alfred Tennyson seemed almost in a sense to bring the history of English poetry to a close. He had outlived all the great poets whose inspiration was drawn from the quickening, dilating forces of the first quarter of the century ; he had long dominated without a rival the poetic realm in the succeeding and quieter epoch ; he had been for fifty years the acknowledged chief of the poet clan, so perfect a representative of English thought, so closely identified with English ideals, as to be looked upon as the natural voice of the nation's noblest spiritual and intellectual life. Tennyson resumed in himself as its highest type the civilization of the Victorian era. And summing as he did in his own person and in his work the gains of the English race throughout its long and splendid history of a thousand years, he must stand for us, as he will assuredly stand for all the future, as the poetic heir of England's aristocratic, intellectual, and heroic traditions. No such inheritance remains for his successors. The new is the age of democracy, and its poets must quarry their marbles from the virgin rock ; Tennyson built with material that was already shaped, and lay ready to his hand. His inspiration came from the past ; upon the past the eye of his poetic imagination was fixed ; in the traditions of the old masters he exercised himself, and in their schools he learnt the secrets of his art. He was of the order of poets who sum up, who bring to an end, while his friend and contemporary, Browning, was of another order—a pioneer poet, an explorer of new lands, the first adventurer in untilled poetic territory. And for this reason, perhaps, it may be justly said that Tennyson belongs to the history of language rather than to the history of thought. He was a polished speaker; master of an exquisite style ; he was not a natural orator, whose words spring forth to wing the impassioned message of the heart. Consider the contemporaries of his youth and of his age, Wordsworth and Browning. Here were poets, charged, it would seem, with oracles for men, but poets the burden of whose message lay heavy upon them, often indeed out-weighted or out-ran their immediate power of utterance. Wordsworth not infrequently found verse unsustainable, and Browning stammered in his haste to speak. But when from either source the word came to be spoken, it was abundantly evident that the revealing prophet was at our doors. Tennyson's revelation, as far as there was a revelation, was personal, the revelation of his own heart. Its sorrows and joys and hopes and aspirations—these were the real themes of his verse ; and because these sorrows and joys and hopes and aspirations were also ours, their perfect expression was a wonder and a delight to us. Here were *Carmina*, verses that might be crooned as "charms" over a heart-dissolving grief to ease its pain, or lilted when language ran to music for very gladness of spirit, or recalled to characterize with magical fitness some natural scene, or to sum in telling phrase a daily experience of every human life. "I sing myself," he might have said with truth, " and in these transcripts of my heart and mind you will find your own."

I have said that in the poetry of Tennyson the past

of English tradition is resumed ; in it the voice of the poet's own time is also heard, for he was, through half a century, the spokesman, the chief speaker of the English race. If in his early volumes, like Keats, he cared only for beauty and languorous melody, cared only for art as art, for poetry as a source of exquisite sensation, when the genius of the world had taken away the veil from his eyes and he saw life plain, his verse took wider range and graver accent. But while he came to represent the thought of his day, and was in a measure too a prophet of the things that were to be, disclosing the tendencies that ripen in due course into creeds, Tennyson never outstepped the intellectual and ethical traditions of his age and country. The English gentleman and scholar are not far off even in poems that breathe revolt, like *Maud*, or like the later *Locksley Hall* "curse the social forms" that delay the day of freedom and of truth. When Science, emboldened by her successes, threatened the gates of the time-honoured citadel of faith, he declined any longer to hymn her praise ; when the dreams of the enthusiast for a new heaven and a new earth seemed about to take shape in revolution, he spoke of law, of freedom that slowly broadens down, and of the red fool-fury of the Seine. Tennyson kept with the main body of English opinion, and was its champion. Thus only in a minor sense was he a shaping or compelling power in social or intellectual development, in the enfranchisement of mind. We may speak more truly of him as a poetic chronicler of the mental life of his time.

A chronicler of the mental life of his time, this we must call him, but we must add, a chronicler who was a consummate artist. And success in poetry of this kind, though far indeed from success in the highest

kind, is neither easy nor the product of every generation.   To chronicle the best ideas of any generation,
it is necessary that one should feel inspired by them ;
that one should find them a source of real power ; that
one should estimate them as of the first importance,
and even find pleasure in them.   But this is not possible for all men ; it is rarely possible for the poet whose
penetrativeness, moral sagacity, and far, sure gaze dis-
close to him the true meanings and real issues of
things.   Such poets, often in advance of their generation, are more likely, save at epochs of rare inspiration, to find the times out of joint, the predominant
current of ideas uninspiring, and the world into which
they have been born an unweeded garden that runs to
seed.   The poetical spirit is an exacting spirit.   A sympathetic spirit, you will say.   Yes, sympathetic, but
exacting.   The needs of Tennyson's nature were such
that he found his age satisfying ; its attitude of mind
was his own attitude ; and thus it was that, as the
chronicler of its mental life, he gained acceptance.
Like Pope, he found the tersest expression for the
dominant moods, the ruling ideas of his time, and became the historian of contemporary thought.   Tennyson, like Pope, took the surest path to immortality ; and
when it is said that he belongs to the history of
language rather than to the history of thought, it is
meant that, thoughtful as he was, and passionate with
the warm human passions of a poet, neither did he
present in his work the full features of the age in
which he lived, nor had he for that age a message of
moment.   Like his age, he was himself in doubt about
many things, and had no unifying conception, no
harmonising hypothesis to offer.   On the minds of his
own contemporaries Tennyson exerted no intellectual

pressure, such as Carlyle exerted, nor did he awaken dulled or sleeping chords in the spiritual life by such strong, animating music as Browning's. His office was to minister to the general mass of readers by holding up the mirror in which their most intimate thoughts and feelings were reflected with charming simplicity, with marvellous exactness.

Tennyson, then, was the spokesman of the English race in an era of art-renaissance, and he that runs may read the cardinal notes of his art—its assimilative power and the *cura et diligentia*, the unwearied devotion he gave to it. Of that assimilative faculty which made his verse so full-flavoured with reminiscences, so dear to scholars, so pleasant on the ears of those familiar with the poetry of an elder day, more needs not to be written. Not a little of what has been written barely conceals the smile of irony beneath the veil of praise. So much that was beautiful, so little that was new! And indeed many of Tennyson's poems are a veritable *cento*, a patchwork from Greek and Italian looms. Is it a cause for censure, you will ask, or must one find in these reminiscences an unqualified delight? To me, and I think I need make no defence of myself, the power possessed by Tennyson of reproducing in his verse the music of strains long familiar, of recalling in phrase and echo the best beauties of poets of long ago — to me this power seems an altogether admirable and delightful power. I cannot wish away a line of his poetry that displays it. To quarrel with *Lucretius* because it is built of materials taken from the *De Rerum Natura*, with passages like that fine one descriptive of

" The gods who haunt
The lucid interspace of world and world"—

to quarrel with such a phrase as that used by Cleopatra in *The Dream of Fair Women*—"I died a queen"—because it is a paraphrase of a fine expression used by Horace of Cleopatra,

> "invidens
> *Privata* deduci superbo
> Non humilis mulier triumpho,"

or with the stanza in which Helen of Troy, in the same poem, cries :

> "I would the white cold heavy-plunging foam,
>   Whirl'd by the wind, had roll'd me deep below,
>   Then when I left my home,"

because if we turn to the sixth *Iliad* we shall find the original—to quarrel with such a line as "This way and that dividing the swift mind," because it is a translation of Virgil's "Atque animum nunc huc celerem, nunc dividit illuc"—to make a quarrel upon causes like these would be to exhibit a temper unworthy of one bidden to the feasts of the gods. Tennyson is indeed full of translations and reminiscences ; he was a plagiarist, as Virgil and Spenser and Milton and Shelley were plagiarists, but a plagiarist of less assurance. If one has a touch of disquietude in the matter, it is due to this lack of assurance in him. A frank expression of indebtedness to his peers of former time could have detracted nothing from his fame. His plagiarisms, if we must call them so, are likely to trouble us less than his anxiety to disprove them. It might well be replied to a critic who complained of these plagiarisms, that the hints taken by Tennyson were not hints given to him alone ; it might be replied that it is too late for criticism to complain of a poetical method honoured in the practice of the best poets of the ancient as of the modern world ; a poetical method which gave us *Lycidas* and *Adonais* and many another lovely poem beside, recalling words sweet on the ears of men long centuries ago, fragrant with the infinite associations and memories that cling around the speech of Homer and Theocritus, of Horace and Virgil and Catullus. If Tennyson failed to be always powerful, he seldom failed to be interesting. And he seldom failed to be interesting because of his close acquaintance with the best writings of the ancients as well as of the moderns, with the masterpieces of Greek art, with the wisest sayings of the philosophers—in a word, with the culture of the world. Tennyson seldom fails to be interesting because of this close acquaintanceship with "the best that has been known and thought in the world," and because his poetry abundantly displays it.

No less conspicuous in his verse than its wealth of reminiscences is the *labor limæ*, the care he devoted to it. The marks of an unwearying labour of love are plainly visible in almost every line of his poetry, whether of his youth or age. Are you curious to learn the secrets of the poetical art ? There is no poet who goes so near betraying them. There is no poet who has so frequently shown a poem upon the stocks, in process of building. In the many versions of a poem like *The Princess*, you are admitted to the studio ; you are shown the first rough draft, the elaborated sketch, the completed picture. The instinct and care for form somewhat obscured in the work of his predecessors—this instinct and care for form, which in the early years of the century had suffered temporary eclipse, were early apparent in Tennyson's poetry. The favouring gale of inspiration and the proud full

sail of Scott's and Byron's verse had seemed sufficient
to their generation, had in the eyes of their readers
left nothing to be desired. The rights of form were
reasserted in the poetry of Coleridge and of Keats,
and the earliest essays of Tennyson in verse foretold
the character of his art, whose final aim was only
reached in a laboured perfection of finish. Passing by
the boyish verses of 1827, indicative of little more than
the presence of strong poetical ambition, the poems of
1832, though still without any grasp of reality, proved
the advent of a writer with undoubted skill in words,
with music in his brain. The feminine daintiness, the
absence of all intensity, of the masculine voice, was
the least hopeful sign of his early work, and seemed
to indicate little real power behind the picture-music,
behind the delicate web of words little real breadth of
poetic imagination.

Even his admirers in those early days would have
welcomed verses that betrayed less anxious correct-
ness, less highly wrought beauty of diction.   The
results appeared due to assiduous culture rather than
to native strength, and it seemed more than doubtful
that the ground could produce a richer or fuller crop.
And indeed in Tennyson there is no such spontaneity as
amazes us in Keats, there is no such " sweet slipping
movement " as in Spenser.   In his more ornate and
decorative verse the artist is too conspicuous ; we admire the skill of the workman more than the quality
of the work.   But let this be as it may, the admirable
poise of his faculties remains to him.   Tennyson's nature was finely balanced, and he rises far above the
poets whose emotion is merely musical.   In the firm
balance of his nature, strong as his artistic instincts
were, in the firm balance of his nature the artist rare-

ly outran the man. The subordination of the matter
to the form is less and less apparent in the succeeding
volumes of his poetry. How different is he in this
from the poets of to-day! The latter-day poets assure us, and the latter-day critics likewise, that art is
all in all, that poetry is style. We have critics not a
few who regard sweetness and strength as attributes of
style, and are ignorant that they are not attributes of
style, but attributes of mind and character, expressed
in style. How fortunate that in Tennyson the balance
was preserved—the balance between the emotions and
the will, between the heart and head, between what is
said and the manner of saying it! Because Tennyson's style is the expression of character, and not a
palace of emptiness, because he is throughout sane
and everywhere guided by a wise knowledge of the
poet's craft, he is a true and great artist. To compare
him with his successors is to gauge the true measure
of his performance. With his successors the balance
is lost, and when a man or a poet has nothing to say,
to think that it can be said finely, what hallucination!
To think that the accent of freshness can be obtained
by torturing language, that the great effects in
poetry, the effects of Sophocles, of Dante and of
Shakespere, their intense significance, can be account-
ed for by a skill in words, an artisan's dexterity! The
great effects in poetry are straightforward effects ; the
great effects of poetry are those in which the emphasis
of expression corresponds to some emphasis of
thought, some intensity of feeling. And it is because
in Tennyson the artist rarely outran the man that we
have confidence in him. If you ask me for the secret of Tennyson's hold upon the mind of his generation, I shall answer you with assurance that it lies in

his accent of sincerity, it lies in his literary integrity, in a wholesomeness in his art. For this integrity we value him, and for this the future will value him. The poetry that cannot make for beauty and grace and harmony in human life, since it has practically no bearing upon life at all, such poetry is as vain a thing as the jargon of the critics who commend it, and as transitory.

As the poetic artist of the nineteenth century who best knew his own limitations, and in whom the balance, the compromise between form and matter in which poetry consists, is best preserved, as poetic chronicler of the mental life of his time, and as the interpreter of that spirit of intellectual hesitation which was characteristic of his contemporaries and leads to eclecticism in matters of faith, Tennyson will be remembered. And he will be remembered, although the greatness of his work must be looked for elsewhere than in its scope or imaginative power. The large comprehensiveness, the wide-eyed vision that takes in the spectacle of human life in its vast whole and in the complexity of its parts, this did not belong to him, nor did he share in all the joys and sorrows of mankind. Tennyson's lyrics sing the joys and sorrows of English folk ; he was above and before all the poet of England, the best lover among her poet-sons. For the rest his attitude was retrospective, and when his fancy ranged, the land of its dearest romance lay in the heroic past. "It was written," he said of that exquisite lyric, *Tears, idle Tears*, "at Tintern Abbey, when the woods were all yellowing with autumn, seen through the ruined windows. It is what I have always felt as a boy, and what as a boy I called the passion of the past. And it is always with me now; it is the distance that charms me in the landscape, the picture and the past, and not the immediate to-day in which I move."*

To the colour-school of English poetry, to.the lineage of the poets of romance, Tennyson belonged. He did not care to draw in outline, to impress by the naked grandeur of conception. From the first, like Keats, he held that poetry should surprise by a fine excess, by a richness and profusion of beauties, that it should be a veritable cloth of gold. From the first he was for such accessories as should lead the senses captive and enthrall the reader with infinite vistas of delight. Yet his is not the bewildering charm of Spenser's fairyland, the luxuriant undergrowth of beauty in enchanted forests. Rather it is the ordered beauty of a noble English garden, of the English landscape that he loved so well. It was said by Wordsworth of Tennyson : " He is not much in sympathy with what I should myself most value in my attempts—viz., the spirituality with which I have endeavoured to view the material universe, and the moral relations under which I have wished to exhibit its most ordinary appearances." It is true that Tennyson was not much in sympathy with such attempts. Few poets indeed have kept with Nature a closer companionship ; her sights and sounds were his most familiar friends. To this close companionship we owe the skilful appropriateness of his backgrounds and the delicate accuracy of their form and colour. Tennyson observed, and observed narrowly ; observed indeed with something akin to the trained scientific eye. There is no need to adduce from his poetry passages

* Cf. *The Ancient Sage*—" On me, when boy, there came what then I call'd," etc.

to prove how loving and how close an eye he kept
upon the world around him.   Readers of Tennyson do
not need to be reminded of such touches as meet us,
for example, in a phrase like that descriptive of the
yew tree answering a random stroke,

> " With fruitful cloud and living smoke"—

such illustrative touches as meet us here,

> " Why lingereth she to clothe her heart with love,
> Delaying as the tender ash delays
> To clothe herself when all the woods are green."

Those who are acquainted with the poetry of
Tennyson know that it is a mine of such wealth ; they
know that he was a true lover of Nature, of her trees
and flowers and waters, and her skies and silent stars.
They know too that he was a bird lover, and that
there are few English birds that have not found mention in his verse.   But for all this Wordsworth was
right.   Tennyson did not, in the same degree as
Wordsworth, "see into the life of things," and when
the elder poet's imagination would have kindled into
the flame of unquenchable poesy, Tennyson remained a
draughtsman and a colourist, but the draughtsman
and colourist who is perhaps the greatest of English
idyllic poets.   His admirers have much to tell us of
his greatness as an epic, of his greatness as a dramatic poet.   It will be sufficient for us to maintain
an attitude of admiration, but an attitude of admiration qualified by some acquaintance with the great
epics and the great dramas of the world.   The truth
is, that Tennyson's versatility is a source of critical
error, just as Byron's brilliancy and versatility were a
source of critical error.   Possessed of a finer judg-

ment but a narrower imaginative range and less strength than Byron, Tennyson essayed, like Byron, song and idyl, epic and drama. Tennyson essayed all these, and on the whole essayed them more successfully than Byron. But as it is merely idle to speak of Byron as a great dramatic or even a great epic poet, it is idle to speak of Tennyson as having achieved greatness in these, the highest departments of the poetic art. The creative artists are few, and though Tennyson was not one of them, though his real power lay in the adornment of familiar themes, in the re-clothing of familiar feelings, so strong and brilliant a writer, so careful and so fine an artist could hardly fail of success, even in fields unsuited to his genius. By reason of his versatility, Tennyson is a difficult poet to characterize. But however his critics may differ upon other points, they will be at one upon this, that his idyllic poems possess a singular and vivid charm, and they will be at one upon this also, that in great measure they possess this charm because in no other poems have the features of English landscape found so admiring and so faithful an interpreter. Here is a poet in whose dealings with Nature there is no mysticism, who sees in her only what all may see, and yet for whom Nature, as seen by the scientific eye, has suffered no loss of beauty, no diminution of her poetic stimulus. For many poets Nature has been the dwelling-place of innumerable spirits, passionful creatures of the flood and field, spirits of forest and stream, lush meadow and gray hill-side. These half-human, half-divine shapes flitted by them in the music of the wind, babbled in the rivulet, or held revel in the cool green depths of their long sea-halls. Upon the minds of their less imaginative readers the appeal made by the

fantastic dreams of such poets was necessarily slight.
The nature-poetry of Wordsworth required for its due
appreciation even a more active and certainly a more
spiritual imagination. In Tennyson's world the demand for any activity of imagination on the part of
the reader is unapparent; his pictures satisfy the
senses and fill the eye. Mark the sharpness of outline, the lucidity and completeness of this, the description of the island in *Enoch Arden*:

> " The mountain wooded to the peak, the lawns
>   And winding glades high up like ways to Heaven,
>   The slender coco's drooping crown of plumes,
>   The lightning flash of insect and of bird,
>   The lustre of the long convolvuluses
>   That coil'd around the stately stems, and ran
>   Ev'n to the limit of the land, the glows
>   And glories of the broad belt of the world ;
>   All these he saw ; but what he fain had seen
>   He could not see, the kindly human face,
>   Nor ever hear a kindly voice, but heard
>   The myriad shriek of wheeling ocean-fowl,
>   The league-long roller thundering on the reef,
>   The moving whisper of huge trees that branch'd
>   And blossom'd in the zenith, or the sweep
>   Of some precipitous rivulet to the wave,
>   As down the shore he ranged, or all day long
>   Sat often in the seaward-gazing gorge,
>   A shipwreck'd sailor waiting for a sail :
>   No sail from day to day, but every day
>   The sunrise broken into scarlet shafts
>   Among the palms and ferns and precipices ;
>   The blaze upon the waters to the east ;
>   The blaze upon his island overhead ;
>   The blaze upon the waters to the west ;
>   Then the great stars that globed themselves in Heaven;
>   The hollower-bellowing ocean, and again
>   The scarlet shafts of sunrise—but no sail."

In the poetry of Tennyson Nature is suffused in a mellow light ; she is at peace, charged with a message of rich but quiet beauty. He sought her society for soothing influences, for her infinite lore and her celestial calm, not, as did Wordsworth, to find a presence that disturbed him with the joy of elevated thoughts.

But just as the reader of Wordsworth will feel the absence of spirituality in Tennyson's transcripts of nature, the readers of Browning will miss in him the spiritual fire by which that poet discovers in nature and life and art not the powers that make for rest and peace, but for restless and upward strife ; they will miss in him the spiritual energy which finds the best hopes of the race in the thought

> " that man is hurled
> From change to change unceasingly,
> His soul's wings never furled."

For Tennyson not passion, not aspirations and enthusiasms are man's guiding angels, but love and duty and allegiance ; and while he seeks for quiet waters and for harbours of refuge for the soul upon the voyage of life, Browning " is glad to know the brine salt on his lips and the large air again," and finds invigorating influences and infinite encouragement in the midst of toil and storm ; *quædam divina voluptas*, a certain divine gladness in the wind and reeling seas.

You will seek in vain in Tennyson for the larger elements, the far horizons of thought, the wide and gracious spaces, the unimagined depths, the austere yet tranquillising sadness, the severe unbroken calm, the magnanimities of the greatest poetry. You will seek in vain for the presence of the higher imagination. The popular verdict will not have it so. It will

affirm that none of the qualities of the highest poetry
are absent from Tennyson's verse. But for those
acquainted, however slightly, with the literature of
the world's past, passage after passage will rise to
mind, passage after passage beside which there is
nothing of Tennyson's to be placed. Take one from
a contemporary :

> " The centre-fire heaves underneath the earth,
>   And the earth changes like a human face ;
>   The molten ore bursts up among the rocks,
>   Winds into the stone's heart, outbranches bright
>   In hidden mines, spots barren river-beds,
>   Crumbles into fine sand where sunbeams bask—
>   God joys therein.   The wroth sea's waves are edged
>   With foam, white as the bitter lip of hate,
>   When, in the solitary waste, strange groups
>   Of young volcanos come up, cyclops-like,
>   Staring together with their eyes on flame—
>   God tastes a pleasure in their uncouth pride.
>   Then all is still ; earth is a wintry clod :
>   But spring-wind, like a dancing psaltress, passes
>   Over its breast to waken it, rare verdure
>   Buds tenderly upon rough banks, between
>   The withered tree-roots and the cracks of frost,
>   Like a smile striving with a wrinkled face ;
>   The grass grows bright, the boughs are swollen with blooms
>   Like chrysalids impatient for the air,
>   The shining dorrs are busy, beetles run
>   Along the furrows, ants make their ado ;
>   Above, birds fly in merry flocks, the lark
>   Soars up and up, shivering for very joy ;
>   Afar the ocean sleeps ; white fishing gulls
>   Flit where the strand is purple with its tribe
>   Of nested limpets ; savage creatures seek
>   Their loves in wood and plain—and God renews
>   His ancient rapture."

I have elsewhere said that Browning was our only

representative of Christian art in an era of classical revival. And he was so because his interest centred in the individual rather than in any terrestrial future of the race, and because in the pursuit of his art, his reach exceeded his grasp, his thought outsped his expression. He passed by, and that deliberately, the possibility of perfection in a limited sphere of endeavour, preferring to follow forever the supreme unapproachable ideal. In Browning's poetry the splendid elevations alternate with the levels of indisputable prose. It was not so with Tennyson. Where inspiration failed, the labour of the artist was redoubled and the verse showed no signs of weakness. Tennyson, to use his own phrase, "respected the limitations," wrought with no material save such as he could fashion to perfection, grasped and outlined his thought with the sharp precision of one who speaks of familiar experiences, and was master of all the keys of his instrument. Tennyson clove the mark at which he aimed, but Browning's arrow, like that of the archer of ancient story, sped, in an arc of light, beyond the ken of the gazers, to be lost in the overarching heaven.

When the critic has put on record his judgments, but one part of his duty is performed. He must put on record his admiration also. And if the office of the poet were to be a minister of sweet pleasure only, I do not know that Tennyson might not be rightly judged the first of the moderns. There is no body of the century's verse wherein for ear and heart a feast of purer, more unalloyed delight is spread. And Tennyson's reward was the reward of acceptance. By the choice of his subjects as well as by the variety of his form, by the simplicity and directness of his method and by the tempered perfection of his art he made his irresistible appeal to his countrymen. Even in his rendering of an old-world story, in his treatment of a Greek myth, he satisfied the modern ear, he created the atmosphere that was the poetic breath of life to the sensitive minds of the time. In his lyrics, where he was most original, he made an almost untouched field of human feeling his own, the field of that vague, wordless autumnal sadness of the spirit, a sadness that seems to have its source in a secret sympathy with some hidden sorrow lying deep in the heart of Nature, the universal mother. Tennyson was born for acceptance as a poet ; under his transmuting touch all material became poetic. He was born for acceptance, and in his strong practical qualities, in his deep-rooted love for the heroic, as displayed in his stirring ballads of action, in his tender domesticities, as well as in his unquenchable patriotism and love of political order, he was a poet after the English heart. He may well spare to others the crowns of their deserving, the people's garland of affection will long be Tennyson's.

That from first to last in Tennyson's poetry the idea of law is paramount, that the central doctrine of his political and social creed was the doctrine of an equable progress under the reign of law—all this has been sufficiently dwelt on by the critics. His philosophy, too, has been sufficiently dwelt on, his ethical and religious teaching. One word more may be added. Of his creed, the creed of optimism, it is inevitable that the inquiry be made, Of what validity is such a creed, reached by a process unknown to logic, supported only by frail trembling desires and emotions that know not the place of their birth?

What is the poet that we should trust him, and who shall be our prophet but the man of science, the revealer of the indisputable fact? There is but one answer to these questions : We are not optimists by nature, neither are we pessimists. To the cry of despair in the poetry of the world, ofttimes an exceeding bitter cry, the heart of man responds no less than to its cry of hope—

" Surgit amari aliquid, quod in ipsis floribus angat."

To the cry of despair in the poetry of the world, let it be fully granted, the heart, indeed, responds, but from the beginning of things one thought has never found a more than momentary place in human minds, one thought has seemed to all men intolerable—that the base and selfish and unjust and craven-hearted have read the riddle of life aright ; that the battle has been and will be to these, and that its pure and merciful and brave and generous souls are the foolish and the vanquished ones of earth. This, even in the foolishness that is our only wisdom, we cannot think. And at the foundations of all poetry and philosophy to which we are accustomed to look for the awakening and the nourishment of the best and highest in man, at the foundations of all poetry and philosophy we find that they are built upon this rock of faith. We shall do well to be on the side of Plato, and of the household of the poets.

LIST OF DATES AND BIBLIOGRAPHY.

1809. Alfred, the fourth son of the Rev. George Clayton Tennyson, LL.D., and Elizabeth Fytche, was born at Somersby Rectory, in Somersby, Lincolnshire. The family consisting of eight sons (Frederick and Charles preceding Alfred) and four daughters. (George, the first-born, died in infancy.)

1811. Arthur Hallam born.

1816. Alfred entered the Grammar School at Louth.

1820. Alfred left the Grammar School at the Christmas vacation.

1826. POEMS BY TWO BROTHERS. "*Hæc nos novimus esse nihil*" (Martial). London : Printed for W. Simpkin & R. Marshall, Stationers, Hall Court, and J. & J. Jackson, Louth, MDCCCXXVII., (post-dated), pp. xii., 228. Published in two sizes, 8vo and 12mo.

1827. Notice of *Poems by Two Brothers*, in the *Literary Chronicle and Weekly Review* (May 19).

1828. Alfred and Charles Tennyson went up to Trinity College, Cambridge, whither Frederick had preceded them.

1829. TIMBUCTOO : A poem which obtained the Chancellor's medal at the Cambridge Commencement. By A. Tennyson, of Trinity College, MDCCCXXIX. Printed in the *Cambridge Chronicle* of July 10, 1829, and in the "*Prolusiones Academicæ præmis annuis dignatæ et in curia Cantabrigiensi recitatæ comitiis maximis, A. D. MDCCCXXIX. Cantabrigiæ ; typis academicis excudit Joannes Smith*, pp. 13.*" Reprinted several times in collections of "Cambridge Prize Poems."

Notice of *Timbuctoo* in *The Athenæum* (July 22).

Burlesqued by W. M. Thackeray in *The Snob* (Cambridge), pp. 18–21.

Reviewed in *The Athenæum* (July 22).

1830. POEMS, CHIEFLY LYRICAL, by Alfred Tennyson. London : Effingham Wilson, Royal Exchange, Cornhill, 1830, 8vo, pp. 154, and leaf of errata. (No Table of Contents.)

Alfred Tennyson and Arthur Hallam made an excursion into the Pyrenees.

In this year Charles Tennyson published *Sonnets and Fugitive Pieces.*

1831. *No More.*⎫   Printed in *The Gem, a Literary An-*
Anacreontics.⎬ *nual.* London : W. Marshall, 1 Holborn
A Fragment.⎭ Bars, MDCCCXXXI.

Sonnet, "Check every outflash, every ruder sally." Printed in *The Englishman's Magazine* (August). Reprinted, 1833, in *Friendship's Offering*, p. 29.

Review of *Poems, chiefly Lyrical,* in *The Westminster Review* (January) ; in *The Tatler* (February 24 and succeeding numbers), by Leigh Hunt, and in *The Englishman's Magazine* (August), by A. H. Hallam (*On Some of the Characteristics of Modern Poetry and on the Lyrical Poems of Alfred Tennyson*).

The Rev. George Clayton Tennyson, the poet's father, died, March 16, aged 52.

1832. POEMS, by Alfred Tennyson. London : Edward Moxon, 64 New Bond Street, MDCCCXXXIII., pp. 163, leaf of contents, title, and half title. Published in winter of 1832 and post-dated.

Sonnet, "There are three things which fill my heart with sighs." Printed in the *Yorkshire Literary Annual* (edited by C. F. Edgar). London : Longmans & Co., p. 127.

Sonnet, "Me, my own fate to lasting sorrow doometh." Printed in *Friendship's Offering*, a literary album. London : Smith, Elder & Co., p. 367.

Review of *Poems* (1833) in *Blackwood's Magazine* (May), by Christopher North (Professor Wilson). Reprinted in works of Professor Wilson, vol. vi., pp. 109-152.

Review of *Poems* (1833) in *Athenæum* (December 1).

Arthur Hallam graduated at Cambridge. A guest at Somersby.

1833. THE LOVER'S TALE, by Alfred Tennyson. London : Edward Moxon, 64 New Bond Street, MDCCCXXXIII., pp. 60. (Suppressed and withdrawn from the press.)

Review of *Poems* (1833) in *The Quarterly* (July), attributed to John Gibson Lockhart, the editor.

Review of *Poems, chiefly Lyrical*, by W. J. Fox in *The Monthly Repository* (January).

Arthur Henry Hallam died at Vienna, September 15.

1834. Mrs. Tennyson removed to Cheltenham, after three years at Boxley, near Maidstone.

1835. Review of *Tennyson's Poems* in *The London Review*, (afterwards merged in *The Westminster Review*) (July), by John Stuart Mill.

Tennyson visited Cumberland.

1836. Charles Tennyson Turner married Louisa Sellwood, sister of Emily, who became the wife of Alfred Tennyson.

1837. ST. AGNES. Printed in *The Keepsake* as *St. Agnes' Eve* (edited by Lady E. S. Wortley). London : Longmans.

Stanzas, "O that 'twere possible." Printed in *The Tribute :* a Collection of Poems by Various Authors (ed. by Lord Northampton). Murray, pp. 244-250.

Notice of Tennyson in *The Edinburgh Review* (October).

Tennyson family left Somersby for High Beech, Essex.

1838. Tennyson appears as a member of the *Anonymous Club*.

1842. POEMS, by Alfred Tennyson. In two volumes. London : Edward Moxon, Dover Street, MDCCCXLII., pp. vii., 233, vii., 231. *Morte d'Arthur, Dora and Other Idylls*, privately printed for the author's use.

Review of 1842 *Poems* in *The Westminster Review* (October), by Richard Monckton Milnes (Lord Houghton).

Review in *The Quarterly* by John Sterling, vol. lxx., pp. 385-416. Reprinted in *Sterling's Remains*, vol. i., pp. 422-462.

Review in *The Examiner* (May).

Review in *Tait's Edinburgh Magazine* (August).

Review in *The London University Magazine* (December).

Review in *The Christian Examiner*, Boston (November).

Cecilia Tennyson married to Edward Law Lushington (October).

1843. POEMS, by Alfred Tennyson. 2 vols. 2d edition. Changes were introduced into *The Blackbird, Walking to the Mail, The Day Dream*, and *The Two Voices*.

Bon Gaultier Ballads, by Theodore Martin and W. E. Aytoun, published in *Tait's* and *Fraser's* magazines.

These contained parodies of several of Tennyson's poems.

Review of *Poems* in *The Edinburgh Review* (July).

Elizabeth Barrett (Browning) introduced to Tennyson.

Tennyson meets Wordsworth.

1844. Portrait and notice of Tennyson in R. H. Horne's *A New Spirit of the Age.* London : Smith, Elder & Co.

Review of Tennyson in *The Democratic Review* (January), New York, by Mrs. Kemble.

Marginalia, by Edgar Allan Poe, in the December number of the same review, p. 580.

1845. POEMS, by Alfred Tennyson. 2 vols. 3d edition. A note to the *Idyll of Dora* and *The Ballad of Lady Clare* omitted.

Review of *Poems* in *Chambers' Edinburgh Review* (July).

Tennyson's name was placed on the Civil List for a pension of £200 a year by Sir Robert Peel.

Tennyson satirised as Poet and Pensioner in *The New Timon : A Romance of London*, by Sir E. B. Lytton. London : Henry Colburn.

Living Poets, and their Services to the Cause of Political Freedom and Human Progress. No. III., Alfred Tennyson. *Lectures addressed chiefly to the Working Classes*, by W. J. Fox. Published from the reporter's notes. London, 1845, vol. i., pp. 248–265.

1846. POEMS, by Alfred Tennyson. 2 vols. 4th edition. *The Golden Year* first printed in this edition (the last in two volumes).

The New Timon and the Poets. A reply to Bulwer Lytton, in *Punch* (February 28).

Afterthought, in *Punch* (March 7).

Keats and Tennyson. Conversations on the Poets, by J. R. Lowell, Cambridge, U. S., p. 104.

1847. THE PRINCESS : A MEDLEY, by Alfred Tennyson. London : Edward Moxon, Dover Street, MDCCCXLVII., pp. 164.

Notice of Tennyson in William Howitt's *Homes and Haunts of the Most Eminent British Poets.* London, 1847, vol. ii., pp. 452–470.

1848. THE PRINCESS : A MEDLEY, by Alfred Tennyson. 2d edition. With a Dedication to Henry Lushington. This edition contains a few slight verbal alterations.

POEMS, by Alfred Tennyson. 5th edition, pp. viii., 372. The first one-volume edition.

Review of *The Princess* in *Quarterly Review* (March), attributed to Sara Coleridge.

Review of *The Princess* in *The North British Review* (May).

1849. Lines to —, "You might have won the poet's fame," in *The Examiner* (March). Reprinted in 4th edition of *Poems*, 1850.

The Living Authors of England (Tennyson, pp. 36–60), by T. Powell, New York.

Review of *Poems* in *Blackwood's Magazine* (April).

Review of *Poems* in *The Westminster Review* (July).

Review of *The Princess* in *The Edinburgh Review* (October).

Review of *The Princess* in *The New Englander*, by Professor Hadley, of Yale.

1850. IN MEMORIAM. London : Edward Moxon, pp. vii., 210. (Anonymous.) The 2d and 3d editions unaltered save by the correction of two misprints.

THE PRINCESS. 3d edition. (Partly rewritten and much altered ; the songs added.)

POEMS. 6th edition, pp. 374. Addition of lines, "You might have won the poet's name."

Lines, "Here often, when a child, I lay reclined." Printed in *The Manchester Athenæum Album*.

Alfred Tennyson married to Emily Sellwood, June 13, in Shiplake Church, Oxfordshire. Settled at Chapel House, Twickenham, after a journey to Italy.

Alfred Tennyson appointed Poet Laureate, November 19, to succeed William Wordsworth, who died April 23.

Tennyson, in *Fraser's Magazine* (September), by Charles Kingsley.

Review of *In Memoriam* in *Tait's Edinburgh Magazine* (August).

Review of *In Memoriam* in Sharpe's *London Magazine* (August).

Review of *In Memoriam* in *The Westminster Review* (October).

Review of *In Memoriam* in *Dublin University Magazine* (August).

1851. THE PRINCESS. 4th edition, pp. 182. Passages added

describing the Prince's *weird seizures*, and the fourth song altered.

IN MEMORIAM. 4th edition. Sec. lix. added ("O Sorrow, wilt thou live with me?").

POEMS. 7th edition. The following poems added, *To the Queen ; Edwin Morris, or the Lake; Come Not when I am Dead*, and *The Eagle*.

Stanzas, "What time I wasted youthful hours," and "Come not when I am dead." Printed in *The Keepsake* (edited by Miss Power). London: David Bogue, p. 22.

Sonnet to W. C. Macready, read by John Forster at the farewell dinner to the actor. Printed in *The Household Narrative of Current Events* (February, March), in *The People's Journal* (April), and elsewhere.

Review of *In Memoriam* in *The People's and Howitt's Journal* (May).

Five papers on Tennyson's *Princess* in the *Christian Socialist* (September to November), by Gerald Massey.

Tennyson presented to the Queen at Buckingham Palace, March 6.

1852. ODE ON THE DEATH OF THE DUKE OF WELLINGTON, by Alfred Tennyson, Poet Laureate. London : Edward Moxon, pp. 16.

Stanzas, "Britons, guard your own," in *The Examiner* (January 31).

Lines, "Third of February, 1852," and "Hands All Round," in *The Examiner* (February 7).

(These three poems were over the signature of "Merlin.")

A Second Gallery of Literary Portraits, Edinburgh, by George Gilfillan (Tennyson, pp. 148–159).

Literary Recreations, by D. L. Richardson. (Criticism of the Day and Tennyson, pp. 291–305.) London : Thacker & Co.

Hallam, Tennyson's eldest son (now Lord Tennyson), born at Twickenham (August).

1853. POEMS. 8th edition, pp. 379. Poem, *Sea Fairies* (1830 vol.) restored ; *A Dream of Fair Women*, and *To the Queen* altered ; *To E. L., on his Travels in Greece*, added.

THE PRINCESS. 5th edition, pp. 183. Passage from the "gallant, glorious chronicle" added in the Prologue.

An Essay on the Characteristic Errors of our Most Distinguished Living Poets, by Nicholas J. Gannon, Dublin, pp. 49.

Sketches of the Poetical Literature of the Past Half Century, by D. M. Moir. Edinburgh and London : Blackwood & Sons. (Tennyson, pp. 307–317.)

Translation : Gedichte übersetzt von W. Hertzberg. Dessau.

Bought, and went to reside at, Farringford, Freshwater, Isle of Wight.

Tennyson visited the Western Highlands, Staffa and Iona.

1854. THE CHARGE OF THE LIGHT BRIGADE. First printed in *The Examiner* (December 9). A thousand copies on a quarto sheet (August, 1855), with a note by the author, printed for distribution among the soldiers before Sebastopol.

Days and Hours, by Frederick Tennyson. London : John W. Parker & Son, West Strand, pp. viii., 346.

Dedication by Frederick Denison Maurice of his *Theological Essays* to Tennyson.

Lionel, Tennyson's second son, born at Farringford.

Translation : In Memoriam aus dem Englischen. Braunschweig.

1855. MAUD, AND OTHER POEMS, by Alfred Tennyson, D.C.L., Poet Laureate. London : Edward Moxon, pp. 154.

Review of *The Poetry of Alfred Tennyson*, by Gerald Massey, in *Hogg's Instructor* (July).

Review of *Maud* in *Blackwood's Magazine* (September).

Review of *Maud* in *Dublin University Magazine* (September).

Review of *Maud* in *The Edinburgh Review* (October).

Review of *Maud* in *Fraser's Magazine* (September).

Review of *Maud* in *The National Review* (October).

Review of *Maud* in *The North American Review* (October), by the Rev. E. E. Hale.

Essay on Tennyson, by George Brimley, published in *Cambridge Essays*. Reprinted in Brimley's *Collected Essays*.

The University of Oxford conferred the D.C.L. upon Tennyson at the May Commencements.

1856. MAUD, AND OTHER POEMS. 2d edition, with considerable alteration and enlargement, pp. 164.

Alfred Tennyson : An Essay. In three parts. By W. Fulford in the *Oxford and Cambridge Magazine*, pp. 7, 73, 136.

English Traits, by Ralph Waldo Emerson. (Tennyson in *Literature* article. Works. Vol. ii., pp. 114–115.)

Tennyson's Maud Vindicated, The Spirit and Purpose of Maud, by R. J. Mann, M.D. London : Jarrold & Son, pp. 78.

Anti-Maud, by a Poet of the People. 2d edition. London : L. Booth, pp. 30.

Defence of *Maud* in an anonymous volume of poems, entitled *Ionica*, in verses entitled *After Reading Maud*, September, 1855.

Review of *Maud* in the *London University Magazine* (May).

Notice of Tennyson in *The National Magazine* (November).

1857. ENID AND NIMUE ; OR, THE TRUE AND THE FALSE. Two idylls privately printed (probably intended for publication and withdrawn for alterations). pp. 139.

POEMS, by A. Tennyson, with engraving of bust by Woolner, and illustrations by various artists. pp. xiii., 375. Edward Moxon, 1857, 8vo.

Notice of Tennyson in the *London University Magazine* (April).

Lectures and Miscellanies, by H. W. Freeland, M.A., London : Longmans & Co. (Tennyson's *In Memoriam*, pp. 194-200.)

Bayard Taylor visited Tennyson at Farringford (June). See Bayard Taylor's *At Home and Abroad*, p. 372.

1858. Two stanzas on the marriage of the Princess Royal, added by Tennyson to the National Anthem, January 28, 1858. Printed in the newspapers of January 29. Notice of Tennyson by the Rev. F. W. Robertson in his *Lectures and Addresses*. London : Smith, Elder & Co., pp. 124–141.

On June 22 Clough "heard Tennyson read a third Arthur poem—the detection of Guinevere, and the last interview with Arthur." (*Remains of A. H. Clough*, vol. i., p. 235.)

Prince Albert visited Tennyson at Farringford.

Tennyson visited Inverary as the guest of the Duke of Argyll.

1859. IDYLLS OF THE KING, by Alfred Tennyson, D.C.L., Poet Laureate. London : Edward Moxon & Co., pp. 261.

Verses, *The War* ("There is a sound of thunder afar"). Printed in *The Times* (May 9), signed "T." Acknowledged by Tennyson, 1891.

Verses, *The Grandmother's Apology*. With an illustration by J. E. Millais. Printed in *Once a Week* (July 16). Now entitled *The Grandmother*.

Tennyson and his Teachers, by Peter Bayne, M.A. James Hogg & Sons, Edinburgh and London, pp. 202–280.

Review of *Idylls of the King* in *The National Review* (October), pp. 368–394.

Review of *Idylls of the King* in *Fraser's Magazine* (September).

Review of *Idylls of the King* in *Edinburgh Review* (July).

Review of *Idylls of the King* in the *North British Review* (August).

Review of *Idylls of the King* in *The New Rugbeian*, by Warner Lee (September), pp. 267–271.

Review of *Idylls of the King* in *Blackwood's Magazine* (November).

Review of *Idylls of the King* in *The Constitutional Press* (September).

Review of *Tennyson's Poems* in *The Quarterly* (October), pp. 454–485.

Review of Tennyson in *Meliora*, a quarterly review of social science (October).

Article on *The Politics of the Poet Laureate*, by D. Owen Maddyn, in *The Constitutional Press* (June).

Article on *Moral Aspects of Mr. Tennyson's Idylls of the King*, by J. M. Ludlow, *Macmillan's Magazine* (November).

Notice of Tennyson's *Maud* in *Macmillan's Magazine* (December), No. 2.

Review of *Tennyson's Poems*, by John Nichol, in *The Westminster Review* (October).

The Poetical Character, Illustrated from the Works of Alfred Tennyson, D.C.L., Poet Laureate, a lecture delivered at Sheffield, December 6, by the Rev. Alfred Gatty, M.A., Vicar of Ecclesfield. London : Bell & Daldy, 1860, pp. 29.

Translation : De Molenaar's-dochter ; door A. J. de Bull. Utrecht.

Tennyson visited Portugal (Vigo, Lisbon, Cintra, and the Monastery of da Cortica) with Mr. F. T. Palgrave. (Account by Mr. Palgrave in *Under the Crown*, a magazine, Nos. 1 and 2.)

Dean Stanley visited Tennyson at Farringford.

Tennyson's bust, by Woolner, presented to Trinity College, Cambridge.

1860. SEA DREAMS: AN IDYLL.   Printed in *Macmillan's Magazine* (January).

SEA DREAMS: AN IDYLL.   Printed in *Macmillan's Magazine* (January).

TITHONUS.   Printed in *Cornhill Magazine*, edited by W. M. Thackeray (February).

Review of *Poetical Works of Alfred Tennyson* in *The North American Review* (January), by C. C. Everett.

Moral Aspects of Tennyson's Idylls of the King, in *Macmillan's Magazine*, by J. M. Ludlow, vol. i., pp. 65–72.

Essay on Tennyson in *Poems and Essays*, by the late William Caldwell Roscoe, edited, with a prefatory memoir, by his brother-in-law, Richard Holt Hutton.   London: Chapman & Hall, vol. ii., pp. 1–37.

Tennyson visited Cornwall.

1861. Stanzas, *The Sailor Boy*.   Printed in *Victoria Regia*, edited by Emily Faithfull, Christmas.

Lines, *Helen's Tower*, printed in quarto pamphlet by Lord Dufferin for private circulation.

Essays on English Literature (Alfred Tennyson, pp. 248–276), by T. McNicholl.   London: Pickering.

Alfred Tennyson (and his wife) visited the Pyrenees, where he had been in the autumn of 1830 with Arthur Hallam. On this journey he wrote the lines, "In the Valley of Cauteretz," which have reference to his former visit with Hallam. On this journey the Tennysons met Arthur Hugh Clough travelling for his health. He died two months later.   (See *Remains of Arthur Hugh Clough*, vol. i., pp. 264–269.)

1862. IDYLLS OF THE KING.   New edition.   With a dedication to the memory of the late Prince Consort.

"ODE: MAY THE FIRST, 1862" (Exhibition Ode).   Sung at the opening of the International Exhibition.   Printed in the daily papers.   Accurate version in *Fraser's Magazine* (June).

POEMS, 1830, 1833.   Privately printed, and suppressed.

A Painter's Camp in the Highlands and Thoughts About Art, by Philip Gilbert Hamerton (Tennyson, *Word Painting and Colour Painting*, vol. ii., pp. 252–269).

An Introduction to English Literature from Chaucer to Tennyson, by Henry Reed.

Index to In Memoriam. London : Edward Moxon & Co., pp. 40.

Analysis of In Memoriam, by the late Rev. F. W. Robertson, of Brighton. London : Smith, Elder & Co.

Tennyson visited Derbyshire and Yorkshire.

1863. A WELCOME (to the Princess Alexandra, March 7). London : Edward Moxon & Co., pp. 4.

ATTEMPTS AT CLASSIC METRES IN QUANTITY, in the *Cornhill Magazine* (December).

An essay *Concerning Cutting and Carving*, by A. K. H. B. (on the changes introduced by Tennyson into his poems), in *Fraser's Magazine* (February).

Remains in Verse and Prose of Arthur Henry Hallam. London : John Murray. The third issue : the first two for private circulation.

1864. ENOCH ARDEN, etc., by Alfred Tennyson, D.C.L., Poet Laureate. London : Edward Moxon & Co., Dover Street, pp. 178. (This volume is dedicated to his wife.)

EPITAPH ON THE LATE DUCHESS OF KENT. Printed in *The Court Journal* (March 19). Also inscribed on Theed's statue at Frogmore.

Review of *Enoch Arden* in *The Westminster Review* (October).

Review of *Enoch Arden* in *Dublin University Magazine* (October).

Review of *Enoch Arden* in *Blackwood's Magazine* (November).

Review of *Enoch Arden* in *The North British Review* (August).

Review of *Enoch Arden* in the *North American Review* (October), by J. Russell Lowell.

Review of *Enoch Arden* in *Harper's Magazine* (October), by George William Curtis.

Review of *Enoch Arden* in the *Nouvelle Revue de Paris* (September), by A. Vermorel.

Wordsworth, Tennyson, and Browning; or, Pure, Ornate, and Grotesque Art, by Walter Bagehot, in *The National Review* (November). Reprinted in Bagehot's "Literary Studies." Edited by R. H. Hutton, 1879. London : Longmans, Green & Co., vol. ii., pp. 338–390.

Alfred Tennyson. A lecture by Henry Edward Watts, delivered at the Town Hall, Prahan, October 10. Melbourne : Samuel Mullen, Collins Street, East, p. 37.

Tennyson's Northern Farmer, in *Macmillan's Magazine* (October), pp. 486–489. By J. M. Ludlow.

Notice of Tennyson's work in H. Taine's *Histoire de la Littérature Anglaise.* Paris, Tom. iv., pp. 431–483.

Garibaldi visited Tennyson at Farringford (April 8), and planted a *Wellingtonea gigantea* in the grounds as a memorial of his visit. See the reference to "the warrior of Caprera" in the poem, *To Ulysses* (*Demeter, and other Poems,* 1889).

(*Sonnets,* by the Rev. Charles [Tennyson] Turner, Vicar of Grasby, Lincoln. London and Cambridge : Macmillan & Co., pp. viii., 102.) Dedicated to Alfred Tennyson.

1865. A Selection from the Works of Alfred Tennyson. London : Edward Moxon & Co., Dover Street, square 12mo, pp. 256. This volume contained seven new poems : *The Captain, On a Mourner, Three Sonnets to a Coquette, Home they brought him slain with spears.* (Rewritten for music. Another version, *Home they brought her warrior dead,* appeared in *The Princess.* The poem is a translation from the Anglo-Saxon *Gudrun* [see Conybeare's *Anglo-Saxon Poetry*]).

The Bibliography of Tennyson. By the Hon. J. Leicester Warren. *Fortnightly Review* (October).

Three Great Teachers of Our Own Time (Carlyle, Tennyson, and Ruskin), by Alexander H. Japp. London : Smith, Elder & Co., pp. 87-186.

Tennyson elected a member of the Royal Society.

Tennyson's mother died February 21, in her eighty-fifth year.

Tennyson visited Weimar and Dresden.

1866. *Tennysoniana : Notes Bibliographical and Critical on Early*

Poems of Alfred and Charles Tennyson. Basil Montague Pickering, Piccadilly, London, W., pp. 170. By R. H. Shepperd. Published anonymously.

Review of *Enoch Arden* in the *London Quarterly Review* (January).

Paper *On a Song in The Princess*, in the *Shilling Magazine* (February), pp. 181–184, by George Grove.

The Last Hundred Years of English Literature. Jena. By Charles Grant. (Tennyson, pp. 147–162.)

Commentary on *Tears, Idle Tears*, in *Macmillan's Magazine* (November).

Translation : Enoch Arden. Oversat of A. Munch. Copenhagen.

Tennyson visited Cambridge.

1867. THE WINDOW ; OR, THE LOVES OF THE WRENS. By Alfred Tennyson, D.C.L., Poet Laureate. Printed at the private press of Sir Ivor Bertie Guest, Bart. (now Lord Wimborne), of Canford Manor, near Wimborne, Dorset, son of Lady Charlotte Guest, editor of the *Mabinogion.* With dedication and note. (These songs were written for music composed by Mr. Arthur [now Sir Arthur] Sullivan, and published in 1870.) The original edition was dedicated as follows : " These little songs, whose almost sole merit—at least till they are wedded to music—is that they are so excellently printed, I dedicate to the printer." Considerable changes were made in later editions.

THE VICTIM, by Alfred Tennyson, D.C.L., Poet Laureate. Published at the same press.

Review of Tennyson's Works in *Afternoon Lectures on Literature and Art* (4th series), by J. K. Ingram, LL.D., Fellow of Trinity College, and Professor of English Literature in the University of Dublin. London : Bell & Daldy, pp. 47–94.

Studies in Tennyson, in *Belgravia*, by W. S.

Lecture on " The Sonnets of Charles and Alfred Tennyson." By Richard Chenevix Trench (Archbishop of Dublin). Printed in *Afternoon Lectures on Literature and Art* (4th series). London : Bell & Daldy, p. 163.

Translation : Enoch Arden. Ubersetzt von R. Schellwien. Quedlinburg.

Idylls of the King. Ubersetzt von W. Scholz. Berlin.
Tennyson visited Dartmoor and Salcombe.

In this year he purchased the Greenhill estate, on Block-
down, in Sussex, three miles distant from the village of
Haslemere, in Surrey. Here was built for him Aldworth
(a summer and autumn residence) from the designs of his
friend, Mr. J. T. Knowles, the editor of *The Nineteenth
Century*.

The Duke of Argyll, Mr. Gladstone, and Lord Houghton
were guests at Farringford in July.

1868. THE VICTIM. Printed in *Good Words* (January).

ON A SPITEFUL LETTER. Printed in *Once a Week* (January).*

WAGES. Printed in *Macmillan's Magazine* (February).

1865–1866 (" I stood on a tower in the wet"). Printed in
Good Words (March). (Since suppressed.)

LUCRETIUS. Printed in *Macmillan's Magazine* (May), and
New York, in *Every Saturday* (May).

Article on *The Arthurian Legends in Tennyson*. By S.
Cheetham, in *The Contemporary Review* (April).

Paper *On Mr. Tennyson's Lucretius*, by Professor R. C.
Jebb, in *Macmillan's Magazine* (June).

Review of *Lucretius* in *London Quarterly Review* (October) ;
also in *Tinsley's Magazine* (July), pp. 610–616.

A Study of the Works of Alfred Tennyson, by Edward
Campbell Tainsh. London : Chapman & Hall. (Enlarged editions published 1870 and 1892.)

*Jerrold, Tennyson, and Macaulay, with Other Critical Es-
says*, by James Hutchison Stirling, LL.D. Edinburgh :
Edmonston & Douglas, pp. 51–111.

Translation : Enoch Arden. Ubersetzt von R. Waldmüller.
Hamburg.

Translation : Dora. Trad. di G. Zanella. Firenze. (*In
versi di Giacomo Zanella*, vol. i.)

(*Small Tableaux*, by the Rev. Charles [Tennyson] Turner,
Vicar of Grasby, Lincoln. London : Macmillan & Co.,
pp. viii., 114.)

Tennyson visited at Farringford by Henry Wadsworth
Longfellow.

---

* In a letter to *Once a Week* Tennyson stated of this poem : " It is no particular
letter that I meant. I have dozens of them from one quarter or another."

1869. THE HOLY GRAIL, AND OTHER POEMS, by Alfred Tennyson, D.C.L., Poet Laureate. London : Strahan & Co., 56 Ludgate Hill, pp. 222. This volume included *The Victim, Wages,* and *Lucretius, The Northern Farmer,* new style, *The Golden Supper, The Higher Pantheism, Flower in the Crannied Wall.*

Pocket edition of Complete Poems. Strahan, London.

A Concordance to the Entire Works of Alfred Tennyson, by D. Barron Brightwell. London : E. Moxon, Son & Co., pp. 477.

Paper on *The Holy Grail* in *The Athenæum* (December).

Notice of Tennyson in an article, "The Poetry of the Period," by Alfred Austin, *Temple Bar* (May).

Mr. Tennyson and Mr. Browning, by Edward Dowden, M.A., Professor of English Literature, Trinity College, Dublin. Printed in *Afternoon Lectures on Literature and Art* (fifth series), pp. 139–179. Reprinted in Professor Dowden's *Studies in Literature,* Kegan Paul, Trench & Co., London.

Paper on *Modern English Poets,* in *The Quarterly* (April), pp. 328–359.

Translation : Enoch Arden. Ubersetzt von F. W. Weber. Leipzig.

Translation : Aylmer's Field. Ubersetzt von F. W. Weber. Leipzig.

Translation : Henoch Arden, door S. J. van den Bergh. Hage.

Tennyson visited North Wales. Elected an Honorary Fellow of Trinity College, Cambridge.

1870. Article, *The Idylls of the King,* by Henry Alford, in *The Contemporary Review* (January).

Paper, *The Epic of Arthur,* in the *Edinburgh Review* (April).

Review of *The Laureate and his Arthuriad* in the *London Quarterly Review* (April).

Modern Men of Letters Honestly Criticised, by J. Hain Friswell. London : Hodder & Stoughton. (Alfred Tennyson, pp. 145–156.)

Paper, *Alfred Tennyson,* in the *Nuova Antologia,* Florence (February), by E. Camerini.

Translation : Enoch Arden. Trad. par M. de la Rive. Paris.

Sir John Simeon, Tennyson's friend and neighbour, died in Switzerland.

The verses, " In the garden at Swainston," were composed at this time.

1871. THE LAST TOURNAMENT,* contributed to *The Contemporary Review* (December).

Article, *The Songs of the Wrens*, by the Rev. H. R. Haweis, in *The Saint Paul's Magazine* (February).

Our Living Poets : An Essay on Criticism, by H. Buxton Forman. London : Tinsley. (Alfred Tennyson, pp. 27–69.)

Mr. Tennyson's Poetry, in *The North British Review* (January), pp. 379–425.

Translation : La Cena d'Oro di Alfredo Tennyson. Trad. di Lodovico Biagi. Firenze.

1872. GARETH AND LYNETTE, etc., by Alfred Tennyson, D.C.L., Poet Laureate. London : Strahan & Co., Ludgate Hill, pp. 136.

Lines for the Opening of the International Exhibition. *Library Edition of Tennyson's Works.* 6 vols. Strahan & Co. (1872–73). (Several of the *Juvenilia* were restored in this edition. It included two early sonnets, *Alexander* and *The Bridesmaid ;* also *The Third of February, 1852* [printed in *Examiner*, January, 1852, over the signature of *Merlin*, and now first acknowledged], *Literary Squabbles* [anonymously printed in *Punch*, March 7, 1846, as *Afterthought*], verses, *To the Queen*, and some additional passages in " *The Idylls of the King*.")

Review of Tennyson's poetry in *Macmillan's Magazine* (December), by Richard Holt Hutton.

Article, *Tennyson's Charm*, by Robert Buchanan, in *The Saint Paul's Magazine* (March).

Tennyson visited Norway.

Translations : Enoch Arden. Aylmer's Field ; Ausgewählte Dichtungen (1870), and *Koenig's Idyllen* (1872), *von*

* As printed in the Review, the two lines, afterwards altered, following :

" He rose, he turn'd, then flinging round her neck,
Claspt it,"

read :

" But while he bowed himself to lay
Warm kisses in the hollow of her throat."

H. A. Feldmann. Hamburg. *Ausgewählte Gedichte, ubersetzt von* M. Rugard. Elbing.

1873. *A Comparative Estimate of Modern English Poets*, by J. Devey. E. Moxon, Son & Co. (Alfred Tennyson, pp. 275–336.)

Article, *Mr. Tennyson as a Botanist*, by J. Hutchison, in *The Saint Paul's Magazine* (October).

Tennyson, by Walter Irving. Edinburgh : Maclachlan & Stewart, pp. 28.

Notes and Marginalia, by J. H. Smith. London.

Article, *Lincolnshire Scenery and Character as Illustrated by Mr. Tennyson*, by the Rev. Drummond Rawnsley, in *Macmillan's Magazine* (December).

Master Spirits, by Robert Buchanan. London : Henry S. King & Co., pp. 349 (*Tennyson, Heine, and De Musset*, pp. 54–88).

Review of *Idylls of the King* in the *Contemporary Review* (May).

Gareth and Lynette, in *The Spectator* and *The Athenæum*.

1874. A WELCOME TO MARIE ALEXANDROVNA, DUCHESS OF EDINBURGH. Printed in *The Times*, and separately on a single sheet.

(Cabinet edition of Tennyson's works. H. S. King & Co. In this edition appeared the poem in memory of Sir John Simeon, *In the Garden at Swainston ;* also *The Voice and the Peak, England and America in 1782*, and an additional passage in *Merlin and Vivien*.)

Translation : Zum Gedächtniss, von Agnes von Bohlen. Berlin.

1875. QUEEN MARY : A DRAMA, by Alfred Tennyson. London : H. S. King & Co., pp. viii., 278.

Prefatory sonnet to Lord Lyttelton's Memoir of W. H. Brookfield, prefixed to a volume of his " Sermons" (" Brooks, for they called you so that knew you best").

(*The Poetical Works of Alfred Tennyson.* H. S. King & Co., 6 vols., 1875-1877. In this edition *Maud* was for the first time entitled *Maud : A Monodrama.* Changes were made in the text of various poems.) Author's edition in 4 vols. H. S. King & Co.

Notes on *Queen Mary*, in *Macmillan's Magazine*.

Review of *Queen Mary* in *The Academy*, by Mr. Andrew Lang.

Review of *Queen Mary* in *The Quarterly Review* (July), pp. 231–248.

Victorian Poets, by Edmund Clarence Stedman.   Boston : Houghton, Mifflin & Co.   London : Chatto & Windus, 1876.   The fifth and sixth chapters deal with the poetry of Tennyson.

The Religion of our Literature : Essays upon Carlyle, Browning, and Tennyson, by George McCrie.   London : Hodder & Stoughton (Tennyson, pp. 110–180).

Article, *Virgil and Tennyson*, in *Blackwood's Magazine* (November), by "A Lincolnshire Rector"—the Rev. Drummond Rawnsley.

Translations : The May Queen, af. A. Falck.   Christiania. *—Enid and Elaine*, translated by L. Gisbert.*—The May Queen, trad. dei* Marchesi Luigi e Raniero de Calboli. Roma.

1876. HAROLD : A DRAMA, by Alfred Tennyson.   London : Henry S. King & Co., 1877 (post-dated), pp. viii., 161.

Queen Mary was produced under the management of Mr. Henry Irving at the Lyceum in April.

Tennyson again visited the Pyrenees.

Browning dedicated the two volumes of his "Selections" "To Alfred Tennyson : In Poetry, illustrious and consummate ; in Friendship, noble and sincere."

Translations : Idilli, Lirichi, Miti, e Legende, Enoc Arden, Quadri Dramatici.   Traduzioni di Carlo Faccioli.   Verona.*—Firenze, Successori le Monnier*, pp. 441 (2d edition, 1879).*—Enoch Arden di Alfredo Tennyson*: *Recats in versi Italiani di* Angelo Saggioni.   Padova, 1876.*—Stabilimenti Prosperini*, pp. 51.   *Nozze Scopoli-Naccari.—Konung Arthur och haus Riddare.*   Upsala.*—Idyller om Kong Arthur, af.* A. Munch.   Copenhagen.*—Enoch Arden : deutsch von* A. Strodtmann.   Berlin.

1877. Prefatory Sonnet to *The Nineteenth Century* (first number, March), edited by Mr. J. T. Knowles.

Sonnet, *Montenegro*, in *The Nineteenth Century* (May).

Sonnet,*To Victor Hugo*, in *The Nineteenth Century* (June).

The Works of A. Tennyson.   7 vols.   H. S. King.

Translation : Achilles over the Trench (Iliad, Book 18), in *The Nineteenth Century* (August).

Lines in memory of Sir John Franklin on the cenotaph in Westminster Abbey.

Review of *Harold* in *The Academy*, by John Addington Symonds.

Article on *Tennyson* in *The International Review*, New York (May), by Bayard Taylor, vol. iv., pp. 397–418.

Longfellow's Sonnet to Tennyson, entitled *Wapentake*, printed in *The Atlantic Monthly* (December).

Translation : Sea Dreams, Aylmer's Field, af. F. L. Mynster.—*Elaine.* A. Hjelmstjerna.

1878. SIR RICHARD GRENVILLE : A BALLAD OF THE FLEET, printed in *The Nineteenth Century* (March) (afterwards named *The Revenge*).

The Poetical Works of Alfred Tennyson, 13 vols. London : Kegan Paul & Co., 1878–1882.

Studies in the Idylls : An Essay on Mr. Tennyson's Idylls of the King, by Henry Elsdale. London : H. S. King & Co., pp. vii., 197.

Article on *Tennyson*, in *The Literary World* (September), by P. Bayne.

Tennyson visited Ireland.

Lionel Tennyson married Miss Eleanor Locker.

1879. THE LOVER'S TALE, by Alfred Tennyson. London : Kegan Paul & Co., pp. 95.

Dedicatory Poem to the Princess Alice.

The Defence of Lucknow, printed in *The Nineteenth Century* (April).

The Falcon, produced at the St. James' Theatre, with Mrs. Kendal in the part of the heroine (December).

Lessons from my Masters (Carlyle, Tennyson, and Ruskin), by Peter Bayne. London : John Clarke & Co., pp. 437.

The Poets Laureate of England, by Walter Hamilton (Alfred Tennyson, pp. 263–300).

Tennysoniana. 2d edition, enlarged (R. H. Shepherd).

Notice of *The Lover's Tale* in *The Academy*, by Edmund Gosse.

Notice of *The Lover's Tale* in *The Congregationalist*, vol. viii., pp. 672–681.

Notice of *The Lover's Tale* in *Fraser's Magazine*, vol. c., pp. 110–116.

Notice of *The Lover's Tale* in *The Canadian Monthly*, vol. xvi., pp. 221–223.

Sketch of the Life of Tennyson in *The Atlantic Monthly*, Vol. cxliv, pp. 356–361, by J. H. Ward.

The Tennyson Birthday Book, edited by Emily Shakspear. London.

The Rev. Charles Tennyson Turner died April 15.

1880. BALLADS, AND OTHER POEMS, by Alfred Tennyson, pp. vi., 184. London : Kegan Paul & Co.

The Works of Alfred Tennyson, with portrait and illustrations, 1 vol., pp. iv., 665. London : Kegan Paul & Co., 1881 (1880).

Poem, *De Profundis*, printed in *The Nineteenth Century* (May).

Lines, *Midnight, June* 30, 1879, prefixed to collected sonnets, old and new, by Charles Tennyson Turner. London : Kegan Paul & Co., pp. xxii., 390.

Two poems (*The City Child* and *Minnie and Winnie*), printed in *St. Nicholas*, an American magazine for children. Set to music by Mrs Tennyson.

Translation : Harald : Ein Drama. Deutsch von A. Graf Wickenburg, pp. 137. Hamburg (printed Altona).

Poets in the Pulpit, by the Rev. H. R. Haweis, London (Tennyson, pp. 33–115).

A New Study of Tennyson, by J. Churton Collins, in *The Cornhill Magazine* (January and July, and July, 1881). Same articles in *Littell's Living Age*, vol. cxlvi.

Sonnet, by Theodore Watts, " To Alfred Tennyson, on his publishing, in his seventy-first year, the most richly various volume of English verse that has appeared in his own century."

Review of *Tennyson's Poems* (with portrait) in the British *Quarterly Review*. The same article in *Littell's Living Age* (December), *Potter's American Monthly*, vol. xvi.

Parody of Tennyson's *Higher Pantheism* in *The Heptalogia ; or, the Seven against Sense*. (A. C. Swinburne.)

1881. DESPAIR, by Alfred Tennyson, printed in *The Nineteenth Century* (November).

The Works of Alfred Tennyson. With Portrait and Illustrations. London : C. Kegan Paul & Co.

THE CUP, produced at the Lyceum Theatre by Henry Irving (January 3).

Alfred Tennyson, his Life and Works, by W. E. Wace. Edinburgh : Macniven & Wallace, pp. vii., 203.

A Key to Tennyson's In Memoriam, by Alfred Gatty, pp. xi., 144. London : D. Bogue. Worksop (printed). (2d edition, new and revised. London : George Bell & Sons, 1882 ; 3d edition, pp. xxvii., 148, 1885.)

Review of *Ballads, and Other Poems,* in *The Edinburgh Review,* vol. cliv., pp. 486–515.

Review of *Ballads, and Other Poems,* in *The International Review,* vol. x., pp. 178–183.

Article on *Tennyson's Ballads* in *The Congregationalist,* vol. x., pp. 53–60.

Article on *The Cup* in *Appleton's Journal* (from *The Saturday Review*), vol. xxv., pp. 253–256.

"The Performance of *The Cup* at the Lyceum," in *Saint James' Magazine,* vol. xlviii., pp. 195–203.

Article on *The Idylls of the King,* by R. W. Boodle, in *The Canadian Monthly,* vol. xix., pp. 379–398.

Article on *Tennyson and Musset* in *The Fortnightly Review* (February), by A. C. Swinburne. (Reprinted in Swinburne's *Miscellanies.*)

Same article in *Eclectic Magazine,* vol. xcvi., pp. 600–616.

A Study of Tennyson, by R. H. Stoddard, in *The North American Review* (July), pp. 82–107.

Article on *Mr. Tennyson's New Volume* in *Macmillan's Magazine* (January), by Sidney Colvin.

Travesty of *Despair,* by A. C. Swinburne, in *The Fortnightly Review,* entitled *Disgust* (October).

Atheism and Suicide. A Reply to Mr. Tennyson, pp. 8, by G. W. Foote. London : Freethought Publishing Co.

The De Profundis of Alfred Tennyson : Remodelled by Metamorphosis. London : E. W. Allen.

Papers on Tennyson in *Colburn's New Monthly Magazine,* vol. clxix., pp. 47–68 ; 131–147 ; 241–257.

Review of *Ballads, and Other Poems. Articolo critico di*

Enrico Nencioni, nel *Fanfulla della Domenica*. Rome. (April.)

Translation: Maria Tudor. Historische Drama i feur Akter. Oversat af. F. L. Mynster (in verse), pp. 280. Kjbenham.

Translation: La Carica della Brigata Lyght. Le Due Sorelle. In Fiori del nord: Versione di Moderne Poesie Tedesche e Inglese di Pietro Turati. Milano, pp. 133–137.

Tennyson elected Vice-President of the Welsh National Eisteddfod.

1882. THE PROMISE OF MAY produced at the Globe Theatre under the management of Mrs. Bernard Beere.

The Charge of the Heavy Brigade, printed in *Macmillan's Magazine* (March).

Lines *To Virgil*, in *The Nineteenth Century* (September).

English Dramatists of To-day, by William Archer. (Tennyson, pp. 334–351.)

A Study of The Princess, by S. E. Dawson. London: Sampson Low & Co., pp. 120 (also Montreal : Dawson Brothers).

A Lecture on *The Religious Significance of Tennyson's Despair*, by Thomas Walker. London: Eliot Stock, pp. 32.

Notice of Tennyson's *Despair* in *The Modern Review*, vol. iii., pp. 462–473. By C. Shakspeare.

Notice of Tennyson's *Despair* in *The Congregationalist*, vol. ii., pp. 824–831. By J. H. Hallowell.

Notice of Tennyson's *Charge of the Heavy Brigade* in *The Literary World*, vol. xiii., p. 97. By W. H. Chamberlain.

Catholic Musings on Tennyson's In Memoriam, in *The Catholic World*, vol. xxxiv., pp. 205–211.

The Literary Career of Tennyson, in *The Literary World*, vol. xiii., pp. 280, 281.

Review of *The Promise of May*, in *The Academy*, vol. xxii., pp. 370, 371, by F. Wedmore.

Review of *The Promise of May* in *The Saturday Review*, vol. liv., pp. 670, 671.

Review of *The Promise of May* in *The Spectator*, vol. lv., pp. 1474, 1475.

An article on *Maud* in *Domenica Litteraria*, Rome (March 19), by Enrico Nencioni.

Translation : Henoch Arden. . . . In het Nederlandsch bewerkt door J. L. Wertheim, pp. 53. Amsterdam.

Tennyson visited Lombardy.

Lines, *Frater Ave atque Vale*, printed in *The Nineteenth Century* (March).

Poems, by Alfred Tennyson, 2 vols. London : Kegan Paul & Co. (50 copies on large paper.)

1883. Article on Tennyson in *The Overland Monthly* (U. S.), vol. i., pp. 17–33, by T. H. Rearden.

Article on Tennyson, with portrait, in *Harper's Monthly Magazine*, vol. lxviii., pp. 21–41, by Anne Thackeray Ritchie.

Paper on *Tennyson and Milton*, in *The Presbyterian Review*, vol. iv., pp. 681–709, by H. J. Van Dyke. (Reprinted in *The Poetry of Tennyson*. London : Elkin Mathews & John Lane.)

Articles on *Tennyson as a Plagiarist*, in *The Literary World*, vol. xiv., p. 291 ; vol. xiv., pp. 272, 273, by E. L. Didier ; vol. xiv., pp. 327, 328, by J. Hooper.

Article on Tennyson's Acceptance of a Peerage in *The Saturday Review*, vol. lvi., pp. 751, 752.

Article on Tennyson's Acceptance of a Peerage in *The Spectator*, vol. lvi., pp. 1577, 1578.

Article on Tennyson's *Poems* in *The Spectator*, vol. lvi., pp. 355–357.

The Earlier and Less-known Poems of Tennyson, by C. E. Mathews. Birmingham, pp. 34.

Articles on *In Memoriam* and *The Idylls of the King* in *Fanfulla della Domenica*, by Enrico Nencioni. Rome. (May and September.)

Translations : Vier Idyllen van Konig Arthur. (A Dutch translation in prose, pp. viii., 116.) Amsterdam.

Poemas . . . *Enoch Arden, Gareth y Lynette, Merlin y Bibiana, La Reina Ginebra, Dora, La Maya, puestos en Castellano* (in prose) *por* D. V. de Arana, *é illustrados con dibujos originales de* D. J. Riudavets, etc., pp. 302. Barcelona.

(Part of the " Biblioteca Verdaguer.")

Maj-dronningen . . . *oversat af.* F. L. Mynster, pp. 12.
(No. 65 of "Den indre Missions Forlagsskrifter.")

Tennyson took a house in Belgrave Square, London, and
lived for some time in town.

Tennyson accompanied Mr. W. E. Gladstone on a sea trip
to Copenhagen. On his return he was offered and accepted a peerage. Gazetted Baron of Aldworth and Farringford, January, 1884.

1884. THE CUP AND THE FALCON, by Alfred, Lord Tennyson,
Poet Laureate. London : Macmillan & Co., pp. 146
(printed in Edinburgh).

BECKET, by Alfred, Lord Tennyson, Poet Laureate. London : Macmillan & Co., pp. 213 (printed in Edinburgh).

Lines, *Early Spring*, in an American periodical, *The
Youth's Companion.*

The following lines, written in youth, were published in a
pamphlet (which also contained a poem by Browning) :

> " Not he that breaks the dams, but he
>   That thro' the channels of the State
>   Conveys the people's wish is great ;
>   His name is pure, his fame is free." *

Introductory verses to *Rosa Rosarum*, by E. V. B. (the
Hon. Mrs. Boyle), published in this year.

Freedom. Printed in *Macmillan's Magazine* for December.

The Works of Alfred, Lord Tennyson (a new and revised
edition in seven vols., and also in one vol.). London :
Macmillan & Co. (printed in Edinburgh).

The Works of Alfred, Lord Tennyson. School edition,
4 parts. London : Macmillan & Co.

THE PASSING OF ARTHUR, by Alfred, Lord Tennyson.
London : Macmillan & Co., pp. 24.

Tennyson's In Memoriam—Its Purpose and Structure,
by J. F. Genung. London : Macmillan & Co., pp. vi.,
199 (also Boston, Mass. : Houghton & Co.).

Lord Tennyson : A Biographical Sketch, by H. J. Jen-
nings. London : Chatto & Windus, pp. vii., 270.

---

* The pamphlet was published in connexion with a Shakespere exhibition at
the Albert Hall in aid of the Chelsea Hospital for Women.

Tennyson's Allusions to Christ, by J. Hogben, in *The Sunday Magazine*, vol. xiii., pp. 761–764.

Articles on Tennyson's *Becket*. *The Academy*, vol. xxvi., pp. 421, 422, by J. W. Mackail.

Articles on Tennyson's *Becket*. *The Saturday Review*, vol. lviii., pp. 757, 758.

Articles on Tennyson's *Becket*. *The Spectator*, vol. lvii., pp. 1699, 1700.

Articles on Tennyson's *Cup and Falcon*. *The Spectator*, vol. lvii., pp. 316, 317.

Articles on Tennyson's *Cup and Falcon*. *The Athenæum*, 1884, vol. i., pp. 319–321.

Article on Tennyson's *Holy Grail*. *The Congregationalist*, vol. xiii., pp. 463–471, by H. Evans.

Article on Tennyson's *In Memoriam* and the Bible. *Quarterly Review*, vol. clviii., pp. 162–183.

(Same article in *Littell's Living Age*, vol. clxii., pp. 549–561.)

The Genesis of Tennyson's Maud. *The North American Review*, vol. cxxxix., pp. 356–361, by R. H. Shepherd.

Letter on Dawson's Study of Tennyson's *Princess*. *The Academy*, vol. xxv., p. 367.

Tennyson on Dawson's Study of The Princess. *The Critic*, vol. iv., pp. 223, 224.

Trifles by Tennyson. *The Critic*, vol. v., pp. 268, 269 ; vol. vi., pp. 301, 302, by W. J. Rolfe.

" A respectful operatic perversion of Tennyson's ' Princess,' in three acts, entitled Princess Ida ; or, Castle Adamant," etc., by W. S. Gilbert. London : Chappel & Co., pp. 48.

Parodies of the Works of American Authors, by Walter Hamilton. London. (Parodies of the poems of Alfred, Lord Tennyson, vol. i.)

Translation : Koenigs Idyllen : In metrum des Orig. übers, von C. Weiser. Leipzig (1883–1886).

Tennyson was elected President of the Society of Authors. Hon. Hallam Tennyson married Miss Audrey Boyle.

1885. TIRESIAS, AND OTHER POEMS, by Alfred, Lord Tennyson, D.C.L., P.L. London : Macmillan & Co., pp. viii., 203 (printed in Edinburgh). This volume bore the following dedication : "To my good friend, Robert Browning, whose genius and geniality will best appreciate what may be best and make most allowance for what may be worst, this volume is affectionately dedicated."

Lyrical Poems. Selected and annotated by F. T. Palgrave. London : Macmillan & Co., pp. vii., 270. (Printed in Edinburgh.)

(Part of the " Golden Treasury Series.")

The Princess : A Medley. Edited with notes by W. J. Rolfe, with illustrations. J. R. Osgood & Co., Boston. (Printed in Cambridge, Mass.)

The Poetical Works of Lord Tennyson. Complete edition from the author's text. Illustrated, etc. New York : T. Y. Crowell & Co., pp. viii., 896. (Printed in Cambridge, Mass.)

The Fleet, printed in *The Times* (April 23).

" *To H. R. H. Princess Beatrice,"* printed in *The Times* (July 23).

Vastness, printed in *Macmillan's Magazine* (November).

A Review of *Tennyson's Poetry* in *The Revue des Deux Mondes,* by Aug. Filon, tom. lxxi., pp. 70–101.

A Review of *Tennyson's Poetry* in *The Contemporary Review,* by Hon. Roden Noel (February).

(Reprinted in *Essays and Poets,* London, pp. 223–255 [1886]).

Same article in *Littell's Living Age,* vol. clxiv., and *Eclectic Magazine,* vol. civ.

Review of *Becket* in *The Catholic World,* by M. F. Egan, vol. xlii., pp. 382–395.

Review of *Becket* in *The Month,* by C. Nicholson, vol. xxxv., pp. 509–520.

Review of *Becket* in *The Athenæum,* 1885, vol. i., pp. 7–9.

Review of *Becket* in *The Theatre,* by F. Hawkins, vol. i., pp. 53–61.

Review of *Becket* in *Macmillan's Magazine,* vol. li., pp. 287–294.

Review of *Becket* in *Blackwood's Magazine,* vol. cxxxviii., pp. 57–66.

Review of *Becket* in *Eclectic Magazine,* vol. cv., pp. 418–425.

The Meaning of The Idylls of the King, by C. B. Pallen, in *The Catholic World,* vol. xli., pp. 43–54.

Article on *The Lyrics of Tennyson*, in *The Spectator*, vol. lviii., pp. 1319, 1320.

Review of *Tiresias, and Other Poems*, in *The Spectator*, vol. lviii., pp. 1649–1651.

Review of *Tiresias, and Other Poems*, in *The Academy*, by T. H. Caine, vol. xxviii., pp. 403–405.

Review of *Tiresias, and Other Poems*, in *The Athenæum*, 1885, vol. ii., pp. 831–834.

Review of *Tiresias, and Other Poems*, in *The Saturday Review*, vol. lx., pp. 810–811.

Review of *Vastness* in *The Spectator*, vol. lviii., pp. 1466, 1467.

Paper on Tennyson in *Urbana Scripta*, by A. Galton. London : Eliot Stock, pp. 36–68.

Translation : Enoch Arden . . . recato in versi Italiani da A. Soggini, p. 109. Firenze. (See 1876.)

1886. LOCKSLEY HALL SIXTY YEARS AFTER, etc., by Alfred, Lord Tennyson, D.C.L., P.L. London and New York : Macmillan & Co., pp. 201 (printed in Edinburgh).

The Poetical Works of Alfred, Lord Tennyson. 10 vols. London and New York : Macmillan & Co. (printed in Edinburgh).

The Dramatic Works of Alfred, Lord Tennyson. 4 vols. Macmillan & Co.

Ode to India and the Colonies. Written for the opening of the Colonial Exhibition in London (May 4).

The Poetry of Tennyson, in *The London Quarterly Review*, vol. lxv., pp. 243–247.

Tennyson or Darwin, by Algernon C. Swinburne, in *Studies in Prose and Verse*, pp. 141–145.

Tennyson as a Conservative, in *The Atlantic Monthly*, vol. lvii., pp. 423–426.

Tennyson's Later Poems, in *The Leisure Hour*, by S. G. Green, vol. xxxv., pp. 99–101.

Review of *Locksley Hall in Youth and Age* in *The Spectator*, vol. lix., pp. 1706, 1707, 1750, 1751.

Review of *Locksley Hall in Youth and Age*, in *The Saturday Review*, vol. lxii., pp. 842, 843.

Philosophy of Locksley Hall, in *The Southern Bivouac*, by T. Canebrake, vol. v., p. 704.

Translation : Il Primo Diverbio . . . *Traduzione* (of the poem entitled *The First Quarrel*), *di* E. Castelnuovo, p. 19. Venezia : Nozze Bordica. Selvatico.

Enoch Arden. Students' *Tauchnitz aufl. mit Wörterbuch, von* Dr. A. Hamann. Leipzig, p. 24.

(Bibliothek der Gesammt-Literatur.)

Tennyson visited Cambridge in August.

Lionel Tennyson died on the voyage home from India (April 20).

(Jack and the Bean-Stalk, by Hallam Tennyson. London : Macmillan & Co. Illustrations from Caldecott.)

1887. *The Jubilee of our Queen* (printed under title, *Carmen Seculare*), in *Macmillan's Magazine* (April). A souvenir poem by Lord Tennyson. Designs by F. Marriott. London : Eyre & Spottiswoode, 16mo.

The Brook. Illustrated by A. Woodruff. London : Macmillan & Co., obl. 8vo.

Vox Clamantis. A comparison analytical and critical between the *Columbus at Seville* of Joseph Ellis . . . and *The Columbus* of the Poet Laureate. London : W. Stewart & Co., p. 32, 4°.

An essay on Tennyson's *Idylls of the King,* by A. Hamann. Berlin, p. 25.

Review of *Locksley Hall Sixty Years After* in *The Church Review,* vol. xlix., pp. 283–289.

Review of *Locksley Hall Sixty Years After* in *The Atlantic Monthly,* vol. lix., pp. 705–708.

Review of *Locksley Hall Sixty Years After* in *The Congregational Review,* vol. i., pp. 97–105.

Review of *Locksley Hall Sixty Years After* in *Blackwood's Magazine,* vol. cxli., pp. 129–131.

Review of *Locksley Hall Sixty Years After* in *The Dial* (Chicago), by W. M. Payne, vol. vii., pp. 246–248.

Review of *Locksley Hall Sixty Years After* in *The New Englander,* by J. R. Bacon, vol. xlvi., pp. 155–167.

Review of *Locksley Hall Sixty Years After* in *The New Princeton Review,* vol. iii., pp. 265–271.

Review of *Locksley Hall Sixty Years After* in *The Academy,* by H. C. Beeching, vol. xxxi., pp. 1, 2.

Review of *Locksley Hall Sixty Years After* in *The Athenæum*, 1887, vol. i., pp. 31–33.

Review of *Locksley Hall Sixty Years After* in *To-Day*, vol. vii., pp. 93–95.

Review of *Locksley Hall Sixty Years After* in *Leisure Hour*, vol. xxxvi., pp. 137–140.

Review of *Locksley Hall* and *Locksley Hall Sixty Years After* and *The Jubilee* in *The Nineteenth Century*, by W. E. Gladstone, vol. xxi., pp. 1–18.

Same article in *Littell's Living Age*, vol. clxxii., and in *Eclectic Magazine*, vol. cviii.

Article on *Locksley Hall and Liberalism* in *The National Review*, by M. Dyncley, vol. viii., pp. 641–647.

Article on *The Palace of Art*—growth of the poem—in *The New Princeton Review*, by H. Van Dyke, vol. iv., pp. 65–74.

A Word about Tennyson, by Walt Whitman, in *The Critic*, vol. x., pp. 1, 2.

Paper, *The Genesis of In Memoriam* in *Walford's Antiquarian Magazine*, by R. A. Shepherd.

Translation: Ausgewählte Dichtungen. Übersetzt von A. Strodtmann. Hildburghausen, 1867. Leipzig, 1887-1890 (Meyer's Volksbücher).

Selections from Tennyson, with notes for the use of Italians, by T. C. Cann. Florence.

Enoch Arden. Trad. par X. Marmier. Paris.

Tennyson visited St. David's and the Channel Islands.

1888. THE COMPLETE WORKS OF ALFRED, LORD TENNYSON. A new edition in 8 vols. Macmillan & Co. (*The Idyll of Geraint* was in this edition divided into *The Marriage of Geraint* and *Geraint and Enid* and some suppressed poems restored.)

Selections from Tennyson, with introduction and notes by F. J. Rowe and W. T. Webb. Macmillan & Co., pp. xiv., 154 (printed in Glasgow).

Tennyson in *Literary Essays*, by R. H. Hutton. 3d edition, pp. 361–436.

Article on *Tennyson* in *The Methodist Review*, by C. J. Little, vol. lxx., pp. 203–221.

Review of *The Idylls of the King* in *The Dublin Review*, by J. M. Stone, vol. ciii., pp. 259–274.

A Companion to In Memoriam, by Elizabeth R. Chapman. London and New York : Macmillan & Co., pp. 72.

Studies on the Legend of the Holy Grail, by Alfred Nutt. London : David Nutt.

Is Tennyson a Spiritualist? in *The Pall Mall Gazette* (December 20).

Dethroning Tennyson, by A. C. Swinburne, in *The Nineteenth Century* (January).

The Tennyson Flora, by L. H. Grindon. (Appendix to the Report of the Manchester Field Naturalists and Archæological Society, 1887.)

Tennysonian Trees, in *The Gardeners' Magazine* (December 29).

Tennyson's Idylls, by A. V. Dorsey, in *The American Magazine* (May).

Tennyson's Idylls, by R. W. Boodle, in *The Canadian Monthly* (April).

Translations : Locksley Hall . . . übersetzt von F. Freiligrath (*Locksley Hall nach sechzig Jahren. Aus dem Englischen, von* J. Feis), pp. 59. Leipzig.

Locksley Hall sechzig Jahre später. Autorisierte übersetzung, von Karl B. Esmarch, p. 32. Gotha.

Enoch Arden frei bearbeitet für die Jugend. Hausbibliothek. Leipzig, pp. 29.

Enoch Arden. Traduction française litterale (in prose), *par* R. Courtois, pp. 33. Paris.

Enoch Arden. Texte Anglais. Annoté par R. Courtois, pp. viii., 41. Paris.

Idylles et Poèmes. Traduction par A. Buisson du Berger. Paris.

Enid metrisch vertaald door D. E. M. van Herwerden *met platen naar* G. Dore, pp. 70. Zwolle.

La Prima Lite. Estratto dal Giornale "La Battaglia Bizantina." *Traduzione di* P. T. Pavolini. Bologna.

1889. DEMETER, AND OTHER POEMS, by Alfred, Lord Tennyson, D.C.L., P.L. London and New York : Macmillan & Co., pp. vi., 175 (printed Edinburgh).

The Throstle in *The New Review* (October). (Published in May as a leaflet, title and one page of text.)

The Works of Alfred, Lord Tennyson in one vol., pp. v. 807. Macmillan & Co.

Idylls of the King, In Twelve Books (first so entitled in this edition).

Interludes, Lyrics, and Idylls, from the poetic and dramatic works of Alfred, Lord Tennyson, pp. 190. Houghton, Mifflin & Co., Boston and New York. (Printed in Cambridge, Mass.)

Poems (To Edward Lear on his Travels in Greece, The Palace of Art, The Daisy). Illustrated by Edward Lear. (With a memoir of Lear by F. Lushington.) London and New York: Boussod, Valadon & Co., pp. iv., 51 (one hundred copies printed and signed by Tennyson).

Lancelot and Elaine, with notes by C. C. Flanagan. 2 parts. Madras. (Being pp. 77-102 of Macmillan's School Edition bound up with notes.)

The Idylls of the King. . . . Illustrated. In shorthand, by A. G. Doughty, ff. 102. Montreal: The Dominion Illustrated Press.

"Prolegomena to *In Memoriam.*" With an index to the poem, pp. vi., 177. Boston and New York: Houghton, Mifflin & Co. (Printed in Cambridge, Mass.)

Ecrivains modernes de l'Angleterre. Deuxième Série. (Alfred Tennyson, p. 349.) By Emile Montégut. (Printed in Paris.) Coulommiers.

Essays on Literature and Ethics, by W. A. O'Connor. (Tennyson's Palace of Art, pp. 25-56.) Manchester.

Lord Tennyson. Studi, di Francesco Rodriguez. Roma, pp. 198.

Alfréd Tennyson. Király. *Idylljei forditatta es bevezette Szasyk.* (with critical introduction), pp. 556. Budapest.

Tennyson's Touch with Nature (illustrated), in *The Sunday Magazine,* by A. Lamont, vol. xviii., pp. 378-387.

Tennyson's Spiritual Service to his Generation, in *The Andover Review,* vol. xii., pp. 291-296.

Paper on *Lord Tennyson,* with portrait, in *Tinsley's Magazine,* pp. 580-584.

Tennyson and Browning, in *The Spectator,* vol. lxiii., pp. 879, 880.

Tennyson as a Prophet, in *The Nineteenth Century,* by F. H. Myers, vol. xxv., pp. 381-396.

(Same article in *Littell's Living Age*, vol. clxxx., and *Eclectic Magazine*, vol. cxii.)

Tennyson at Eighty. Sonnet to Tennyson on his birthday, by Theodore Watts, in *The Athenæum*, vol. ii., p. 191.

Tennyson at Eighty. Sonnet by the Rev. H. D. Rawnsley, in *Macmillan's Magazine* (August), vol. lx., p. 293.

To Lord Tennyson, lines by Lewis Morris, in *Macmillan's Magazine* (August).

A Poem, by Alfred Austin, in *The Spectator*, vol. lxiii., p. 175.

Article in *The Critic*, vol. xv., pp. 69, 70.

Article in *The Critic*, vol. xv., pp. 105–107, by Edmund Gosse.

Article on *The Bible in Tennyson*, with portrait of Tennyson, by H. Van Dyke, in *The Century Magazine*, vol. xvi., pp. 515–522.

Article on *Tennyson's First Flight*, in *Scribner's Magazine*, by H. Van Dyke.

Both reprinted in *The Poetry of Tennyson*, by Henry Van Dyke. New York : Charles Scribner's Sons, pp. xiii., 296.

The Two Locksley Halls, by T. R. Lounsbury, in *Scribner's Magazine*, vol. vi., pp. 250–256.

Review of *Demeter, and Other Poems*, in *The Academy*, by H. B. Garrod, vol. xxxvi., pp. 413, 414.

Review of *Demeter, and Other Poems*, in *The Athenæum*, 1889, vol. ii., pp. 883–885.

Review of *Demeter, and Other Poems*, in *The Spectator*, vol. lxiii., pp. 883, 884.

The Undertones of Tennyson, in *The Spectator*, vol. lxii. pp. 165, 166.

Tennyson's Art and Genius, in *The Baptist Review* (January) (U. S.), by Eugene Parsons.

The Poets Laureate of England, in *The Methodist Recorder* (February and March), by the Rev. G. Lester.

Homes and Haunts of Alfred, Lord Tennyson, by George P. Napier. (Illustrated.) Pp. xvi., 204. (One hundred copies for private circulation.) Published Glasgow : J. Maclehose & Sons, 1892.

Translations : Enoch Arden. Traduit de l'Anglais par E. Duglin, pp. 32. Beauvais.

Enoch Arden. Ubersetzung aus den Englischen von H. Griebenow, pp. 35. Halle.

1890. *The Poetical Works of Alfred, Lord Tennyson.* A new edition in one volume, pp. viii., 535. Also an edition containing the dramas. London and New York : Macmillan & Co., 1 vol., pp. v., 842.

Tennyson Pictures, by W. Paget and H. Dicksee (with short criticisms of the poems illustrated). London : E. Nister (Nuremburg printed), obl. 4°.

In Tennyson Land, by John C. Walters. Illustrated. London : George Redway, pp. viii., 108.

The Laureate's Country, by Alfred J. Church, with illustrations from drawings by E. Hull. London : Seeley & Co., pp. 111, fol.

The Makers of Modern English, by W. J. Dawson (Tennyson, pp. 169–269). London.

Article on *Lord Tennyson* in *Nuova Antologia* (Rome), pp. 318–340, by F. Rodriguez.

Tennyson's Ballad, *The Voyage of Maeldune,* with music by C. U. Stanford. London : Novello, Ewer & Co.

Views and Reviews, by W. E. Henley. (Tennyson, pp. 154-158). London.

A Study of Tennyson's English. Modern Language Notes, vol. iv.

Tennyson and After ? in *The Fortnightly Review,* vol. liii., pp. 621–637.

(Same article in *The Eclectic Magazine,* vol. cxv.)

Tennyson and Browning, in *The Edinburgh Review,* vol. clxxii., pp. 301–316.

Tennyson and Browning, in *The Leisure Hour,* vol. xxxix., pp. 231–234.

Tennyson and the Questionings of Our Age, in *The Arena,* by J. T. Brixby, vol. ii., pp. 57–71.

Review of *Demeter, and Other Poems,* in *The National Review,* by Alfred Austin, vol. xiv., pp. 694–702.

Review of *Demeter, and Other Poems,* in *The Atlantic Monthly,* vol. lxv., pp. 421–423.

Review of *Demeter, and Other Poems*, in *Poet Lore*, by
C. Porter, vol. ii., pp. 201–207.

Tennyson's In Memoriam, in *The New Englander*, vol. liii.,
p. 492.

Love Passages in Tennyson, in *The New Englander*, by W.
Higgs, vol. liii., pp. 126–142, and pp. 276–283.

Tennyson's Philosophy of the Future Life, in *The Baptist
Quarterly Review*, by J. W. White, vol. xii., pp. 158–
182.

Tennyson's School Days, in *The Pall Mall Gazette*, by C. J.
Caswell (June 19).

Paper on *Tennyson* in *The Examiner* (New York), by E.
Parsons (February).

" In King Arthur's Capital" in *Igdrasil* (the journal of
Ruskin Reading Guild), by J. C. Walters (November).

" Christmas with Lord Tennyson" in *The Fireside Magazine*, by Rev. G. Lester (December).

" An Arthurian Journey" in *The Atlantic Monthly* (June).

Poem on *Tennyson*, in *The Atlantic Monthly*, by T. B.
Aldrich (March).

(*The Isles of Greece, Sappho and Alcæus*, by Frederick
Tennyson.   London and New York: Macmillan & Co.,
pp. xiv., 443.)

Tennyson's portrait, by G. F. Watts, given to Trinity College, Cambridge.

1891. *To Sleep* printed in *The New Review* (March).   Reprinted in *The Foresters*.

Pearl, an English poem of the fourteenth century.   Edited
with a modern rendering by J. Gollanez, *with introductory
lines by Lord Tennyson* and a frontispiece by Holman
Hunt.   London : D. Nutt, pp. lii., 142.

Lines in a volume of his *Poems* presented to Princess Louise
of Schleswig-Holstein.

Lines on the christening of the daughter of the Duchess of
Fife.

The Poetical Works of Alfred, Lord Tennyson.   A new edition in one volume, revised, with new portrait.   Macmillan & Co., pp. 842.

The Coming of Arthur and *The Passing of Arthur*, with
introductions and notes by F. J. Rowe.   Macmillan &
Co., pp. xliii., 78.

Aylmer's Field, with introduction and notes by F. J. Rowe and W. T. Webb. Macmillan & Co., pp. xxxi., 70.

Enoch Arden, with introduction and notes by W. T. Webb. Macmillan & Co., pp. xxxiii., 60.

Tennyson for the Young, with introduction and notes by A. Ainger. Macmillan & Co., pp. xiii., 120.

Illustrations of Tennyson, by J. Churton Collins. London : Chatto & Windus, pp. ix., 186.

Nature in Books, by P. A. Graham. (Tennyson, Art and Scenery, pp. 44–65.) London.

Victorian Poets, by Amy Sharp. (Tennyson, pp. 1–39.) London.

A Vision of Fair Women, a dramatic paraphrase (in verse) based upon Tennyson's *Dream of Fair Women*. Boston : W. H. Baker & Co., pp. 15.

Tennyson's Foresters, in *The Athenæum*, by Theodore Watts, vol. ii., pp. 461, 493, 494. (Same article in *The Critic*, vol. xix., pp. 238, 239.)

The Childhood of Tennyson, illustrated, in *The Art Journal*, by P. A. Graham, vol. xliii., pp. 13–18 and 46–50.

A Day with Tennyson, in *The Forum*, by E. Arnold, vol. xii., pp. 536–548.

Illustrations of Animal Life in the Poems of Tennyson, in *The Cornhill Magazine*, vol. lxiii., pp. 145–151. (Same article in *Littell's Living Age*, vol. clxxxviii.)

Tennyson's Farmers of Lincolnshire, in *The Westminster Review*, by J. J. Davis, vol. cxxxvi., pp. 132–137. (Same article in *Littell's Living Age*, vol. cxci.)

The Quotableness of Tennyson, in *The Chautauquan*, by E. Parsons, vol. xiii., pp. 334–337.

Article on *St. Agnes' Eve* in *Poet Lore*, by A. S. Cook, vol. iii., pp. 10–17.

The Study of Tennyson, in *The Century Magazine*, by H. Van Dyke, vol. xx., pp. 502–510.

Reprinted in *The Poetry of Tennyson*. London : Elkin Mathews.

The Literary Genealogy of Ulysses, in *Poet Lore*, by A. S. Cook, vol. iii., pp. 499–504.

Lord Tennyson's Birthday, in *Notes and Queries* (March 14), by C. J. Caswell.

A Comitia of Errors in *Birmingham Weekly Mercury*, by
C. J. Caswell, April 11. .

Translation : Maud, Ein Gedicht . . . übersetzt von F. W.
Weber. *Zweite verbesserte auflage*, pp. 108. Paderborn.

(*Daphne, and Other Poems*, by Frederick Tennyson. Macmillan & Co., pp. 522.)

Tennyson spent part of the spring on a Mediterranean
cruise, and in the same year visited Devonshire.

1892. Lines on " THE DEATH OF THE DUKE OF CLARENCE AND
AVONDALE," printed in *The Nineteenth Century* (February).

THE FORESTERS, produced at Daly's Theatre, New York
(March 19), with Mr. Drew and Miss Ada Rehan as Robin
Hood and Marian.

On the same day a single formal performance of *The Foresters*, to secure copyright, was given at the Lyceum in London.

The Foresters : Robin Hood and Maid Marian, by Alfred,
Lord Tennyson (a play in four acts, in verse and prose).
London and New York : Macmillan & Co., pp. 155.

THE DEATH OF ŒNONE, AKBAR'S DREAM, AND OTHER
POEMS, by Alfred, Lord Tennyson. London and New
York : Macmillan & Co.. pp. vi., 113, published in
October.

(Also an edition with five steel portraits of the author, pp.
vi., 111.)

Gareth and Lynette, with introduction and notes by G. C.
Macaulay. Macmillan & Co., pp. xxxv., 108.

The Princess, with introduction and notes by Percy M. Wallace. Macmillan & Co., pp. lii., 233.

The Marriage of Geraint ; Geraint and Enid, with introduction and notes by G. C. Macaulay. Macmillan &
Co., pp. xlv., 125.

Idylls of the King (in twelve books). Macmillan & Co.,
pp. 421.

" In Memoriam : Alfred, Lord Tennyson, born 5 August,
1809, died 6 October, 1892," "Crossing the Bar" [and]
" A Poem." London (?), 1892, s. sh. 8°.

Phases of Thought and Criticism, by Brother Azarias. Boston. (*The Spiritual Sense of In Memoriam*, pp. 183–
264.)

The Golden Guess, essays, etc., by J. V. Cheney (Tennyson
and his Critics, pp. 161–201).

A Sermon (Heb. xiii. 7),ꞌ preached by H. M. Butler,
Dean of Gloucester, in the Chapel of Trinity College,
Cambridge, in reference to the death of Lord Tennyson.
London : Macmillan & Bowes, pp. 15.

Tennyson and our Imperial Heritage, by W. H. P. Gres-
well. London : Gower & Co., pp. 23.

Tennyson and In Memoriam, an appreciation and a study,
by Joseph Jacobs. London : D. Nutt., pp. viii., 108.

*Alfred, Lord Tennyson : A Brief Study of his Life and
Poetry*, by Arthur Jenkinson. London : J. Nisbet & Co.,
pp. x., 127.

A Lecture : *Tennyson's Idylls of the King*, by W. M. Mac-
Phail. London: Hitchcock, pp. 36.

Popular Studies of Nineteenth Century Poets, by J. M.
Mather. London. (*Tennyson the Moodist*, pp. 125–
152.)

*Tennyson's Life and Poetry, and Mistakes Concerning Ten-
nyson*, by E. Parsons. Chicago : The Craig Press, pp. 29.
(Enlarged edition, 1893.)

Poets the Interpreters of their Age, by Anna Swanwick.
London. (Tennyson, pp. 380–387.)

*In Memory of Alfred, Lord Tennyson, the English Theocri-
tus*, etc. (verses, with portrait), by E. S. Sterne. London.

Sermonettes from Tennyson, by A. Taylor, pp. 68. Birmingham.

Shadows of the Stage, by William Winter. Edinburgh.
(Tennyson's *Foresters*, pp. 269–285.) Second series,
1893 (Tennyson, pp. 359–367).

" Funeral of the Right Hon. Lord Tennyson, Westminster
Abbey, October 12, 1892" (order of service [including the
text of two poems by Lord Tennyson, " Crossing the
Bar" and " The Silent Voices"]). London: Harrison &
Sons, s. sh. fol.

Records of Tennyson, Ruskin, and Browning, by A.
Thackeray Ritchie, pp. 245. London : Macmillan & Co. ;
New York : Harper & Brothers, pp. 190.

TENNYSON DIED OCTOBER 6.

Article on *Tennyson*, in *The Academy*, by Joseph Jacobs

(October 15), vol. xlii., pp. 335–337. (Reprinted in *Tennyson and In Memoriam* [D. Nutt].)

Article on *Tennyson*, in *The Athenæum*, by Theodore Watts (October 8 and 22), vol. ii., pp. 482, 483 and 555, 556.

Article on *Tennyson*, in *The Andover Review*, by S. H. Thayer (November), vol. xviii., pp. 460–478.

Article on *Tennyson*, in *La Nouvelle Revue*, by F. Lobee (November 1), pp. 173–181.

Article on *Tennyson*, in *Daheim*, with portrait, by K. Koenig (November 19), pp. 102–104.

Article on *Tennyson*, in *Blackwood's Magazine* (November), vol. clii., pp. 748–768.

Article on *Tennyson*, in the *Catholic World*, with portrait, by M. F. Egan (November), vol. lvi., pp. 149–157.

Article on *Tennyson*, in *The Contemporary Review*, by Stopford A. Brooke (December), vol. lxii., pp. 761–785.

Article on *Tennyson*, in *The Critic* (October 15 and 29), with portrait, pp. 203, 204, 237, by H. Van Dyke ; also articles (November 5 and 12), pp. 254–257 and 285–290.

Article on *Tennyson*, in *The Cosmopolitan*, by G. Stewart (December), vol. xiv., p. 169.

Article on *Tennyson*, in *The Dial*, Chicago (October 16), vol. xiii., pp. 231–234.

Article on *Tennyson*, in *Revue Bleue*, by Mary Darmesteter, tom. xlix., pp. 619–623.

Article on *Tennyson*, in *Gentleman's Magazine*, U.S. (November), pp. 535–540.

Article on *Tennyson*, in *Literary World*, Boston (October 22), vol. xxxiii., pp. 372, 373.

Article on *Tennyson*, in *Macmillan's Magazine*, by A. Ainger (November), vol. lxvii., pp. 76–80.

Article on *Tennyson*, in *The Nation*, by J. W. Chadwick (October 13), vol. lv., pp. 276–278.

Article on *Tennyson*, in *The Spectator* (October 8), vol. lxix., pp. 484, 485.

Article on *Tennyson*, in *The Saturday Review*, vol. lxxiv., pp. 405, 406.

Article on *Tennyson*, in *The Westminster Review* (December), vol. cxxxviii., pp. 589–596.

Article on *Tennyson*, in *The Review of Reviews*, by W.
T. Stead (illustrated), vol. vi., pp. 435-447.

Article on *Tennyson*, in *The New Review*, by Edmund
Gosse and Herbert Paul (November), vol. vii., pp. 513-532.
(Same article *Littell's Living Age*, vol. cxcv.)

Poem in *The Spectator* (October 15), by G. H. Warren,
p. 528.

Poem in *The London Illustrated News*, by William Watson
(October 8).

Love and Duty in Tennyson and Browning, in *Poet Lore*, by
E. F. R. Stitt, vol. iv., pp. 271-274.

Tennyson and Whittier, with portraits, in *The Arena*, by
W. J. Fowler, vol. vii., pp. 1-11.

Relations of Tennyson and Whitman to Science, in *The
Dial*, Chicago, by J. Burroughs, vol. xiv., pp. 168, 169.

Aspects of Tennyson (1st paper), in *The Nineteenth Century*, by H. D. Traill, vol. xxxii., pp. 952-956. (Same
article in *Littell's Living Age*, vol. cxcvi.)

Bibliography of Tennyson, in *The Critic*, vol. xxi., p. 211.

Review of *Death of Œnone, and Other Poems*, in *The Academy*, by L. Johnson (November 5), vol. xlii., pp. 403,
404.

Review of *Death of Œnone, and Other Poems*, in *Poet Lore*
(December), vol. iv., pp. 640-643.

Review of *Death of Œnone, and Other Poems*, in *Athenæum*
(November 19), vol. ii., pp. 695-697.

Review of *Death of Œnone, and Other Poems*, in *Saturday
Review* (November 5), vol. lxxiv., pp. 536, 537.

Early French Estimates of Tennyson, in *The Athenæum*
(October 22), vol. ii., pp. 554, 555.

Fancy of Tennyson, in *The Spectator* (April 2), vol. lxviii.,
pp. 458, 459.

Review of Tennyson's *Foresters* in *The Academy*, by W.
Watson (April 9), vol. xli., pp. 341, 342.

Review of Tennyson's *Foresters* in *The Saturday Review*,
vol. lxxiii., pp. 391, 392.

Review of Tennyson's *Foresters* in *The Athenæum* (April
16), vol. i., pp. 491-493.

Review of Tennyson's *Foresters* in *The Gentleman's Magazine*, U. S. (May), vol. xlviii., pp. 528-532.

Maid Marian on the Stage, in *The Theatre*, by A. W. Walkley, vol. xxviii., pp. 227–231.

Notice of the *Funeral of Tennyson* in *The Literary World* (November 5), vol. xxiii., pp. 388, by J. R. Macquoid.

Notice of the *Funeral of Tennyson* in *Littell's Living Age* (November 19), vol. cxcv., p. 510.

Notice of the *Funeral of Tennyson* in *The Spectator* (October 15), vol. lxix., pp. 516, 517.

Notice of the *Funeral of Tennyson* in *The Critic* (November 26), pp. 286–290.

The Genius of Tennyson, in *The Spectator* (October 15), vol. lxix., pp. 522–524.

(Same article in *The Eclectic Magazine*, vol. cxix., and *Littell's Living Age*, vol. cxcv.)

Homes of Tennyson at Aldworth and Farringford, in *The English Illustrated Magazine*, by Grant Allen, vol. x., pp. 145–156.

In the Laureate's Footsteps, in *Good Words* (illustrated), by G. Winterwood, vol. xxxiii., pp. 670–678.

The Celtic Element in The Lady of Shalott, in *Poet Lore*, by A. R. Brown (August and September), vol. iv., pp. 408–415.

The Latest Verses of Tennyson, in *The Gentleman's Magazine*, U. S. (December), vol. xlix., pp. 641, 642.

The Literary Sensitiveness of Tennyson, in *The National Review*, by Alfred Austin (December), vol. xx., pp. 454–460.

(Same article in *Eclectic Magazine*, vol. cxx.)

Art and Architecture in Tennyson's Poems, in *The American Architect* (November 5), vol. xxxviii., p. 87.

Poetical Tributes to Tennyson, poems in *The Nineteenth Century*, by the editor, T. H. Huxley, F. W. H. Myers, and others (November), vol. xxxii., pp. 831–844.

Poetical Tributes to Tennyson in *The Spectator*, by D. Beale (October 29), vol. lxix., p. 595.

Tennysoniana, in *The Athenæum* (October 15, November 26), vol. ii., p. 517, pp. 741, 742.

Tennysoniana, in *The Critic* (December 3), vol. xxi., pp. 315, 316.

Tennysoniana, in *The Dial*, Chicago, vol. xiii., pp. 265–267.

The Theology of Tennyson, in *The Spectator*, vol. lxix., pp. 642, 643.

(Same article in *Eclectic Magazine*, vol. cxix.)

Visit to Tennyson, in *The Critic*, by W. J. Rolfe, vol. xxi., pp. 285, 286.

Tennyson's Works, in *The Spectator*, vol. lxviii., pp. 201, 202.

Enoch Arden. Texte Anglais publié avec une notice sur la vie et les œuvres de Tennyson, une étude sur la versification du prème des notes . . . et des appendices par A. Beljame, pp. 120. Paris.

Enoch Arden . . . avec . . . des notes . . .par A. Beljame. Paris.

1893. *Poems by Two Brothers.* A reprint of the 1827 edition. With facsimiles of part of the MS. and a preface by Hallam, Lord Tennyson, pp. xix., 251. London : Macmillan & Co.

Poems . . . illustrated (reprinted from the edition of 1857), pp. xiii., 374. Macmillan & Co.

The Holy Grail. With introduction and notes by G. C. Macaulay, pp. xl., 86. Macmillan & Co.

Selections from Tennyson. With introduction and notes by J. F. Rowe and W. T. Webb. 2 parts. Macmillan & Co.

Maud : A Monodrama, pp. 69. Macmillan & Co. 4°.

Becket. As arranged for the stage by Henry Irving. Macmillan & Co.

Tennyson's Heroes and Heroines. Illustrated by Marcus Stone. London : Tuck & Sons.

The Teaching of Tennyson, by E. H. Blakeney. Reprinted from *The Churchman*, pp. 8.

Essays, Addresses, etc., by the Rev. T. C. Finlayson. (Tennyson's *In Memoriam*, pp. 1-35.) Macmillan & Co.

The Scenery of Tennyson's Poems. Etchings after drawings by various artists. With introduction and descriptive letterpress by B. Francis. London : J. & E. Bumpus.

Questions at Issue, by Edmund Gosse. (Tennyson, pp. 175-198.)

" The Poems of A. H. Hallam, together with his Essay on the Lyrical Poems of Alfred Tennyson." Edited, with an introduction, by R. Le Gallienne, pp. xxxix., 139. E. Mathews and John Lane.

Seers and Singers, by A. D. Innes. (Tennyson, pp. 26–49.)

Essays on Lord Tennyson's *Idylls of the King*, by Harold Littledale, pp. x., 308.

New Studies in Tennyson, including a Commentary on *Maud*, by Morton Luce (2d edition), pp. 96. Clifton : J. Barker & Son.

The Poets and the Poetry of the Century. (Frederick Tennyson to Clough.) (Alfred Tennyson, by A. H. Japp, pp. 67–102.)

Science and a Future Life, by F. W. H. Myers. (Tennyson as prophet, pp. 127–165.)

Tennyson as a Thinker, by Henry Salt, pp. 56. London : W. Reeves.

Death of Tennyson, by John Parnell (in verse), a single sheet. London.

Alfred, Lord Tennyson and his Friends. A series of twenty-five portraits in photogravure from the negatives of Mrs. J. M. Cameron and H. H. H. Cameron. Reminiscences by A. Thackeray Ritchie. With introduction by H. H. H. Cameron. London : T. F. Unwin, folio.

Tennyson : Poet, Philosopher, Idealist. Studies on the life, work, and teaching of the Poet Laureate (Tennysonian chronology). With portrait, pp. viii., 370. London : Kegan Paul & Co.

Alfred, Lord Tennyson, by Arthur Waugh (2d edition, enlarged), pp. x., 332. London : Heinemann.

English Poetry from Blake to Browning, by W. Macneile Dixon. (Tennyson, Arnold, Browning, pp. 188–200.) London : Methuen & Co.

Article on *Tennyson*, in *Harper's Magazine*, by A. Fields (January), vol. lxxxvi., pp. 309–312.

Article on *Tennyson*, in *The Church Quarterly*, vol. xxxv., pp. 485–506.

Tennyson and Browning as Spiritual Forces, in *The New World*, by C. C. Everett (June), vol. ii., pp. 240–256.

Tennyson and the Meaning of Life, in *The Nineteenth Century*, by F. W. H. Myers (January), vol. xxxiii., pp. 93–111.

Tennyson on the Future Life, in *The Spectator* (March 4), vol. lxx., p. 283.

Tennyson as a Nature Poet, in *The Nineteenth Century*. by Theodore Watts (May), vol. xxxiii., pp. 836-856. (Same article, June and July.)

Tennyson as the Poet of Evolution, in *The Nineteenth Century*, by Theodore Watts (October), vol. xxxiv., pp. 657-672. (Same article, December.)

Tennyson as the Religious Exponent of his Age, in *The Sunday Magazine*, by J. Wedgwood (January), vol. xxii., pp. 34-38.

Aspects of Tennyson. One of a series of articles in *The Nineteenth Century*, by the editor (January), vol. xxxiii., pp. 164-168. (Same article in *Littell's Living Age*, vol. cxcvi.)

At the Laureate's Funeral. A poem in *The National Review* by the Duke of Argyll (January), vol. xx., pp. 581-586.

The Real Thomas Becket, in *The Nineteenth Century*, by Agnes Lambert, vol. xxxiii., pp. 273-292.

"*Becket* at the Lyceum Theatre," in *The Spectator* (February 25), vol. lxx., p. 253.

"*Becket* at the Lyceum Theatre," in *The Academy*, by F. Wedmore (February 18), vol. xliii., pp. 158, 159.

"*Becket* at the Lyceum Theatre," in *The Saturday Review* (February 11), vol. lxxv., pp. 146-147.

"*Becket* at the Lyceum Theatre," in *The Art Journal* (illustrated), by J. Hatton (April), vol. xlv., pp. 105-109.

Tennyson's Classical Poems, in *The Nineteenth Century*, by H. Paul (March), vol. xxxiii., pp. 436-453. (Same article, May.)

A Word with Dissenters about Tennyson, in *The Dial*, Chicago, by P. Shorey (February 16), vol. xiv., pp. 102, 103.

The Earliest Poems of Tennyson, in *The Critic* (May 2), vol. xxii., pp. 333-335.

Tennyson's Elaine and Shakespere's Miranda, in *Poet Lore*, by S. D. Davies (January), vol. v., p. 15.

How to Study In Memoriam, in *Poet Lore*, by H. A. Clarke (November), vol. v., pp. 574-582.

The Two Locksley Halls, in *Poet Lore* (January), vol. v., p. 34.

Tennyson's Place in Poetry, in *The Dial*, Chicago, by E. E. Hale (February 16), vol. xiv., pp. 101, 102.

Poem on *Tennyson*, in *The Nineteenth Century*, by A. C. Swinburne (January), vol. xxxiii., pp. 1–3. (Same in *Eclectic Magazine*, vol. cxx.)

Review of *The Poetry of Tennyson* in *The Quarterly Review*, vol. clxxvi., pp. 1–39.

Recollections of Tennyson, in *The Century Magazine*, by J. A. Symonds (May), vol. xlvi., pp. 32–37.

The Study of Tennyson in Class, in *Education*, by H. M. Reynolds (February), vol. xiii., p. 359.

Talks with Tennyson, in *The Contemporary Review*, by A. G. Weld, vol. lxiii., pp. 394–397.

Tennysoniana, in *The Sunday Magazine* (January, February, March), vol. xxii., pp. 50–53, 122–125, 201–205.

The Voice of Tennyson, in *The Century Magazine*, by H. Van Dyke, vol. xlv., pp. 539–544.

Was Tennyson Consistent? in *The American Catholic Quarterly*, by G. P. Lathrop, vol. xviii., p. 101.

Was Tennyson either Gnostic or Agnostic? in *The Spectator* (January 7), vol. lxx., p. 10. (Same article in *Littell's Living Age*, vol. cxcvi.)

Translations: Des Koenigs. Idyllen metrisch vertaald door J. H. F. Le Comte, pp. 296. Rotterdam.

Aylmer's Field . . . Deutsch von H. Griebenow, pp. 49. Halle.

1894.   *Tennyson: His Art and Relation to Modern Life*, by Stopford A. Brooke, pp. vi., 490. London: Isbister & Co.

Tennyson's Idylls of the King and Arthurian Story from the XVIth Century, by M. W. Maccallum. Glasgow: Maclehose & Sons, pp. xiv., 435.

'Tis Sixty Years Since; or, The Two Locksley Halls, by H. S. Wilson. London: Kegan Paul & Co., pp. 45.

Article on *Tennyson* in *The New Review*, by Francis Adams (March), pp. 311–323.

Tennyson and Dante, in *Temple Bar*, by Francis St. J. Thackeray (July), pp. 387–397.

Tennyson as a Humorist, in *The Nineteenth Century*, by H. D. Traill, vol. xxxv., pp. 761–774.

New Lights on Tennyson, in *The Sunday Magazine*, by H. V. Taylor (May), pp. 344–347.

The Religion of Tennyson, in *The Arena*, by W. H· Savage (April), pp. 582–592.

Turncoat of Tennyson, in *The Westminster Review*, by J. J. Davies (November), pp. 558–566.

The Trees and Flowers of Tennyson, in *Temple Bar* (November), pp. 358–366.

A Visit to the Tennysons in 1839, in *Blackwood's Magazine*, by B. Teeling (May), pp. 605–621.

Translation : Balladen und lyrische Gedichte übertaagen von Sophie von Harbon, pp. viii., 208. Charlottenburg.

The Works of Alfred, Lord Tennyson, Poet Laureate, the complete single vol. edition, containing the last alterations. London : Macmillan & Co.

A CATALOGUE OF BOOKS
AND ANNOUNCEMENTS OF
METHUEN AND COMPANY
PUBLISHERS : LONDON
36 ESSEX STREET
W.C.

CONTENTS

SEPTEMBER 1902

MESSRS. METHUEN'S
ANNOUNCEMENTS

THE COMPLETE WORKS OF CHARLES LAMB. Edited by E. V. LUCAS. With numerous Illustrations. *In Seven Volumes. Demy 8vo. 7s. 6d. each.*

This new edition of the works of Charle and Mary Lamb, in five volumes (to be followed by two volumes containing the Letters), will be found to contain a large quantity of new matter both in prose and verse—several thousand words in all. Mr. E. V. Lucas, the editor, has attempted in the notes, not only to relate Lamb's writings to his life, but to account for all his quotations and allusions— an ideal of thoroughness far superior to any that previous editors have set before themselves. A Life of Lamb by Mr. Lucas will follow next year.

THE LIFE AND LETTERS OF OLIVER CROMWELL. By THOMAS CARLYLE. With an Introduction by C. H. FIRTH, M.A., and Notes and Appendices by Mrs. S. C. LOMAS. *Three Volumes. 6s. each.* [*Methuen's Standard Library.*

This edition is brought up to the standard of modern scholarship by the addition of numerous new letters of Cromwell, and by the correction of many errors which recent research has discovered.

CRITICAL AND HISTORICAL ESSAYS. By LORD MACAULAY. Edited by F. C. MONTAGUE, M.A. *Three Volumes. Crown 8vo. 6s. each.* [*Methuen's Standard Library.*

The only edition of this book completely annotated.

IN MEMORIAM, MAUD, AND THE PRINCESS. Edited by J. CHURTON COLLINS, M.A. *Crown 8vo. 6s.*
[*Methuen's Standard Library.*

THE FRENCH REVOLUTION. By THOMAS CARLYLE. Edited by C. R. L. FLETCHER, Fellow of Magdalen College, Oxford. *Three Volumes. Crown 8vo. 6s. each.*
[*Methuen's Standard Library.*

This edition is magnificently equipped with notes.

LORD STRATHCONA: THE STORY OF HIS LIFE. By BECKLES WILLSON. Illustrated. *Demy 8vo. 7s. 6d.*

OTHELLO. Edited by H. C. HART. *Demy 8vo. 3s. 6d.*
[*The Arden Shakespeare.*

ROBERT HARLEY, EARL OF OXFORD. By E. S. ROSCOE. Illustrated. *Demy 8vo. 7s. 6d.*

WALTER RALEIGH. By Miss J. A. TAYLOR. With 12 Illustrations. *Cloth, 3s. 6d. ; leather, 4s. net.*
[*Little Biographies.*

LORD TENNYSON. By A. C. BENSON, M.A. With 12 Illustrations. *Cloth, 3s. 6d. ; leather, 4s. net.*
[*Little Biographies.*

ERASMUS. By E. F. H. CAPEY, M.A. With Illustrations. *Cloth, 3s. 6d.; leather, 4s net.*
[*Little Biographies.*

CHRISTMAS BOOKS By W. M. THACKERAY. Edited by STEPHEN GWYNN. *Pot 8vo, cloth, 1s. 6d. net; leather, 2s. 6d. net.*
[*The Little Library.*

ESMOND. By W. M. THACKERAY. Edited by STEPHEN GWYNN. *Two Volumes. Pott 8vo, cloth, 1s. 6d. net ; leather, 2s. 6d. net.*
[*The Little Library.*

CHRISTMAS BOOKS. By CHARLES DICKENS. Edited by STEPHEN GWYNN. *Two Volumes. Pott 8vo, cloth, 1s. 6d. net; leather, 2s. 6d. net.*
[*The Little Library.*

THE INGOLDSBY LEGENDS. Edited by J. B. ATLAY. *Two Volumes. Pott 8vo, cloth, 1s. 6d. net ; leather, 2s. 6d. net.*
[*The Little Library.*

A LITTLE BOOK OF ENGLISH SONNETS. Edited by J. B. B. NICHOLS. *Pott 8vo, cloth, 1s. 6d. net ; leather, 2s. 6d. net.*
[*The Little Library.*

THE SCARLET LETTER. By NATHANIEL HAWTHORNE. Edited by PERCY DEARMER. *Pott 8vo, cloth, 1s. 6d. net ; leather, 2s. 6d. net.*
[*The Little Library.*

THE INHERITANCE. By SUSAN FERRIER. *Two Volumes. Pott 8vo, cloth, 1s. 6d. net ; leather, 2s. 6d. net.*
[*The Little Library.*

PARIS. By HILAIRE BELLOC. Illustrated. *Crown 8vo. 6s.*

CORNWALL. By A. L. SALMON. Illustrated by B. C. BOULTER. *Pott 8vo, cloth, 3s. ; leather, 3s. 6d. net.*
[*The Little Guides.*

KENT. By G. CLINCH. Illustrated by F. D. BEDFORD. *Pott 8vo, cloth, 3s.; leather, 3s. 6d. net.* [*The Little Guides.*

BRITTANY. By S. BARING - GOULD. Illustrated by J. WYLIE. *Pott 8vo, cloth, 3s. ; leather, 3s. 6d. net.*
[*The Little Guides.*

THE ENGLISH LAKES. By F. G. BRABANT, M.A. Illustrated by E. H. NEW. *Pott 8vo, cloth 3s. ; leather, 3s. 6d. net.*
[*The Little Guides.*

ON COMMANDO. By D. S. VAN WARMELO. With Portrait. *Crown 8vo. 3s 6d.*

THE HEART OF JAPAN. By C. L. BROWNELL. Illustrated. *Crown 8vo. 6s.*
A lively description of Japan and the Japanese.

OLD PICTURE-BOOKS. By A. W. POLLARD, M.A. With many Illustrations. *Demy 8vo.*

A KEY TO THE TIME ALLUSIONS IN THE DIVINE COMEDY. By G. PRADEAU. With a Dial. *Small quarto. 3s. 6d.*

THE STRUGGLE FOR PERSIA. By CAPTAIN DONALD STUART. With a Map. *Crown 8vo. 6s.*

THE VISIT TO LONDON. Described in verse by E. V. LUCAS, and in coloured pictures by F. D. BEDFORD. *Small 4to. 6s.*
This charming book describes the introduction of a country child to the delights and sights of London. It is the result of a well-known partnership between author and artist.

THE BOOK OF THE COUNTRY AND THE GARDEN. By H. M. BATSON. Illustrated by F. CARRUTHERS GOULD and A. C. GOULD. *Demy 8vo. 10s. 6d.*

MODERN SPIRITUALISM. By FRANK PODMORE. *Two Volumes. 8vo. 21s. net.*
A History and a Criticism.

ANCIENT COFFERS AND CUPBOARDS : THEIR HISTORY AND DESCRIPTION. With many Illustrations. By FRED ROE. *Quarto. £3, 3s. net.*

THE INNER AND MIDDLE TEMPLE. By H. H. L. BELLOT, M.A. With numerous Illustrations. *Crown 8vo. 6s. net.*
This book is not only a history of the Temple and of its many associations, but it is also a guide to its buildings. It is full of interesting anecdotes, and is abundantly illustrated.

SIDELIGHTS ON THE GEORGIAN PERIOD. By GEORGE PASTON. With many illustrations. *Demy 8vo. 10s. 6d.*

THE AUTOBIOGRAPHY OF A 'NEWSPAPER GIRL.' By E. L. BANKS. With Portrait of the Author. *Crown 8vo. 6s.*

THE DEVOTIONS OF ST. ANSELM. Edited by C. C. J. WEBB, M.A. *Pott 8vo, cloth, 2s. ; leather, 2s. 6d. net.*
[*The Library of Devotion.*

THE DEVOTIONS OF BISHOP ANDREWES. By F. E. BRIGHTMAN, M.A., of Pusey House, Oxford. *Crown 8vo. 6s.*
This elaborate work has been in preparation for many years, and is the most complete edition that has ever been published of the famous devotions. It contains a long Introduction, with numerous Notes and References.

COMPARATIVE THEOLOGY. By J. A. MacCulloch.
Crown 8vo. 6s. [*The Churchman's Library.*

SECOND STRINGS. By A. D. Godley, M.A. *F'cap. 8vo.*
2s. 6d.
A volume of light verse.

Educational Books

DESIGNING AND WEAVING. By A. F. Barker. Illustrated. *Demy 8vo.*

AGRICULTURAL GEOLOGY By J. E. Marr, F.R.S. With numerous Illustrations. *Crown 8vo.*

ARITHMETIC AND MENSURATION FOR THE WORK-SHOP AND TECHNICAL SCHOOL. By C. T. Millis, M.I.M.E., Principal of the Borough Polytechnic College. With Diagrams. *Crown 8vo.*

EASY DICTATION AND SPELLING. By W. Williamson, B.A., Headmaster of the West Kent Grammar School, Brockley. *Fcap. 8vo. 1s.*

THE ROSE READER. By Edward Rose. With Four coloured and other Illustrations. *Crown 8vo. 2s. 6d. And in 4 Parts.* Parts I. and II., *6d. each*; Part III., *8d.* ; Part IV., *10d.*

JUNIOR ENGLISH EXAMINATION PAPERS. By W. Williamson, B.A., Headmaster West Kent Grammar School, Brockley. *Fcap. 8vo. 1s.* [*Junior Examination Series.*

JUNIOR ARITHMETIC EXAMINATION PAPERS. By W. S. Beard, Headmaster Modern School, Fareham. *Fcap. 8vo. 1s.* [*Junior Examination Series.*

THE ACTS OF THE APOSTLES. Edited by A. E. Rubie, M.A., Headmaster Royal Naval School, Eltham. *Crown 8vo. 2s.*
[*Methuen's Junior School Books.*

THE GOSPEL ACCORDING TO ST. LUKE. Edited by W. Williamson, B.A., Headmaster of the West Kent Grammar School, Brockley. *Crown 8vo. 1s. 6d.* [*Methuen's Junior School Books.*

A JUNIOR FRENCH GRAMMAR. By L. A. Sornet and M. J. Acatos, Modern Language Masters at King Edward's School, Birmingham. [*Methuen's Junior School Books.*

THE STUDENTS' PRAYER BOOK. Part I. Morning and Evening Prayer and Litany. Edited by W. H. Flecker, M.A., D.C.L., Headmaster of the Dean Close School, Cheltenham. *Crown 8vo. 2s. 6d.*

A JUNIOR CHEMISTRY. By E. A. TYLER, B.A., F.C.S.,
Science Master at Framlingham College. With 73 Illustrations.
Crown 8vo. 2s. 6d.   [*Methuen's Junior School Books.*

JUNIOR ALGEBRA EXAMINATION PAPERS. By S. W.
FINN, M.A. *Crown 8vo. 1s.*

The Little Blue Books for Children

Edited by E. V. LUCAS.

Illustrated: Square Fcap. 8vo. 2s. 6d.

Messrs. METHUEN are publishing a series of children's books under
the above general title. The new volumes are :

A SCHOOL YEAR. By NETTA SYRETT.

THE PEELES AT THE CAPITAL. By T. HILBERT.

THE TREASURE OF PRINCEGATE PRIORY. By T. COBB.

Fiction

TEMPORAL POWER : A STUDY IN SUPREMACY. By MARIE
CORELLI. *Crown 8vo. 6s.*

THE SEA LADY. By H. G. WELLS. *Crown 8vo. 6s.*

A FIVE YEARS' TRYST AND OTHER STORIES. By Sir
WALTER BESANT. *Crown 8vo. 6s.*

THE HOLE IN THE WALL. By ARTHUR MORRISON,
Author of 'A Child of the Jago,' etc. *Crown 8vo. 6s.*

OLIVIA'S SUMMER. By Mrs. M. E. MANN, Author of 'The
Patten Experiment.' *Crown 8vo. 6s.*

A BAYARD FROM BENGAL. By F. ANSTEY, Author of 'Vice
Versâ.' Illustrated by BERNARD PARTRIDGE. *Crown 8vo. 3s. 6d.*

A VOLUME OF STORIES. By 'Q.' *Crown 8vo. 6s.*

THE RIVER. By EDEN PHILLPOTTS. *Crown 8vo 6s.*

A ROMAN MYSTERY. By RICHARD BAGOT. *Crown 8vo. 6s.*

JAIR THE APOSTATE. By A. G. HALES. Illustrated by
A. H. BUCKLAND. *Crown 8vo. 6s.*

FELIX. By R. HICHENS, Author of 'Flames,' etc. *Crown
8vo. 6s.*

CHILDREN OF THE BUSH. By HARRY LAWSON. *Crown
8vo. 6s.*

THE FOUNDING OF FORTUNES. By JANE BARLOW
Author of 'Irish Idylls.' *Crown 8vo. 6s.*

THE CREDIT OF THE COUNTY. By W. E. NORRIS.
Illustrated by N. TENISON. *Crown 8vo. 6s.*

THE LIGHTNING CONDUCTOR : Being the Romance of a
Motor Car. By Mr. and Mrs. C. N. WLLIAMSON. *Crown 8vo. 6s.*

HONEY. By HELEN MATHERS, Author of 'Comin' thro' the
Rye.' *Crown 8vo. 6s.*

HOLY MATRIMONY. By DOROTHEA GERARD, Author of
'Lady Baby.' *Crown 8vo. 6s.*

MISS QUILLET. By S. BARING-GOULD, Author of 'Mehalah.'
Illustrated by G. GRENVILLE MANTON. *Crown 8vo. 6s.*

BARBARA'S MONEY. By ADELINE SERGEANT, Author of
'The Story of a Penitent Soul.' *Crown 8vo. 6s.*

JIM TWELVES. By W. F. SHANNON, Author of 'The Mess
Deck.' *Crown 8vo. 3s. 6d.*

THE ADVENTURES OF SIR JOHN SPARROW. By
HAROLD BEGBIE. *Crown 8vo. 6s.*

THE FATE OF VALSEC. By J. BLOUNDELLE BURTON.
Crown 8vo. 6s.

PAPA. By Mrs. C. N. WILLIAMSON, Author of 'The Barn-
stormers.' *Crown 8vo. 6s.*

MRS. CLYDE. By JULIEN GORDON. *Crown 8vo. 6s.*

THE BRANDED PRINCE. By WEATHERBY CHESNEY,
Author of 'John Topp, Pirate.' *Crown 8vo. 6s.*

A PRINCESS OF THE HILLS. By Mrs. BURTON HARRISON.
Illustrated. *Crown 8vo. 6s.*

THE TWICKENHAM PEERAGE. By RICHARD MARSH,
Author of 'The Beetle.' *Crown 8vo. 6s.*

THE PUPPET CROWN. By HAROLD MACGRATH. Illustrated. *Crown 8vo. 6s.*

ASTED FIRES. By HUME NISBET. *Crown 8vo. 6s.*

WITH ESSEX IN IRELAND. By the Hon. EMILY LAW-
LESS. *Cheaper Edition. Crown 8vo. 6s.*
A cheaper edition of a book which won considerable popularity in a more expensive
form some years ago.

THE INCA'S TREASURE. By ERNEST GLANVILLE.
Illustrated by A. H. BUCKLAND. *Crown 8vo. 3s. 6d.*

The Novelist

Messrs. METHUEN are issuing under the above general title a Monthly
Series of Novels by popular authors at the price of Sixpence. Each
Number is as long as the average Six Shilling Novel.

No. XXXII. THE KLOOF BRIDE. By ERNEST GLANVILLE.

Methuen's Sixpenny Library

THE MILL ON THE FLOSS. By GEORGE ELIOT.
PETER SIMPLE. By CAPTAIN MARRYAT.
MARY BARTON. By MRS. GASKELL.
PRIDE AND PREJUDICE. By JANE AUSTEN.
NORTH AND SOUTH. By MRS. GASKELL.
JACOB FAITHFUL. By CAPTAIN MARRYAT.
SHIRLEY. By CHARLOTTE BRONTË.

MESSRS. METHUEN'S
PUBLICATIONS

---◆---

PART I.—GENERAL LITERATURE

Jacob Abbot. THE BEECHNUT BOOK. Edited by E. V. LUCAS. Illustrated. *Square Fcap 8vo.* 2s. 6d.
[Little Blue Books.

W. F. Adeney, M.A. See Bennett and Adeney.

Æschylus. AGAMEMNON, CHOEPHOROE, EUMENIDES. Translated by LEWIS CAMPBELL, LL.D., late Professor of Greek at St. Andrews. 5s.
[Classical Translations.

G. A. Aitken. See Swift.

William Alexander, D.D., Archbishop of Armagh. THOUGHTS AND COUNSELS OF MANY YEARS. Selected from the writings of Archbishop ALEXANDER. *Square Pott 8vo.* 2s. 6d.

St. Anselm, THE DEVOTIONS OF. Edited by C. C. J. WEBB, M.A. *Pott 8vo. Cloth,* 2s. ; *leather,* 2s. 6d. net.
[Library of Devotion.

Aristophanes. THE FROGS. Translated into English by E. W. HUNTINGFORD, M.A., Professor of Classics in Trinity College, Toronto. *Crown 8vo.* 2s. 6d.

Aristotle. THE NICOMACHEAN ETHICS. Edited, with an Introduction and Notes, by JOHN BURNET, M.A., Professor of Greek at St. Andrews. *Demy 8vo.* 15s. net.

'We have seldom, if ever, seen an edition of any classical author in which what is held in common with other commentators is so clearly and shortly put, and what is original is (with equal brevity) of such value and interest.'—*Pilot.*

J. B. Atkins. THE RELIEF OF LADY-SMITH. With 16 Plans and Illustrations. *Third Edition. Crown 8vo.* 6s.

St. Augustine, THE CONFESSIONS OF. Newly Translated, with an Introduction and Notes, by C. BIGG, D.D., late Student of Christ Church. *Third Edition. Pott 8vo. Cloth,* 2s ; *leather,* 2s. 6d. net.
[Library of Devotion.

'The translation is an excellent piece of English, and the introduction is a masterly exposition. We augur well of a series which begins so satisfactorily.'—*Times.*

Jane Austen. PRIDE AND PREJUDICE. Edited by E. V. LUCAS. *Two Volumes. Pott 8vo. Each volume, cloth,* 1s. 6d.; *leather,* 2s. 6d. net. [Little Library.

NORTHANGER ABBEY. Edited by E. V. LUCAS. *Pott 8vo. Cloth,* 1s. 6d.; *leather,* 2s. 6d. net. [Little Library.

Constance Bache. BROTHER MUSICIANS. Reminiscences of Edward and Walter Bache. With 16 Illustrations. *Crown 8vo.* 6s. net.

R. S. S. Baden-Powell, Major-General. THE DOWNFALL OF PREMPEH. A Diary of Life in Ashanti, 1895. With 21 Illustrations and a Map. *Third Edition. Large Crown 8vo.* 6s.

THE MATABELE CAMPAIGN, 1896. With nearly 100 Illustrations. *Fourth and Cheaper Edition. Large Crown 8vo.* 6s.

Graham Balfour. THE LIFE OF ROBERT LOUIS STEVENSON. *Second Edition. Two Volumes. Demy 8vo.* 25s. net.

'The biographer has performed his labour of love with exemplary skill, with unfailing good taste, and with an enthusiastic admiration for the genius of the writer and a whole-souled affection for the man.'—
Daily Telegraph.

'The story has all the charm of a revelation. It is written with admirable taste and simplicity.'—*Pall Mall Gazette.*

Mr. Balfour has done his work extremely well—done it, in fact, as Stevenson himself would have wished it done, with care and skill and affectionate appreciation. His own personal tribute in the last chapter of the second volume is an admirable piece of writing, the tribute of a relative and admirer, but none the less faithful and discerning.'—*Westminster Gazette.*

S. Baring-Gould, Author of 'Mehalah,' etc.
THE LIFE OF NAPOLEON BONA-PARTE. With over 450 Illustrations in the Text, and 12 Photogravure Plates. *Gilt top. Large quarto.* 36s.
'The main feature of this gorgeous volume is its great wealth of beautiful photogravures and finely-executed wood engravings, constituting a complete pictorial chronicle of Napoleon I.'s personal history.'—*Daily Telegraph.*

THE TRAGEDY OF THE CÆSARS. With numerous Illustrations from Busts, Gems, Cameos, etc. *Fifth Edition. Royal 8vo. 15s.*
'A most splendid and fascinating book on a subject of undying interest. It is brilliantly written, and the illustrations are supplied on a scale of profuse magnificence.' —*Daily Chronicle.*

A BOOK OF FAIRY TALES. With numerous Illustrations and Initial Letters by ARTHUR J. GASKIN. *Second Edition. Crown 8vo. Buckram.* 6s.

OLD ENGLISH FAIRY TALES. With numerous Illustrations by F. D. BEDFORD. *Second Edition. Cr. 8vo. Buckram.* 6s.
'A charming volume.'—*Guardian.*

THE CROCK OF GOLD. Fairy Stories. *Crown 8vo.* 6s.
'Twelve delightful fairy tales. —*Punch.*

THE VICAR OF MORWENSTOW: A Biography. A new and Revised Edition. With Portrait. *Crown 8vo.* 3s. 6d.
A completely new edition of the well-known biography of R. S. Hawker.

DARTMOOR: A Descriptive and Historical Sketch. With Plans and numerous Illustrations. *Crown 8vo.* 6s.
'A most delightful guide, companion and instructor.'—*Scotsman.*

THE BOOK OF THE WEST. With numerous Illustrations. *Two volumes.* Vol. I. Devon. *Second Edition.* Vol. II. Cornwall. *Second Edition. Crown 8vo.* 6s. each.
'Bracing as the air of Dartmoor, the legend weird as twilight over Dozmare Pool, they give us a very good idea of this enchanting and beautiful district.'—*Guardian.*

A BOOK OF BRITTANY. With numerous Illustrations. *Crown 8vo.* 6s.
Uniform in scope and size with Mr. Baring-Gould's well-known books on Devon, Cornwall, and Dartmoor.

OLD COUNTRY LIFE. With 67 Illustrations. *Fifth Edition. Large Cr. 8vo.* 6s.

AN OLD ENGLISH HOME. With numerous Plans and Illustrations. *Cr. 8vo.* 6s.

HISTORIC ODDITIES AND STRANGE EVENTS. *Fifth Edition. Cr. 8vo.* 6s.

YORKSHIRE ODDITIES AND STRANGE EVENTS. *Fifth Edition. Crown 8vo.* 6s.

STRANGE SURVIVALS AND SUPER-STITIONS. *Second Edition. Cr. 8vo.* 6s.

A GARLAND OF COUNTRY SONG: English Folk Songs with their Traditional Melodies. Collected and arranged by S. BARING-GOULD and H. F. SHEPPARD. *Demy 4to.* 6s.

SONGS OF THE WEST: Traditional Ballads and Songs of the West of England, with their Melodies. Collected by S. BARING-GOULD, M.A., and H. F. SHEPPARD, M.A. In 4 Parts. *Parts I., II., III.,* 3s. *each. Part IV.,* 5s. *In One Volume, French Morocco,* 15s.
'A rich collection of humour, pathos, grace, and poetic fancy.'—*Saturday Review.*

S. E. Bally. A FRENCH COMMERCIAL READER. With Vocabulary. *Second Edition. Crown 8vo.* 2s.
[Commercial Series.

FRENCH COMMERCIAL CORRE-SPONDENCE. With Vocabulary. *Third Edition. Crown 8vo.* 2s.
[Commercial Series.

A GERMAN COMMERCIAL READER. With Vocabulary. *Crown 8vo.* 2s.
[Commercial Series.

GERMAN COMMERCIAL CORRE-SPONDENCE. With Vocabulary. *Crown 8vo.* 2s. 6d. [Commercial Series.

W. E. Barnes, D.D. ISAIAH. *Two Volumes. Fcap. 8vo.* 2s. *net each.* Vol. I. With Map. [Churchman's Bible.

Mrs. P. A. Barnett. A LITTLE BOOK OF ENGLISH PROSE. *Pott 8vo. Cloth,* 1s. 6d. *net ; leather,* 2s. 6d. *net.*
[Little Library.

R. R. N. Baron, M.A. FRENCH PROSE COMPOSITION. *Crown 8vo.* 2s. 6d. *Key,* 3s. *net.*

H. M. Barron, M.A., Wadham College, Oxford. TEXTS FOR SERMONS ON VARIOUS OCCASIONS AND SUB-JECTS. With a Preface by Canon SCOTT HOLLAND. *Crown 8vo* 3s. 6d.

C. F. Bastable, M.A., Professor of Economics at Trinity College, Dublin. THE COMMERCE OF NATIONS. *Second Edition. Crown 8vo 2s. 6d.*
[Social Questions Series.

H. M. Batson. See Edward FitzGerald.

A. Hulme Beaman. PONS ASINORUM; OR, A GUIDE TO BRIDGE. *Second Edition. Fcap. 8vo. 2s.*

A practical guide, with many specimen games, to the game of Bridge.

Peter Beckford. THOUGHTS ON HUNTING. Edited by J. OTHO PAGET, and Illustrated by G. H. JALLAND. *Demy 8vo. 10s. 6d.*

William Beckford. THE HISTORY OF THE CALIPH VATHEK. Edited by E. DENISON ROSS. *Pott 8vo. Cloth, 1s. 6d. net; leather, 2s 6d. net.* [Little Library.

H. C. Beeching, M.A. See Tennyson.

Jacob Behmen. THE SUPERSENSUAL LIFE. Edited by BERNARD HOLLAND. *Fcap. 8vo. 3s. 6d.*

W. H. Bennett, M.A., A PRIMER OF THE BIBLE. *Second Edition. Crown 8vo. 2s. 6d.*

'The work of an honest, fearless, and sound critic, and an excellent guide in a small compass to the books of the Bible.' —*Manchester Guardian.*

W. H. Bennett and W. F. Adeney. A BIBLICAL INTRODUCTION. *Crown 8vo. 7s. 6d.*

'It makes available to the ordinary reader the best scholarship of the day in the field of Biblical introduction. We know of no book which comes into competition with it.' —*Manchester Guardian.*

A. C. Benson, M.A. THE LIFE OF LORD TENNYSON. With 12 Illustrations. *Fcap. 8vo. Cloth, 3s. 6d.; Leather, 4s. net.* [Little Biographies.

R. M. Benson. THE WAY OF HOLINESS: a Devotional Commentary on the 119th Psalm. *Crown 8vo. 5s.*

M. Bidez. See Parmentier.

C. Bigg, D.D. See St. Augustine, à Kempis, and William Law.

C. R. D. Biggs, B.D. THE EPISTLE TO THE PHILIPPIANS. Edited by. *Fcap. 8vo. 1s. 6d. net.* [Churchman's Bible.

'Mr. Biggs' work is very thorough, and he has managed to compress a good deal of information into a limited space.' —*Guardian.*

T. Herbert Bindley, B.D. THE OECUMENICAL DOCUMENTS OF THE FAITH. With Introductions and Notes. *Crown 8vo. 6s.*
A historical account of the Creeds.

William Blake. See Little Library.

B. Blaxland, M.A. THE SONG OF SONGS. Being Selections from ST. BERNARD. *Pott 8vo. Cloth, 2s.; leather, 2s. 6d. net.* [Library of Devotion.

George Body, D.D. THE SOUL'S PILGRIMAGE: Devotional Readings from his published and unpublished writings. Selected and arranged by J. H. BURN, B.D. *Pott 8vo. 2s. 6d.*

A. Boisragon, Captain. THE BENIN MASSACRE. *Second Edition. Crown 8vo. 3s. 6d.*

Cardinal Bona. A GUIDE TO ETERNITY. Edited with an Introduction and Notes, by J. W. STANBRIDGE, B.D., late Fellow of St. John's College, Oxford. *Pott 8vo. Cloth, 2s.; leather, 2s. 6d. net.* [Library of Devotion.

F. C. Boon, B.A. A COMMERCIAL GEOGRAPHY OF FOREIGN NATIONS. *Crown 8vo. 2s.* [Commercial Series.

George Borrow. LAVENGRO. Edited by F. HINDES GROOME. *Two Volumes. Pott 8vo. Each volume, cloth, 1s. 6d. net; leather, 2s. 6d. net.* [Little Library.

J. Ritzema Bos. AGRICULTURAL ZOOLOGY. Translated by J. R. AINSWORTH DAVIS, M.A. With an Introduction by ELEANOR A. ORMEROD, F.E.S. With 155 Illustrations. *Cr. 8vo. 3s. 6d.*

C. G. Botting, B.A. JUNIOR LATIN EXAMINATION PAPERS. *Fcap. 8vo. 1s.* [Junior Examination Series.

E. M. Bowden. THE EXAMPLE OF BUDDHA: Being Quotations from Buddhist Literature for each Day in the Year. *Third Edition. 16mo. 2s. 6d.*

E. Bowmaker. THE HOUSING OF THE WORKING CLASSES. *Crown 8vo. 2s. 6d.* [Social Questions Series.

F. G. Brabant, M.A. SUSSEX. Illustrated by E. H. NEW. *Pott 8vo. Cloth, 3s.; leather, 3s. 6d. net.* [Little Guides.

'A charming little book; as full of sound information as it is practical in conception.' —*Athenæum.*

'Accurate, complete, and agreeably written'—*Literature.*

Miss M. Brodrick and Miss Anderson Morton. A CONCISE HANDBOOK OF EGYPTIAN ARCHÆOLOGY. With many Illustrations. *Crown 8vo. 3s. 6d.*

E. W. Brooks. See F. J. Hamilton.

O. Browning, M.A. A SHORT HISTORY OF MEDIÆVAL ITALY, A.D. 1250-1530. *In Two Volumes. Crown 8vo. 5s. each.*
VOL. I. 1250-1409.—Guelphs and Ghibellines.
VOL. II. 1409-1530.—The Age of the Condottieri.

J. Buchan. See Isaak Walton.

Miss Bulley. See Lady Dilke.

John Bunyan. THE PILGRIM'S PROGRESS. Edited, with an Introduction, by C. H. FIRTH, M.A. With 39 Illustrations by R. ANNING BELL. *Cr. 8vo. 6s.*
'The best "Pilgrim's Progress."'—*Educational Times.*

G. J. Burch, M.A., F.R.S. A MANUAL OF ELECTRICAL SCIENCE. With numerous Illustrations. *Crown 8vo. 3s.* [University Extension Series.

Gelett Burgess. GOOPS AND HOW TO BE THEM. With numerous Illustrations. *Small 4to. 6s.*

A. E. Burn, B.D., Examining Chaplain to the Bishop of Lichfield. AN INTRODUCTION TO THE HISTORY OF THE CREEDS. *Demy 8vo. 10s. 6d.* [Handbooks of Theology.
'This book may be expected to hold its place as an authority on its subject.'—*Spectator.*

J. H. Burn, B.D., F.R.S.E. A MANUAL OF CONSOLATION FROM THE SAINTS AND FATHERS. *Pott 8vo. Cloth, 2s.; leather, 2s. 6d. net.* [Library of Devotion.

Robert Burns. THE POEMS OF ROBERT BURNS. Edited by ANDREW LANG and W. A. CRAIGIE. With Portrait. *Second Edition. Demy 8vo, gilt top. 6s.*

J. B. Bury. LL.D. See Gibbon.

Alfred Caldecott, D.D. THE PHILOSOPHY OF RELIGION IN ENGLAND AND AMERICA. *Demy 8vo. 10s. 6d.* [Handbooks of Theology.
'Dr. Caldecott treats the subject as we have long hoped it would eventually be treated.'—*Church Times.*
'A lucid and informative account, which certainly deserves a place in every philosophical library.'—*Scotsman.*

D S. Calderwood, Headmaster of the Normal School, Edinburgh. TEST CARDS IN EUCLID AND ALGEBRA. In three packets of 40, with Answers. 1s. each. Or in three Books, price 2d., 2d., and 3d.

R. M. and A. J. Carlyle, M.A. BISHOP LATIMER. With Portrait. *Crown 8vo. 3s. 6d.* [Leaders of Religion.

C. C. Channer and M. E. Roberts. LACE-MAKING IN THE MIDLANDS, PAST AND PRESENT. With 16 full-page Illustrations. *Crown 8vo. 2s. 6d.*
'An interesting book, illustrated by fascinating photographs.'—*Speaker.*

Lord Chesterfield, THE LETTERS OF, TO HIS SON. Edited, with an Introduction, by C. STRACHEY, and Notes by A. CALTHROP. *Two Volumes. Crown 8vo. 6s. each.* [Methuen's Standard Library.

F. W. Christian. THE CAROLINE ISLANDS. With many Illustrations and Maps. *Demy 8vo. 12s. 6d. net.*

Cicero. DE ORATORE I. Translated by E. N. P. MOOR, M.A. *Crown 8vo. 3s. 6d.* [Classical Translations.

SELECT ORATIONS (Pro Milone, Pro Murena, Philippic II., In Catilinam). Translated by H. E. D. BLAKISTON, M.A., Fellow and Tutor of Trinity College, Oxford. *Crown 8vo. 5s.* [Classical Translations.

DE NATURA DEORUM. Translated by F. BROOKS, M.A., late Scholar of Balliol College, Oxford. *Crown 8vo. 3s. 6d.* [Classical Translations.

DE OFFICIIS. Translated by G. B. GARDINER, M.A. *Crown 8vo. 2s. 6d.* [Classical Translations.

F. A. Clarke, M.A. BISHOP KEN. With Portrait. *Crown 8vo. 3s. 6d.* [Leaders of Religion.

E. H. Colbeck, M.D. DISEASES OF THE HEART. With numerous Illustrations. *Demy 8vo. 12s.*

W. G. Collingwood, M.A. THE LIFE OF JOHN RUSKIN. With Portraits. *Cheap Edition. Crown 8vo. 6s.*

J. C. Collins, M.A. See Tennyson.

W. E. Collins, M.A. THE BEGINNINGS OF ENGLISH CHRISTIANITY. With Map. *Crown 8vo. 3s. 6d.* [Churchman's Library.

A. M. Cook, M.A. See E. C. Marchant.

R. W. Cooke-Taylor. THE FACTORY SYSTEM. *Crown 8vo. 2s. 6d.* [Social Questions Series.

Marie Corelli. THE PASSING OF THE GREAT QUEEN : A Tribute to the Noble Life of Victoria Regina. *Small 4to. 1s.*

A CHRISTMAS GREETING. *Sm. 4to. 1s.*

Rosemary Cotes. DANTE'S GARDEN. With a Frontispiece. *Second Edition. Fcap. 8vo. cloth 2s. 6d.; leather, 3s. 6d. net.*

Harold Cox, B.A. LAND NATIONAL-IZATION. *Crown 8vo. 2s. 6d.*
[Social Questions Series.

W. J. Craig. See Shakespeare.

W. A. Craigie. A PRIMER OF BURNS. *Crown 8vo. 2s. 6d.*

Mrs. Craik. JOHN HALIFAX, GEN-TLEMAN. Edited by ANNIE MATHE-SON. *Two Volumes. Pott 8vo. Each Volume, Cloth, 1s. 6d. net ; leather, 2s. 6d. net.* [Little Library.

Richard Crashaw, THE ENGLISH POEMS OF. Edited by EDWARD HUT-TON. *Pott 8vo. Cloth, 1s. 6d. net ; leather, 2s. 6d. net.* [Little Library.

F. G. Crawford. See Mary C. Danson

C. G. Crump, M.A. See Thomas Ellwood.

F. H. E. Cunliffe, Fellow of All Souls' College, Oxford. THE HISTORY OF THE BOER WAR. With many Illustrations, Plans, and Portraits. *In 2 vols. Vol. I., 15s.*

E. L. Cutts, D.D. AUGUSTINE OF CANTERBURY. With Portrait. *Crown 8vo. 3s. 6d.* [Leaders of Religion.

The Brothers Dalziel. A RECORD OF FIFTY YEARS' WORK. With 150 Illustrations. *Large 4to. 21s. net.*

The record of the work of the celebrated Engravers, containing a Gallery of beautiful Pictures by F. Walker, Sir J. Millais, Lord Leighton, and other great Artists. The book is a history of the finest black-and-white work of the nineteenth century.

'The book is abundantly illustrated, and shows that wood engraving was at its best.'—*Scotsman.*

'A store of genial reminiscences. The designs of the various masters are exquisitely engraved. A worthy record of a period that is gone.'—*Standard.*

G. W. Daniell, M.A. BISHOP WILBER-FORCE With Portrait. *Crown 8vo. 3s. 6d.* [Leaders of Religion.

Mary C. Danson and F. G. Crawford. FATHERS IN THE FAITH. *Small 8vo. 1s. 6d.*

Dante Alighieri. LA COMMEDIA DI DANTE. The Italian Text edited by PAGET TOYNBEE, Litt.D., M.A. *Demy 8vo. Gilt top. 8s. 6d. Also, Crown 8vo. 6s.* [Methuen's Standard Library.

THE INFERNO OF DANTE. Translated by H. F. CARY. Edited by PAGET TOYNBEE, Litt.D., M.A. *Pott 8vo. Cloth, 1s. 6d. net ; leather, 2s. 6d. net.* [Little Library.

THE PURGATORIO OF DANTE. Translated by H. F. CARY. Edited by PAGET TOYNBEE, Litt.D., M.A. *Pott 8vo. Cloth, 1s. 6d. net ; leather, 2s. 6d. net.* [Little Library.

THE PARADISO OF DANTE. Translated by H. F. CARY. Edited by PAGET TOYNBEE, Litt.D., M.A. *Post 8vo. Cloth, 1s. 6d. net ; leather, 2s. 6d. net.* [Little Library.

See also Paget Toynbee.

A. C. Deane. Edited by. A LITTLE BOOK OF LIGHT VERSE. *Pott 8vo. Cloth, 1s. 6d. net ; leather, 2s. 6d. net* [Little Library.

Leon Delbos. THE METRIC SYSTEM. *Crown 8vo. 2s.*

A theoretical and practical guide, for use in schools and by the general reader.

Demosthenes : THE OLYNTHIACS AND PHILIPPICS. Translated upon a new principle by OTHO HOLLAND. *Crown 8vo. 2s. 6d.*

Demosthenes. AGAINST CONON AND CALLICLES. Edited with Notes and Vocabulary, by F. DARWIN SWIFT, M.A. *Fcap. 8vo. 2s.*

Charles Dickens.
THE ROCHESTER EDITION.
Crown 8vo. Each Volume, cloth, 3s. 6d. With Introductions by GEORGE GISSING, Notes by F. G. KITTON, and Topographical Illustrations.

THE PICKWICK PAPERS. With Illustrations by E. H. NEW. *Two Volumes.*

'As pleasant a copy as any one could desire. The notes add much to the value of the edition, and Mr. New's illustrations are also historical. The volumes promise well for the success of the edition.'—*Scotsman.*

NICHOLAS NICKLEBY. With Illustrations by R. J. WILLIAMS. *Two Volumes.*

BLEAK HOUSE. With Illustrations by BEATRICE ALCOCK. *Two Volumes.*

OLIVER TWIST. With Illustrations by E. H. NEW.

THE OLD CURIOSITY SHOP. With Illustrations by G. M. BRIMELOW *Two Volumes.*

BARNABY RUDGE. With Illustrations by BEATRICE ALCOCK. *Two Volumes.*

G. L. Dickinson, M.A., Fellow of King's College, Cambridge. THE GREEK VIEW OF LIFE. *Second Edition. Crown 8vo. 2s. 6d.* [University Extension Series.

H. N. Dickson, F.R.S.E., F.R.Met. Soc. METEOROLOGY. The Elements of Weather and Climate. Illustrated. *Crown 8vo. 2s. 6d.* [University Extension Series.

Lady Dilke, Miss Bulley, and **Miss Whitley.** WOMEN'S WORK. *Crown 8vo.* 2s. 6d. [Social Questions Series.

P. H. Ditchfield, M.A., F.S.A. ENGLISH VILLAGES. Illustrated. *Crown 8vo.* 6s.
'A book which for its instructive and pictorial value should find a place in every village library.'—*Scotsman.*
'One of the best books on village antiquities we have seen.'—*Outlook.*

THE STORY OF OUR ENGLISH TOWNS. With Introduction by AUGUSTUS JESSOP, D.D. *Second Edition. Crown 8vo.* 6s.

OLD ENGLISH CUSTOMS: Extant at the Present Time. An Account of Local Observances, Festival Customs, and Ancient Ceremonies yet Surviving in Great Britain. *Crown 8vo.* 6s.

W. M. Dixon, M.A. A PRIMER OF TENNYSON. *Second Edition. Crown 8vo.* 2s. 6d.
'Much sound and well-expressed criticism. The bibliography is a boon.'—*Speaker.*

ENGLISH POETRY FROM BLAKE TO BROWNING. *Second Edition. Crown 8vo.* 2s. 6d.
[University Extension Series.

E. Dowden, Litt.D. See Shakespeare.

J. Dowden, D.D., Lord Bishop of Edinburgh. THE WORKMANSHIP OF THE PRAYER BOOK: Its Literary and Liturgical Aspects. *Second Edition. Crown 8vo.* 3s. 6d.
[Churchman's Library.

S. R. Driver, D.D., Canon of Christ Church, Regius Professor of Hebrew in the University of Oxford. SERMONS ON SUBJECTS CONNECTED WITH THE OLD TESTAMENT. *Crown 8vo.* 6s.
'A welcome companion to the author's famous "Introduction."'—*Guardian.*

S. J. Duncan (Mrs. COTES), Author of 'A Voyage of Consolation.' ON THE OTHER SIDE OF THE LATCH. *Second Edition. Crown 8vo.* 6s.

J. T. Dunn, D.Sc., **and V. A. Mundella.** GENERAL ELEMENTARY SCIENCE. With 114 Illustrations. *Crown 8vo.* 3s. 6d. [Methuen's Science Primers.

The Earl of Durham. A REPORT ON CANADA. With an Introductory Note. *Demy 8vo.* 7s. 6d. net.
A reprint of the celebrated Report which Lord Durham made to the British Government on the state of British North America in 1839. It is probably the most important utterance on British colonial policy ever published.

W. A. Dutt. NORFOLK. Illustrated by B. C. BOULTER. *Pott 8vo. Cloth,* 3s.; *leather,* 3s. 6d. net. [Little Guides.

Clement Edwards. RAILWAY NATIONALIZATION. *Crown 8vo.* 2s. 6d. [Social Questions Series.

W. Douglas Edwards. COMMERCIAL LAW. *Crown 8vo.* 2s. [Commercial Series.

H. E. Egerton, M.A. A HISTORY OF BRITISH COLONIAL POLICY. *Demy 8vo.* 12s. 6d.
'It is a good book, distinguished by accuracy in detail, clear arrangement of facts, and a broad grasp of principles.'—*Manchester Guardian.*

Thomas Ellwood, THE HISTORY OF THE LIFE OF. Edited by C. G. CRUMP, M.A. *Crown 8vo.* 6s.
[Methuen's Standard Library.
This edition is the only one which contains the complete book as originally published. It has a long Introduction and many Footnotes.

E. Engel. A HISTORY OF ENGLISH LITERATURE: From its Beginning to Tennyson. Translated from the German. *Demy 8vo.* 7s. 6d. net.
This is a very complete and convenient sketch of the evolution of our literature from early days. The treatment is biographical as well as critical, and is rendered more interesting by the quotation of characteristic passages from the chief authors.

W. H. Fairbrother, M.A. THE PHILOSOPHY OF T. H. GREEN. *Second Edition. Crown 8vo.* 3s. 6d.

Susan Ferrier. MARRIAGE. Edited by Miss GOODRICH FREER and Lord IDDESLEIGH. *Two Volumes. Pott 8vo. Each volume, cloth,* 1s. 6d. net; *leather,* 2s. 6d. net. [Little Library.

C. H. Firth, M.A. CROMWELL'S ARMY: A History of the English Soldier during the Civil Wars, the Commonwealth, and the Protectorate. *Crown 8vo.* 7s. 6d.
An elaborate study and description of Cromwell's army by which the victory of the Parliament was secured. The 'New Model' is described in minute detail, and the author, who is one of the most distinguished historians of the day, has made great use of unpublished MSS.

G. W. Fisher, M.A. ANNALS OF SHREWSBURY SCHOOL. With numerous Illustrations. *Demy 8vo.* 10s. 6d.

Edward FitzGerald. THE RUBAIYAT OF OMAR KHAYYAM. With a Commentary by H. M. BATSON, and a Biography of Omar by E. D. ROSS. 6s.

E. A. FitzGerald. THE HIGHEST ANDES. With 2 Maps, 51 Illustrations, 13 of which are in Photogravure, and a Panorama. *Royal 8vo.* 30*s. net.*

W. Warde Fowler. M.A.   See Gilbert White.

J. F. Fraser. ROUND THE WORLD ON A WHEEL. With 100 Illustrations. *Crown 8vo.* 6*s.*
'A classic of cycling, graphic and witty.' —*Yorkshire Post.*

W. French, M.A., Principal of the Storey Institute, Lancaster.   PRACTICAL CHEMISTRY. Part I. With numerous Diagrams. *Crown 8vo.* 1*s. 6d.*
[Textbooks of Technology.
'An excellent and eminently practical little book.'—*Schoolmaster.*

Ed. von Freudenreich. DAIRY BACTERIOLOGY. A Short Manual for the Use of Students. Translated by J. R. AINSWORTH DAVIS, M.A. *Second Edition. Revised. Crown 8vo.* 2*s. 6d.*

H. W. Fulford, M.A.   THE EPISTLE OF ST. JAMES   Edited by.   *Fcap. 8vo.* 1*s. 6d. net.*   [Churchman's Bible.

Mrs. Gaskell. CRANFORD. Edited by E. V. LUCAS.   *Pott 8vo.   Cloth, 1s. 6d. net ; leather, 2s. 6d. net.*   [Little Library.

H. B. George, M.A., Fellow of New College, Oxford.   BATTLES OF ENGLISH HISTORY. With numerous Plans. *Third Edition. Crown 8vo.* 6*s.*
'Mr. George has undertaken a very useful task—that of making military affairs intelligible and instructive to non-military readers—and has executed it with a large measure of success.'—*Times.*

H. de B. Gibbins, Litt.D., M.A.   INDUSTRY IN ENGLAND: HISTORICAL OUTLINES. With 5 Maps. *Second Edition. Demy 8vo.* 10*s. 6d.*

A COMPANION GERMAN GRAMMAR. *Crown 8vo.* 1*s. 6d.*

THE INDUSTRIAL HISTORY OF ENGLAND. *Eighth Edition.* Revised. With Maps and Plans. *Crown 8vo.* 3*s.*
[University Extension Series.

THE ECONOMICS OF COMMERCE. *Crown 8vo.* 1*s. 6d.*   [Commercial Series.

COMMERCIAL EXAMINATION PAPERS. *Crown 8vo.* 1*s. 6d.*
[Commercial Series.

BRITISH COMMERCE AND COLONIES FROM ELIZABETH TO VICTORIA. *Third Edition. Crown 8vo.* 2*s.*
[Commercial Series.

ENGLISH SOCIAL REFORMERS. *Second Edition. Crown 8vo.* 2*s. 6d.*
[University Extension Series.

H. de B. Gibbins, D.Litt., M.A., and **R. A. Hadfield,** of the Hecla Works, Sheffield. A SHORTER WORKING DAY. *Crown 8vo.* 2*s. 6d.*   [Social Questions Series.

Edward Gibbon. THE DECLINE AND FALL OF THE ROMAN EMPIRE. A New Edition, edited with Notes, Appendices, and Maps, by J. B. BURY, LL.D., Fellow of Trinity College, Dublin. *In Seven Volumes. Demy 8vo. Gilt top.* 8*s. 6d. each. Also, Crown 8vo.* 6*s. each.*
'At last there is an adequate modern edition of Gibbon. . . . The best edition the nineteenth century could produce.'—*Manchester Guardian.*
'A great piece of editing.'—*Academy.*

MEMOIRS OF MY LIFE AND WRITINGS. By EDWARD GIBBON. Edited, with an Introduction and Notes, by G. BIRKBECK HILL, LL.D. *Crown 8vo.* 6*s.*
'An admirable edition of one of the most interesting personal records of a literary life. Its notes and its numerous appendices are a repertory of almost all that can be known about Gibbon.'—*Manchester Guardian.*

E. C. S. Gibson, D.D., Vicar of Leeds. THE BOOK OF JOB. With Introduction and Notes. *Demy 8vo,* 6*s.*
[Commentaries on the R.V.
'The publishers are to be congratulated on the start the series has made.'—*Times.*
'Dr. Gibson's work is worthy of a high degree of appreciation. To the busy worker and the intelligent student the commentary will be a real boon ; and it will, if we are not mistaken, be much in demand. The Introduction is almost a model of concise, straightforward, prefatory remarks on the subject treated.'—*Athenæum.*

THE XXXIX. ARTICLES OF THE CHURCH OF ENGLAND. With an Introduction. *Third and Cheaper Edition in One Volume. Demy 8vo.* 12*s. 6d.*
[Handbooks of Theology.
'We welcome with the utmost satisfaction a new, cheaper, and more convenient edition of Dr. Gibson's book. It was greatly wanted. Dr. Gibson has given theological students just what they want, and we should like to think that it was in the hands of every candidate for orders.'—*Guardian.*

THE LIFE OF JOHN HOWARD. With 12 Illustrations. *Pott 8vo.   Cloth, 3s.; leather, 3s. 6d. net.*   [Little Biographies.

See also George Herbert.

George Gissing. See Dickens.

A. D. Godley, M.A., Fellow of Magdalen College, Oxford. LYRA FRIVOLA. *Third Edition. F'cap. 8vo. 2s. 6d.*

VERSES TO ORDER. *Cr. 8vo. 2s. 6d. net.*

Miss Goodrich-Freer. See Susan Ferrier.

P. Anderson Graham. THE RURAL EXODUS. *Crown 8vo. 2s. 6d.*
[Social Questions Series.

F. S. Granger, M.A., Litt.D. PSYCHOLOGY. *Second Edition. Crown 8vo. 2s. 6d.* [University Extension Series.

THE SOUL OF A CHRISTIAN. *Crown 8vo. 6s.*
A book dealing with the evolution of the religious life and experiences.
'A remarkable book.'—*Glasgow Herald.*
See also University Extension Series.

E. M'Queen Gray. GERMAN PASSAGES FOR UNSEEN TRANSLATION. *Crown 8vo. 2s. 6d.*

P. L. Gray, B.Sc., formerly Lecturer in Physics in Mason University College, Birmingham. THE PRINCIPLES OF MAGNETISM AND ELECTRICITY: an Elementary Text-Book. With 181 Diagrams. *Crown 8vo. 3s. 6d.*

G. Buckland Green, M.A., Assistant Master at Edinburgh Academy, late Fellow of St. John's College, Oxon. NOTES ON GREEK AND LATIN SYNTAX. *Crown 8vo. 3s. 6d.*
Notes and explanations on the chief difficulties of Greek and Latin Syntax, with numerous passages for exercise.

E. T. Green, M.A. THE CHURCH OF CHRIST. *Crown 8vo. 6s.*
[Churchman's Library.

R. A. Gregory. THE VAULT OF HEAVEN. A Popular Introduction to Astronomy. With numerous Illustrations. *Crown 8vo. 2s. 6d.*
[University Extension Series.

W. Hall Griffin, M.A. SELECTIONS FROM THE EARLY POEMS OF ROBERT BROWNING. Edited by. *Pott 8vo. Cloth, 1s. 6d. net; leather, 2s. 6d. net.* [Little Library.

C. H. Grinling. A HISTORY OF THE GREAT NORTHERN RAILWAY, 1845-95. With Illustrations. *Demy 8vo. 10s. 6d.*
'Mr. Grinling has done for a Railway what Macaulay did for English History.'—*The Engineer.*

F. Hindes Groome. See George Borrow.

M. L. Gwynn. A BIRTHDAY BOOK. *Royal 8vo. 12s.*
This is a birthday-book of exceptional dignity, and the extracts have been chosen with particular care.

Stephen Gwynn. See Thackeray.

John Hackett, B.D. A HISTORY OF THE ORTHODOX CHURCH OF CYPRUS. With Maps and Illustrations. *Demy 8vo. 15s. net.*

A. C. Haddon, Sc.D., F.R.S. HEADHUNTERS, BLACK, WHITE, AND BROWN. With many Illustrations and a Map. *Demy 8vo. 15s.*
A narrative of adventure and exploration in Northern Borneo. It contains much matter of the highest scientific interest.

R. A. Hadfield. See H. de B. Gibbins.

R. N. Hall and W. G. Neal. THE ANCIENT RUINS OF RHODESIA. With numerous Illustrations. *Demy 8vo. 21s. net.*
This book contains descriptions of two hundred ruins of temples and forts, and of their types and ages of architecture. It describes also the Sabæan and Phœnician occupations of Rhodesia; King Solomon's gold, ancient burials, ancient gold-mining, etc. It is profusely illustrated, and contains many maps and plans.

F. J. Hamilton, D.D., **and E. W. Brooks.** ZACHARIAH OF MITYLENE. Translated into English. *Demy 8vo. 12s. 6d. net.*
[Byzantine Texts.

D. Hannay. A SHORT HISTORY OF THE ROYAL NAVY, FROM EARLY TIMES TO THE PRESENT DAY. Illustrated. *Two Volumes. Demy 8vo. 7s. 6d. each.* Vol. I. 1200-1688.

A. T. Hare, M.A. THE CONSTRUCTION OF LARGE INDUCTION COILS. With numerous Diagrams. *Demy 8vo. 6s.*

Clifford Harrison. READING AND READERS. *Fcap. 8vo. 2s. 6d.*
'An extremely sensible little book.'—*Manchester Guardian.*

Sven Hedin, Gold Medallist of the Royal Geographical Society. THROUGH ASIA. With 300 Illustrations from Sketches and Photographs by the Author, and Maps. *Two Volumes. Royal 8vo. 36s. net.*
'One of the greatest books of the kind issued during the century. It is impossible to give an adequate idea of the richness of the contents of this book, or of its abounding attractions as a story of travel unsurpassed in geographical and human interest. Much of it is a revelation. Altogether the work is one which in solidity, novelty, and interest must take a first rank among publications of its class.'—*Times.*

T. F. Henderson. A LITTLE BOOK OF SCOTTISH VERSE. *Pott 8vo. Cloth, 1s. 6d. net; leather, 2s. 6d. net.*
[Little Library.

See also D. M. Moir.

W. E. Henley. ENGLISH LYRICS. *Crown 8vo. Gilt top. 3s. 6d.*

W. E. Henley and C. Whibley. A BOOK OF ENGLISH PROSE. *Crown 8vo. Buckram, gilt top. 6s.*

H. H. Henson, M.A., Fellow of All Souls', Oxford, Canon of Westminster. APOSTOLIC CHRISTIANITY : As Illustrated by the Epistles of St. Paul to the Corinthians. *Crown 8vo. 6s.*

LIGHT AND LEAVEN : HISTORICAL AND SOCIAL SERMONS. *Crown 8vo. 6s.*

DISCIPLINE AND LAW. *Fcap. 8vo. 2s. 6d.*

George Herbert. THE TEMPLE. Edited, with an Introduction and Notes, by E. C. S. GIBSON, D.D., Vicar of Leeds. *Pott 8vo. Cloth, 2s.; leather, 2s. 6d. net.*
[Library of Devotion.

This edition contains Walton's Life of Herbert, and the text is that of the first edition.

Herodotus : EASY SELECTIONS. With Vocabulary. By A. C. LIDDELL, M.A. *Fcap. 8vo. 1s. 6d.*

W. A. S. Hewins, B.A. ENGLISH TRADE AND FINANCE IN THE SEVENTEENTH CENTURY. *Crown 8vo.*
[University Extension Series.

T. Hilbert. THE AIR GUN : or, How the Mastermans and Dobson Major nearly lost their Holidays. Illustrated. *Square Fcap. 8vo. 2s. 6d.* [Little Blue Books.

Clare Hill, Registered Teacher to the City and Guilds of London Institute. MILLINERY, THEORETICAL, AND PRACTICAL. With numerous Diagrams. *Crown 8vo. 2s.*
[Textbooks of Technology.

Henry Hill, B.A., Headmaster of the Boy's High School, Worcester, Cape Colony. A SOUTH AFRICAN ARITHMETIC. *Crown 8vo. 3s. 6d.*

This book has been specially written for use in South African schools.

G. Birkbeck Hill, LL.D. See Gibbon.

Howard C. Hillegas. WITH THE BOER FORCES. With 24 Illustrations. *Second Edition. Crown 8vo. 6s.*

S. L. Hinde. THE FALL OF THE CONGO ARABS. With Plans, etc. *Demy 8vo. 12s. 6d.*

L. T. Hobhouse, Fellow of C.C.C., Oxford. THE THEORY OF KNOWLEDGE. *Demy 8vo. 21s.*

J. A. Hobson, M.A. PROBLEMS OF POVERTY : An Inquiry into the Industrial Condition of the Poor. *Fourth Edition. Crown 8vo. 2s. 6d.*
[Social Questions Series and University Extension Series.

THE PROBLEM OF THE UNEMPLOYED. *Crown 8vo. 2s. 6d.*
[Social Questions Series.

T. Hodgkin, D.C.L. GEORGE FOX, THE QUAKER. With Portrait. *Crown 8vo. 3s. 6d.* [Leaders of Religion.

Chester Holcombe. THE REAL CHINESE QUESTION. *Crown 8vo. 6s.*

'It is an important addition to the materials before the public for forming an opinion on a most difficult and pressing problem.'—*Times.*

Sir T. H. Holdich, K.C.I.E. THE INDIAN BORDERLAND : being a Personal Record of Twenty Years. Illustrated. *Demy 8vo. 15s. net*

'Interesting and inspiriting from cover to cover, it will assuredly take its place as the classical work on the history of the Indian frontier.'—*Pilot.*

Canon Scott Holland. LYRA APOSTOLICA. With an Introduction. Notes by H. C. BEECHING, M.A. *Pott 8vo. Cloth, 2s.; leather, 2s. 6d. net.*
[Library of Devotion.

G. J. Holyoake. THE CO-OPERATIVE MOVEMENT TO-DAY. *Second Edition. Crown 8vo. 2s. 6d.*
[Social Questions Series.

Horace : THE ODES AND EPODES. Translated by A. GODLEY, M.A., Fellow of Magdalen College, Oxford. *Crown 8vo. 2s.* [Classical Translations.

E. L. S. Horsburgh, M.A. WATERLOO : A Narrative and Criticism. With Plans. *Second Edition. Crown 8vo. 5s.*

'A brilliant essay—simple, sound, and thorough.'—*Daily Chronicle.*

THE LIFE OF SAVONAROLA. With Portraits and Illustrations. *Fcap. 8vo. Cloth, 3s. 6d.; leather, 4s. net.*
[Little Biographies.

R. F. Horton, D.D. JOHN HOWE. With Portrait. *Crown 8vo. 3s. 6d.*
[Leaders of Religion.

Alexander Hosie. MANCHURIA. With Illustrations and a Map. *Demy 8vo. 10s. 6d. net.*

G. Howell. TRADE UNIONISM—NEW AND OLD. *Third Edition. Crown 8vo. 2s. 6d.* [Social Questions Series.

H. G. Hutchinson. THE GOLFING PIL-GRIM. *Crown 8vo. 6s.*

A. W. Hutton, M.A. CARDINAL MANNING. With Portrait. *Crown 8vo. 3s. 6d.* [Leaders of Religion.

See also TAULER.

Edward Hutton. See Richard Crashaw.

R. H. Hutton. CARDINAL NEWMAN. With Portrait. *Crown 8vo. 3s. 6d.* [Leaders of Religion.

W. H. Hutton, M.A. THE LIFE OF SIR THOMAS MORE. With Portraits. *Second Edition. Crown 8vo. 5s.*

WILLIAM LAUD. With Portrait. *Second Edition. Crown 8vo. 3s. 6d.* [Leaders of Religion.

Henrik Ibsen. BRAND. A Drama. Translated by WILLIAM WILSON. *Third Edition. Crown 8vo. 3s. 6d.*

Lord Iddesleigh. See Susan Ferrier.

W. R. Inge, M.A., Fellow and Tutor of Hertford College, Oxford. CHRISTIAN MYSTICISM. The Bampton Lectures for 1899. *Demy 8vo. 12s. 6d. net.*

'It is fully worthy of the best traditions connected with the Bampton Lectureship.'—*Record.*

A. D. Innes, M.A. A HISTORY OF THE BRITISH IN INDIA. With Maps and Plans. *Crown 8vo. 7s. 6d.*

'Written in a vigorous and effective style . . . a thoughtful and impartial account.'—*Spectator.*

'Mr. Innes has done a difficult piece of work well. He has taken the history into his mind; given it shape, feature, and vitality there; therefore it comes alive and fresh from his mind.'—*Scotsman.*

S. Jackson, M.A. A PRIMER OF BUSINESS. *Third Edition. Crown 8vo. 1s. 6d.* [Commercial Series.

F. Jacob, M.A. JUNIOR FRENCH EXAMINATION PAPERS. *Fcap. 8vo. 1s.* [Junior Examination Series.

J. Stephen Jeans. TRUSTS, POOLS, AND CORNERS. *Crown 8vo. 2s. 6d.* [Social Questions Series.

R. L. Jefferson. A NEW RIDE TO KHIVA. Illustrated. *Crown 8vo. 6s*

E. Jenks, M.A., Professor of Law at University College, Liverpool. ENGLISH LOCAL GOVERNMENT. *Crown 8vo. 2s. 6d.* [University Extension Series.

C. S. Jerram, M.A. See Pascal.

Augustus Jessopp, D.D. JOHN DONNE. With Portrait. *Crown 8vo. 3s. 6d.* [Leaders of Religion.

F. B. Jevons, M.A., Litt.D., Principal of Hatfield Hall, Durham. EVOLUTION. *Crown 8vo. 3s. 6d.* [Churchman's Library.

AN INTRODUCTION TO THE HISTORY OF RELIGION. *Second Edition. Demy 8vo. 10s. 6d.* [Handbooks of Theology.

'The merit of this book lies in the penetration, the singular acuteness and force of the author's judgment. He is at once critical and luminous, at once just and suggestive. A comprehensive and thorough book.'—*Birmingham Post.*

Sir H. H. Johnston, K.C.B. BRITISH CENTRAL AFRICA. With nearly 200 Illustrations and Six Maps. *Second Edition. Crown 4to. 18s. net.*

H. Jonés. A GUIDE TO PROFESSIONS AND BUSINESS. *Crown 8vo. 1s. 6d.* [Commercial Series.

F. W. Joyce, M.A. THE LIFE OF SIR FREDERICK GORE OUSELEY. *7s. 6d.*

Lady Julian of Norwich. REVELATIONS OF DIVINE LOVE. Edited by GRACE WARRACK. *Crown 8vo. 6s.*

A partially modernised version, from the MS. in the British Museum of a book which Dr. Dalgairns terms 'One of the most remarkable books of the Middle Ages.' Mr. Inge in his Bampton Lectures on Christian Mysticism calls it 'The beautiful but little known *Revelations.*'

M. Kaufmann. SOCIALISM AND MODERN THOUGHT. *Crown 8vo. 2s. 6d.* [Social Questions Series.

J. F. Keating, D.D. THE AGAPE AND THE EUCHARIST. *Crown 8vo. 3s. 6d.*

John Keble. THE CHRISTIAN YEAR. With an Introduction and Notes by W. LOCK, D.D., Warden of Keble College. Illustrated by R. ANNING BELL. *Second Edition. Fcap. 8vo. 3s. 6d; padded morocco, 5s.*

'The present edition is annotated with all the care and insight to be expected from Dr. Lock.'—*Guardian.*

LYRA INNOCENTIUM. Edited, with Introduction and Notes, by WALTER LOCK, D.D., Warden of Keble College, Oxford. *Pott 8vo. Cloth, 2s.; leather, 2s. 6d. net.* [Library of Devotion.

'This sweet and fragrant book has never been published more attractively.'—*Academy.*

THE CHRISTIAN YEAR. With Introduction and Notes by WALTER LOCK, D.D., Warden of Keble College. *Second Edition. Pott 8vo. Cloth,* 2s. *; leather,* 2s. 6d. *net.* [Library of Devotion.

Thomas à Kempis. THE IMITATION OF CHRIST. With an Introduction by DEAN FARRAR. Illustrated by C. M. GERE. *Second Edition. Fcap. 8vo.* 3s. 6d. *net ; padded morocco,* 5s.
'Amongst all the innumerable English editions of the "Imitation," there can have been few which were prettier than this one, printed in strong and handsome type, with all the glory of red initials.'—*Glasgow Herald.*

THE IMITATION OF CHRIST. A Revised Translation by C. BIGG, D.D., Canon of Christ Church. With an Introduction. *Crown 8vo.* 3s. 6d.
A new edition, carefully revised and set in large type, of Dr. Bigg's well-known version.
'Dignified, harmonious, and scholarly.' —*Church Review.*

THE IMITATION OF CHRIST. A Revised Translation, with an Introduction by C. BIGG, D.D., late Student of Christ Church. *Second Edition. Pott 8vo. Cloth,* 2s. *; leather,* 2s. 6d. *net.*
[Library of Devotion.
A practically new translation of this book which the reader has, almost for the first time, exactly in the shape in which it left the hands of the author.

James Houghton Kennedy, D.D., Assistant Lecturer in Divinity in the University of Dublin. ST. PAUL'S SECOND AND THIRD EPISTLES TO THE CORINTHIANS. With Introduction, Dissertations and Notes. *Crown 8vo.* 6s.

C. W. Kimmins, M.A. THE CHEMISTRY OF LIFE AND HEALTH. Illustrated. *Crown 8vo.* 2s. 6d.
[University Extension Series.

A. W. Kinglake. EOTHEN. With an Introduction and Notes. *Pott 8vo. Cloth,* 1s. 6d. *net ; leather,* 2s. 6d. *net.*
[Little Library.

Rudyard Kipling. BARRACK-ROOM BALLADS. 73rd Thousand. *Crown 8vo.* 6s. *; leather,* 6s. *net.*
'Mr. Kipling's verse is strong, vivid, full of character. . . . Unmistakable genius rings in every line.'—*Times.*
'The ballads teem with imagination, they palpitate with emotion. We read them with laughter and tears : the metres throb in our pulses, the cunningly ordered words tingle with life ; and if this be not poetry, what is !'—*Pall Mall Gazette.*

THE SEVEN SEAS. 62nd Thousand. *Crown 8vo. Buckram, gilt top,* 6s. *; leather,* 6s. *net.*
'The Empire has found a singer ; it is no depreciation of the songs to say that statesmen may have, one way or other, to take account of them.'—
Manchester Guardian.

F. G. Kitton. See Dickens.

W. J. Knox Little. See St. Francis de Sales.

Charles Lamb, THE ESSAYS OF ELIA. With over 100 Illustrations by A. GARTH JONES, and an Introduction by E. V. LUCAS. *Demy 8vo.* 10s. 6d.
'This edition is in many respects of peculiar beauty.'—*Daily Chronicle.*
'It is in every way an admirable edition and the illustrations are delightful.'—
Literature.

ELIA, AND THE LAST ESSAYS OF ELIA. Edited by E. V. LUCAS. *Pott 8vo. Cloth,* 1s. 6d. *net ; leather,* 2s. 6d. *net.*
[Little Library.

THE KING AND QUEEN OF HEARTS: An 1805 Book for Children. Illustrated by WILLIAM MULREADY. A new edition, in facsimile, edited by E. V. LUCAS. 1s. 6d.
This little book is a literary curiosity, and has been discovered and identified as the work of Charles Lamb by E. V. Lucas. It is an exact facsimile of the original edition, which was illustrated by Mulready.

Professor Lambros. ECTHESIS CHRONICA. Edited by. *Demy 8vo.* 7s. 6d. *net.* [Byzantine Texts.

Stanley Lane-Poole. THE LIFE OF SIR HARRY PARKES. *A New and Cheaper Edition. Crown 8vo.* 6s.
A HISTORY OF EGYPT IN THE MIDDLE AGES. Fully Illustrated. *Crown 8vo.* 6s.

F. Langbridge, M.A. BALLADS OF THE BRAVE : Poems of Chivalry, Enterprise, Courage, and Constancy. *Second Edition. Crown 8vo.* 2s. 6d.
'The book is full of splendid things.'—*World.*

William Law. A SERIOUS CALL TO A DEVOUT AND HOLY LIFE. Edited, with an Introduction, by C. BIGG, D.D., late Student of Christ Church. *Pott 8vo. Cloth,* 2s. *; leather,* 2s. 6d. *net.*
[Library of Devotion.
This is a reprint, word for word and line for line, of the *Editio Princeps.*

G. S. Layard. THE LIFE OF MRS. LYNN LINTON. Illustrated. *Demy 8vo.* 12s. 6d.
'Mrs. Lynn Linton is here presented to us in all her moods. She lives in the book ; she is presented to us so that we really know her.'—*Literature.*

Captain Melville Lee. A HISTORY OF POLICE IN ENGLAND. *Crown 8vo.* 7s. 6d.

'A learned book, comprising many curious details to interest the general reader as well as the student who will consult it for exact information.'—*Daily News.*

'The book rests on accurate research and gives a vast array of facts and statistics.'—*Glasgow Herald.*

V. B. Lewes, M.A. AIR AND WATER. Illustrated. *Crown 8vo.* 2s. 6d. [University Extension Series.

Walter Lock, D.D., Warden of Keble College. ST. PAUL, THE MASTER-BUILDER. *Crown 8vo.* 3s. 6d.

See also Keble and Oxford Commentaries.

JOHN KEBLE. With Portrait. *Crown 8vo.* 3s. 6d. [Leaders of Religion.

E. V. Lucas. See Jane Austen and Mrs. Gaskell and Charles Lamb.

Lucian. SIX DIALOGUES (Nigrinus, Icaro-Menippus, The Cock, The Ship, The Parasite, The Lover of Falsehood). Translated by S. T. Irwin, M.A., Assistant Master at Clifton; late Scholar of Exeter College, Oxford. *Crown 8vo.* 3s. 6d. [Classical Translations.

L. W. Lyde, M.A. A COMMERCIAL GEOGRAPHY OF THE BRITISH EMPIRE. *Third Edition. Crown 8vo.* 2s. [Commercial Series.

Hon. Mrs. Lyttelton. WOMEN AND THEIR WORK. *Crown 8vo.* 2s. 6d.

'Thoughtful, interesting, practical.'— *Guardian.*

'The book is full of sound precept given with sympathy and wit.'—*Pilot.*

J. E. B. M'Allen, M.A. THE PRINCIPLES OF BOOKKEEPING BY DOUBLE ENTRY. *Crown 8vo.* 2s. [Commercial Series.

F. MacCunn. JOHN KNOX. With Portrait. *Crown 8vo.* 3s. 6d. [Leaders of Religion.

A. M. Mackay. THE CHURCHMAN'S INTRODUCTION TO THE OLD TESTAMENT. *Crown 8vo.* 3s. 6d. [Churchman's Library.

'The book throughout is frank and courageous.'—*Glasgow Herald.*

Laurie Magnus, M.A. A PRIMER OF WORDSWORTH. *Crown 8vo.* 2s. 6d.

J P. Mahaffy, Litt.D. A HISTORY OF THE EGYPT OF THE PTOLEMIES. Fully Illustrated. *Crown 8vo.* 6s.

F. W. Maitland, LL.D., Downing Professor of the Laws of England in the University of Cambridge. CANON LAW IN ENGLAND. *Royal 8vo.* 7s. 6d.

H. E. Malden, M.A. ENGLISH RECORDS. A Companion to the History of England. *Crown 8vo.* 3s. 6d.

THE ENGLISH CITIZEN: HIS RIGHTS AND DUTIES. *Crown 8vo.* 1s. 6d.

E. C. Marchant, M.A., Fellow of Peterhouse, Cambridge, and Assistant Master at St. Paul's School. A GREEK ANTHOLOGY. *Crown 8vo.* 3s. 6d.

E. C. Marchant, M.A., and **A. M. Cook,** M.A. PASSAGES FOR UNSEEN TRANSLATION. *Crown 8vo.* 3s. 6d.

'We know no book of this class better fitted for use in the higher forms of schools.' —*Guardian.*

J. E. Marr, F.R.S., Fellow of St. John's College, Cambridge. THE SCIENTIFIC STUDY OF SCENERY. Illustrated. *Crown 8vo.* 6s.

'A volume, moderate in size and readable in style, which will be acceptable alike to the student of geology and geography, and to the tourist.'—*Athenæum.*

A. J. Mason. THOMAS CRANMER. With Portrait. *Crown 8vo.* 3s. 6d. [Leaders of Religion.

George Massee. THE EVOLUTION OF PLANT LIFE: Lower Forms. With Illustrations. *Crown 8vo.* 2s. 6d. [University Extension Series.

C. F. G. Masterman, M.A. TENNYSON AS A RELIGIOUS TEACHER. *Crown 8vo.* 6s.

'A thoughtful and penetrating appreciation, full of interest and suggestion.'— *World.*

Annie Matheson. See Mrs. Craik.

Emma S. Mellows. A SHORT STORY OF ENGLISH LITERATURE. *Crown 8vo.* 3s. 6d.

'A lucid and well-arranged account of the growth of English literature.'—*Pall Mall Gazette.*

L. C. Miall, F.R.S. See Gilbert White.

E. B. Michell. THE ART AND PRACTICE OF HAWKING. With 3 Photogravures by G. E. LODGE, and other Illustrations. *Demy 8vo.* 10s. 6d.

J. G. Millais. THE LIFE AND LETTERS OF SIR JOHN EVERETT MILLAIS, President of the Royal Academy. With 319 Illustrations, of which 9 are Photogravure. 2 *vols. Royal 8vo.* 20s. *net.*

'This splendid work.'—*World.*

'Of such absorbing interest is it, of such completeness in scope and beauty. Special tribute must be paid to the extraordinary completeness of the illustrations.'—*Graphic.*

J. G. Milne, M.A. A HISTORY OF ROMAN EGYPT. Fully Illustrated. *Crown 8vo.* 6s.

P. Chalmers Mitchell, M.A. OUTLINES OF BIOLOGY. Illustrated. *Second Edition. Crown 8vo.* 6s.

A text - book designed to cover the Schedule issued by the Royal College of Physicians and Surgeons.

D. M. Moir. MANSIE WAUCH. Edited by T. F. HENDERSON. *Pott 8vo. Cloth,* 1s. 6d. *net ; leather,* 2s. 6d. *net.*
[Little Library.

H. E. Moore. BACK TO THE LAND : An Inquiry into the cure for Rural Depopulation. *Crown 8vo.* 2s. 6d.
[Social Questions Series.

W. R. Morfill, Oriel College, Oxford. A HISTORY OF RUSSIA FROM PETER THE GREAT TO ALEXANDER II. With Maps and Plans. *Crown 8vo.* 7s. 6d.

This history, is founded on a study of original documents, and though necessarily brief, is the most comprehensive narrative in existence. Considerable attention has been paid to the social and literary development of the country, and the recent expansion of Russia in Asia.

R. J. Morich, late of Clifton College. GERMAN EXAMINATION PAPERS IN MISCELLANEOUS GRAMMAR AND IDIOMS. *Fifth Edition. Crown 8vo.* 2s. 6d.
[School Examination Series.

A KEY, issued to Tutors and Private Students only, to be had on application to the Publishers. *Second Edition. Crown 8vo.* 6s. *net.*

Miss Anderson Morton. See Miss Brodrick.

H. C. G. Moule, D.D. CHARLES SIMEON. With Portrait. *Crown 8vo.* 3s. 6d. [Leaders of Religion.

M. M. Pattison Muir, M.A. THE CHEMISTRY OF FIRE. The Elementary Principles of Chemistry. Illustrated. *Crown 8vo.* 2s. 6d.
[University Extension Series.

V. A. Mundella, M.A. See J. T. Dunn.

W. G. Neal. See R. N. Hall.

H. W. Nevinson. LADYSMITH : The Diary of a Siege. With 16 Illustrations and a Plan. *Second Edition. Crown 8vo.* 6s.

James Northcote, R.A., THE CONVERSATIONS OF, AND JAMES WARD. Edited by ERNEST FLETCHER. With many Portraits. *Demy 8vo.* 10s. 6d.

'Mr. Fletcher's book will range and rank with Hazlitt's.'—*Globe.*

'Every reader, with any taste for art, will find the book engrossing.'—*Yorkshire Post.*

A. H. Norway, Author of ' Highways and Byways in Devon and Cornwall.' NAPLES : PAST AND PRESENT. With 40 Illustrations by A. G. FERARD. *Crown 8vo.* 6s.

Standish O'Grady. THE STORY OF IRELAND. *Crown 8vo.* 2s. 6d.

Mrs. Oliphant. THOMAS CHALMERS. With Portrait. *Crown 8vo.* 3s. 6d.
[Leaders of Religion.

C. W. Oman, M.A., Fellow of All Souls', Oxford. A HISTORY OF THE ART OF WAR. Vol. II.: The Middle Ages, from the Fourth to the Fourteenth Century. Illustrated. *Demy 8vo.* 21s.

' The whole art of war in its historic evolution has never been treated on such an ample and comprehensive scale, and we question if any recent contribution to the exact history of the world has possessed more enduring value.'—*Daily Chronicle.*

Prince Henri of Orleans. FROM TONKIN TO INDIA. Translated by HAMLEY BENT, M.A. With 100 Illustrations and a Map. *Crown 4to, gilt top.* 25s.

R. L. Ottley, M.A., late Fellow of Magdalen College, Oxon., and Principal of Pusey House. THE DOCTRINE OF THE INCARNATION. *Second and cheaper Edition. Demy 8vo.* 12s. 6d.
[Handbooks of Theology.

'A clear and remarkably full account of the main currents of speculation. Scholarly precision . . . genuine tolerance . . . intense interest in his subject—are Mr. Ottley's merits.'—*Guardian.*

LANCELOT ANDREWES. With Portrait. *Crown 8vo.* 3s. 6d.
[Leaders of Religion.

J. H. Overton, M.A. JOHN WESLEY. With Portrait. *Crown 8vo.* 3s. 6d.
[Leaders of Religion.

M. N. Oxford, of Guy's Hospital. A HANDBOOK OF NURSING. *Crown 8vo.* 3s. 6d.

' The most useful work of the kind that we have seen. A most valuable and practical manual.'—*Manchester Guardian.*

W. C. C. Pakes. THE SCIENCE OF HYGIENE. With numerous Illustrations. *Demy 8vo.* 15s.

'A thoroughgoing working text-book of its subject, practical and well-stocked.'— *Scotsman.*

Prof. Léon Parmentier and M. Bidez. EVAGRIUS. Edited by. *Demy 8vo.* 10s. 6d. net. [Byzantine Texts.

H. W. Paul. See Laurence Sterne.

E. H. Pearce, M.A. THE ANNALS OF CHRIST'S HOSPITAL. With many Illustrations. *Demy 8vo.* 7s. 6d.

'A well-written, copious, authentic history.'— *Times.*

R. E. Peary, Gold Medallist of the Royal Geographical Society. NORTHWARD OVER THE GREAT ICE. With over 800 Illustrations. *Royal 8vo.* 32s. net.

'His book will take its place among the permanent literature of Arctic exploration.' — *Times.*

Sidney Peel, late Fellow of Trinity College, Oxford, and Secretary to the Royal Commission on the Licensing Laws. PRACTICAL LICENSING REFORM. *Second Edition. Crown 8vo.* 1s. 6d.

M. Perugini. SELECTIONS FROM WILLIAM BLAKE. *Pott 8vo.* Cloth, 1s. 6d. net; leather, 2s. 6d. net.
[Little Library.

J. P. Peters, D.D. THE OLD TESTAMENT AND THE NEW SCHOLARSHIP. *Crown 8vo.* 6s.
[Churchman's Library.

'Every page reveals wide reading, used with sound and scholarly judgment.' — *Manchester Guardian.*

W. M. Flinders Petrie, D.C.L., LL.D., Professor of Egyptology at University College. A HISTORY OF EGYPT, FROM THE EARLIEST TIMES TO THE PRESENT DAY. Fully Illustrated. *In six volumes. Crown 8vo.* 6s. each.

'A history written in the spirit of scientific precision so worthily represented by Dr. Petrie and his school cannot but promote sound and accurate study, and supply a vacant place in the English literature of Egyptology.'— *Times.*

VOL. I. PREHISTORIC TIMES TO XVITH DYNASTY. *Fourth Edition.*
VOL. II. THE XVIITH AND XVIIITH DYNASTIES. *Third Edition.*
VOL. IV. THE EGYPT OF THE PTOLEMIES. J. P. MAHAFFY, Litt.D.
VOL. V. ROMAN EGYPT. J. G. MILNE, M.A.
VOL. VI. EGYPT IN THE MIDDLE AGES. STANLEY LANE-POOLE, M.A.

RELIGION AND CONSCIENCE IN ANCIENT EGYPT. Fully Illustrated. *Crown 8vo.* 2s. 6d.

SYRIA AND EGYPT, FROM THE TELL EL AMARNA TABLETS. *Crown 8vo.* 2s. 6d.

EGYPTIAN TALES. Illustrated by TRISTRAM ELLIS. *In Two Volumes. Crown 8vo.* 3s. 6d. each.

EGYPTIAN DECORATIVE ART. With 120 Illustrations. *Crown 8vo.* 3s. 6d.

'In these lectures he displays rare skill in elucidating the development of decorative art in Egypt.'— *Times.*

Philip Pienaar. WITH STEYN AND DE WET. *Second Edition. Crown 8vo.* 3s. 6d.

A narrative of the adventures of a Boer telegraphist of the Orange Free State during the war.

Plautus. THE CAPTIVI. Edited, with an Introduction, Textual Notes, and a Commentary, by W. M. LINDSAY, Fellow of Jesus College, Oxford. *Demy 8vo.* 10s. 6d. net.

For this edition all the important MSS. have been re-collated. An appendix deals with the accentual element in early Latin verse. The Commentary is very full

'A work of great erudition and fine scholarship.'— *Scotsman.*

THE CAPTIVI. Adapted for Lower Forms, by J. H. FREESE, M.A., late Fellow of St. John's, Cambridge. 1s. 6d.

J. T. Plowden-Wardlaw, B.A., King's College, Cambridge. EXAMINATION PAPERS IN ENGLISH HISTORY. *Crown 8vo.* 2s. 6d.
[School Examination Series.

M. C. Potter, M.A., F.L.S. A TEXTBOOK OF AGRICULTURAL BOTANY. Illustrated. *2nd Edition. Crown 8vo.* 4s. 6d. [University Extension Series.

L. L. Price, M.A., Fellow of Oriel College, Oxon. A HISTORY OF ENGLISH POLITICAL ECONOMY. *Third Edition. Crown 8vo.* 2s. 6d.
[University Extension Series.

"Q." THE GOLDEN POMP. A Procession of English Lyrics. Arranged by A. T. QUILLER COUCH. *Crown 8vo. Buckram.* 6s.

R. B. Rackham, M.A. THE ACTS OF THE APOSTLES. With Introduction and Notes. *Demy 8vo.* 12s. 6d.
[Oxford Commentaries.

'A really helpful book. Both introduction and commentary are marked by common sense and adequate knowledge.'— *Guardian.*

B. W. Randolph, D.D., Principal of the Theological College, Ely. THE PSALMS OF DAVID. With an Introduction and Notes. *Pott 8vo. Cloth, 2s.; leather, 2s. 6d. net.*   [Library of Devotion.

A devotional and practical edition of the Prayer Book version of the Psalms.

Hastings Rashdall, M.A., Fellow and Tutor of New College, Oxford. DOCTRINE AND DEVELOPMENT. *Crown 8vo. 6s.*

W. Reason, M.A. UNIVERSITY AND SOCIAL SETTLEMENTS. *Crown 8vo. 2s. 6d.*   [Social Questions Series.

Charles Richardson. THE ENGLISH TURF. With numerous Illustrations and Plans. *Demy 8vo. 15s.*

'From its sensible introduction to its very complex index, this is about the best book that we are likely for some time to see upon the subject with which it deals.'— *Athenæum.*

M. E. Roberts. See C. C. Channer.

A. Robertson, D.D., Principal of King's College, London. REGNUM DEI. The Bampton Lectures of 1901. *Demy 8vo. 12s. 6d. net.*

'A notable volume. Its chief value and interest is in its historic treatment of its great theme.'—*Daily News.*

'It is altogether a solid piece of work and a valuable contribution to the history of Christian thought.'—*Scotsman.*

Sir G. S. Robertson, K.C.S.I. CHITRAL: The Story of a Minor Siege. With numerous Illustrations, Map and Plans. *Second Edition. Demy 8vo. 10s. 6d.*

'A book which the Elizabethans would have thought wonderful. More thrilling, more piquant, and more human than any novel.'—*Newcastle Chronicle.*

J. W. Robertson-Scott. THE PEOPLE OF CHINA. With a Map. *Crown 8vo. 3s. 6d.*

A. W. Robinson, Vicar of All Hallows, Barking. THE EPISTLE TO THE GALATIANS. Explained. *Fcap. 8vo. 1s. 6d. net.*   [Churchman's Bible.

'The most attractive, sensible, and instructive manual for people at large, which we have ever seen.'—*Church Gazette.*

Cecilia Robinson. THE MINISTRY OF DEACONESSES. With an Introduction by the Lord Bishop of Winchester. *Crown 8vo. 3s. 6d.*

C. Rodwell, B.A. NEW TESTAMENT GREEK. A Course for Beginners. With a Preface by WALTER LOCK, D.D., Warden of Keble College. *Fcap. 8vo. 3s. 6d.*

Edward Rose. THE ROSE READER. With numerous Illustrations. *Crown 8vo. 2s. 6d. Also in 4 Parts. Parts I. and II. 6d. each; Part III. 8d.; Part IV. 10d.*

A reader on a new and original plan.

The distinctive feature of this book is the entire avoidance of irregularly-spelt words until the pupil has thoroughly mastered the principle of reading, and learned its enjoyment. The reading of connected sentences begins from the first page, before the entire alphabet is introduced.

E. Denison Ross, M.A. See W. Beckford, A. W. Kinglake, and F. H. Skrine.

A. E. Rubie, M.A., Head Master of the Royal Naval School, Eltham. THE GOSPEL ACCORDING TO ST. MARK. Edited by. With three Maps. *Crown 8vo. 1s. 6d.*   [Methuen's Junior School Books.

W. Clark Russell. THE LIFE OF ADMIRAL LORD COLLINGWOOD. With Illustrations by F. BRANGWYN. *Fourth Edition. Crown 8vo. 6s.*

'A book which we should like to see in the hands of every boy in the country.'— *St. James's Gazette.*

Viscount St. Cyres. THE LIFE OF FRANÇOIS DE FENELON. Illustrated. *Demy 8vo. 10s. 6d.*

'A work of high historical and lively interest.'—*Outlook.*

'A most interesting life of a most interesting personage.'—*Scotsman.*

'We have in this admirable volume a most valuable addition to our historical portrait gallery.'—*Daily News.*

St. Francis de Sales. ON THE LOVE OF GOD. Edited by W. J. KNOX-LITTLE, M.A. *Pott 8vo. Cloth, 2s.; leather, 2s. 6d. net.*   [Library of Devotion.

J. Sargeaunt, M.A. ANNALS OF WESTMINSTER SCHOOL. With numerous Illustrations. *Demy 8vo. 7s. 6d.*

C. Sathas. THE HISTORY OF PSELLUS. *Demy 8vo. 15s. net.*   [Byzantine Texts.

H. G. Seeley, F.R.S. DRAGONS OF THE AIR. With many Illustrations. *Crown 8vo. 6s.*

A popular history of the most remarkable flying animals which ever lived. Their relations to mammals, birds, and reptiles, living and extinct, are shown by an original series of illustrations. The scattered remains preserved in Europe and the United States have been put together accurately to show the varied forms of the animals. The book is a natural history of these extinct animals which flew by means of a single finger.

V. P. Sells, M.A. THE MECHANICS OF DAILY LIFE. Illustrated. *Crown 8vo. 2s. 6d.* [University Extension Series.

Edmund Selous. TOMMY SMITH'S ANIMALS. Illustrated by G. W. ORD. *Second Edition. Fcap. 8vo. 2s. 6d.*

'A quaint, fascinating little book : a nursery classic.'—*Athenæum.*

William Shakespeare.

THE ARDEN EDITION.

'No edition of Shakespeare is likely to prove more attractive and satisfactory than this one. It is beautifully printed and paged and handsomely and simply bound.'— *St. James's Gazette.*

Demy 8vo. 3s. 6d. each volume. General Editor, W. J. CRAIG. An Edition of Shakespeare in single Plays. Edited with a full Introduction, Textual Notes, and a Commentary at the foot of the page. The first volumes are :—

HAMLET. Edited by EDWARD DOWDEN, Litt.D.

ROMEO AND JULIET. Edited by EDWARD DOWDEN, Litt.D.

KING LEAR. Edited by W. J. CRAIG.

JULIUS CAESAR. Edited by M. MACMILLAN, M.A.

THE TEMPEST Edited by MORTON LUCE.

A. Sharp. VICTORIAN POETS. *Crown 8vo. 2s. 6d.* [University Extension Series.

J. S. Shedlock. THE PIANOFORTE SONATA : Its Origin and Development. *Crown 8vo. 5s.*

'This work should be in the possession of every musician and amateur. A concise and lucid history and a very valuable work for reference.'—*Athenæum.*

Arthur Sherwell, M.A. LIFE IN WEST LONDON. *Third Edition. Crown 8vo. 2s. 6d.* [Social Questions Series.

F. H. Skrine and E. D. Ross. THE HEART OF ASIA. With Maps and many Illustrations by VERESTCHAGIN. *Large Crown 8vo. 10s. 6d. net.*

'This volume will form a landmark in our knowledge of Central Asia. . . . Illuminating and convincing.'—*Times.*

Evan Small, M.A. THE EARTH. An Introduction to Physiography. Illustrated. *Crown 8vo. 2s. 6d.* [University Extension Series.

Nowell C. Smith, Fellow of New College, Oxford. SELECTIONS FROM WORDSWORTH. *Pott 8vo. Cloth, 1s. 6d. net; leather, 2s. 6d. net.* [Little Library.

Sophocles. ELECTRA AND AJAX. Translated by E. D. A. MORSHEAD, M.A., Assistant Master at Winchester. *2s. 6d.* [Classical Translations.

R. Southey. ENGLISH SEAMEN (Howard, Clifford, Hawkins, Drake, Cavendish). Edited, with an Introduction, by DAVID HANNAY. *Second Edition. Crown 8vo.*

'A brave, inspiriting book.'—*Black and White.*

C. H. Spence, M.A., Clifton College. HISTORY AND GEOGRAPHY EXAMINATION PAPERS. *Second Edition. Crown 8vo. 2s. 6d.* [School Examination Series.

W. A. Spooner, M.A., Fellow of New College, Oxford. BISHOP BUTLER. With Portrait. *Crown 8vo. 3s. 6d.* [Leaders of Religion.

J. W. Stanbridge, B.D., Rector of Bainton, Canon of York, and sometime Fellow of St. John's College, Oxford. A BOOK OF DEVOTIONS. *Pott 8vo. Cloth, 2s. ; leather, 2s. 6d. net.* [Library of Devotion.

'It is probably the best book of its kind. It deserves high commendation.'—*Church Gazette.*

See also Cardinal Bona.

'Stancliff.' GOLF DO'S AND DONT'S. *Fcap. 8vo. 1s.*

A. M. M. Stedman, M.A.

INITIA LATINA : Easy Lessons on Elementary Accidence. *Fifth Edition. Fcap. 8vo. 1s.*

FIRST LATIN LESSONS. *Sixth Edition. Crown 8vo. 2s.*

FIRST LATIN READER. With Notes adapted to the Shorter Latin Primer and Vocabulary. *Fifth Edition revised. 18mo. 1s. 6d.*

EASY SELECTIONS FROM CÆSAR. Part 1. The Helvetian War. *Second Edition. 18mo. 1s.*

EASY SELECTIONS FROM LIVY. Part 1. The Kings of Rome. *18mo. Second Edition. 1s. 6d.*

EASY LATIN PASSAGES FOR UNSEEN TRANSLATION. *Eighth Edition. Fcap. 8vo. 1s. 6d.*

EXEMPLA LATINA. First Lessons in Latin Accidence. With Vocabulary. *Crown 8vo. 1s.*

EASY LATIN EXERCISES ON THE SYNTAX OF THE SHORTER AND REVISED LATIN PRIMER. With Vocabulary. *Eighth and Cheaper Edition, re-written. Crown 8vo. 1s. 6d.* KEY *3s. net. Original Edition. 2s. 6d.*

THE LATIN COMPOUND SENTENCE: Rules and Exercises. *Second Edition. Crown 8vo. 1s. 6d.* With Vocabulary. *2s.*

NOTANDA QUAEDAM: Miscellaneous Latin Exercises on Common Rules and Idioms. *Fcap. 8vo. 1s. 6d.* With Vocabulary. *2s.* Key, *2s. net.*

LATIN VOCABULARIES FOR REPETITION: Arranged according to Subjects. *Tenth Edition. Fcap. 8vo. 1s. 6d.*

A VOCABULARY OF LATIN IDIOMS. *18mo. Second Edition. 1s.*

STEPS TO GREEK. *Second Edition, revised. 18mo. 1s.*

A SHORTER GREEK PRIMER. *Crown 8vo. 1s. 6d.*

EASY GREEK EXERCISES. By C. G. BOTTING, B.A. *Crown 8vo. 2s.*

EASY GREEK PASSAGES FOR UNSEEN TRANSLATION. *Third Edition, revised. Fcap. 8vo. 1s. 6d.*

GREEK VOCABULARIES FOR REPETITION. Arranged according to Subjects. *Third Edition. Fcap. 8vo. 1s. 6d.*

GREEK TESTAMENT SELECTIONS. For the use of Schools. With Introduction, Notes, and Vocabulary. *Third Edition. Fcap. 8vo. 2s. 6d.*

STEPS TO FRENCH. *Fifth Edition. 18mo. 8d.*

FIRST FRENCH LESSONS. *Fifth Edition, revised. Crown 8vo. 1s.*

EASY FRENCH PASSAGES FOR UNSEEN TRANSLATION. *Fourth Edition, revised. Fcap. 8vo. 1s. 6d.*

EASY FRENCH EXERCISES ON ELEMENTARY SYNTAX. With Vocabulary. *Second Edition. Crown 8vo. 2s. 6d.* KEY. *3s. net.*

FRENCH VOCABULARIES FOR REPETITION: Arranged according to Subjects. *Tenth Edition. Fcap. 8vo. 1s.*

FRENCH EXAMINATION PAPERS IN MISCELLANEOUS GRAMMAR AND IDIOMS. *Eleventh Edition. Crown 8vo. 2s. 6d.* [School Examination Series.

A KEY, issued to Tutors and Private Students only, to be had on application to the Publishers. *Fifth Edition. Crown 8vo. 6s. net.*

GENERAL KNOWLEDGE EXAMINATION PAPERS. *Third Edition. Crown 8vo. 2s. 6d.* [School Examination Series.

KEY (*Second Edition*) issued as above. *7s. net.*

GREEK EXAMINATION PAPERS IN MISCELLANEOUS GRAMMAR AND IDIOMS. *Sixth Edition. Crown 8vo. 2s. 6d.* [School Examination Series.

KEY (*Second Edition*) issued as above. *6s. net.*

LATIN EXAMINATION PAPERS IN MISCELLANEOUS GRAMMAR AND IDIOMS *Tenth Edition. Crown 8vo. 2s. 6d.* [School Examination Series.

KEY (*Fourth Edition*) issued as above. *6s. net.*

R. Elliott Steel, M.A., F.C.S. THE WORLD OF SCIENCE. Including Chemistry, Heat, Light, Sound, Magnetism, Electricity, Heat, Zoology, Physiology, Astronomy, and Geology. 147 Illustrations. *Second Edition. Crown 8vo. 2s. 6d.*

PHYSICS EXAMINATION PAPERS. *Crown 8vo. 2s. 6d.* [School Examination Series.

C. Stephenson, of the Technical College, Bradford, and **F. Suddards**, of the Yorkshire College, Leeds. ORNAMENTAL DESIGN FOR WOVEN FABRICS. *Demy 8vo. Second Edition. 7s. 6d.*

J. Stephenson, M.A. THE CHIEF TRUTHS OF THE CHRISTIAN FAITH. *Crown 8vo. 3s. 6d.*

An attempt to present in clear and popular form the main truths of the Faith. The book is intended for lay workers in the Church, for educated parents and for teachers generally.

Laurence Sterne. A SENTIMENTAL JOURNEY. Edited by H. W. PAUL. *Pott 8vo. Cloth, 1s. 6d. net; leather, 2s. 6d. net.* [Little Library.

W. Sterry, M.A. ANNALS OF ETON COLLEGE. With numerous Illustrations. *Demy 8vo. 7s. 6d.*

R. L. Stevenson. THE LETTERS OF ROBERT LOUIS STEVENSON TO HIS FAMILY AND FRIENDS. Selected and Edited, with Notes and Introductions, by SIDNEY COLVIN. *Sixth and Cheaper Edition. Crown 8vo. 12s.*

LIBRARY EDITION. *Demy 8vo. 2 vols. 25s. net.*

'Irresistible in their raciness, their variety, their animation . . . of extraordinary fascination. A delightful inheritance, the truest record of a "richly compounded spirit" that the literature of our time has preserved.'—*Times.*

VAILIMA LETTERS. With an Etched Portrait by WILLIAM STRANG. *Third Edition. Crown 8vo. Buckram. 6s.*

THE LIFE OF R. L. STEVENSON. See G. Balfour.

E. D. Stone, M.A., late Assistant Master at Eton. SELECTIONS FROM THE ODYSSEY. *Fcap. 8vo. 1s. 6d.*

Charles Strachey. See Chesterfield.

A. W. Streane, D.D. ECCLESIASTES. Explained. *Fcap. 8vo. 1s. 6d. net.*
[Churchman's Bible.
'Scholarly, suggestive, and particularly interesting.'—*Bookman.*

Clement E. Stretton. A HISTORY OF THE MIDLAND RAILWAY. With numerous Illustrations. *Demy 8vo. 12s. 6d.*

H. Stroud, D.Sc., M.A., Professor of Physics in the Durham College of Science, Newcastle-on-Tyne. PRACTICAL PHYSICS. Fully Illustrated. *Crown 8vo. 3s. 6d.*
[Textbooks of Technology.

F. Suddards. See C. Stephenson.

Jonathan Swift. THE JOURNAL TO STELLA. Edited by G. A. AITKEN. *Crown 8vo. 6s.*
[Methuen's Standard Library.

J. E. Symes, M.A. THE FRENCH REVOLUTION. *Crown 8vo. 2s. 6d.*
[University Extension Series.

Tacitus. AGRICOLA. With Introduction, Notes, Map, etc. By R. F. DAVIS, M.A., late Assistant Master at Weymouth College. *Crown 8vo. 2s.*

GERMANIA. By the same Editor. *Crown 8vo. 2s.*

AGRICOLA AND GERMANIA. Translated by R. B. TOWNSHEND, late Scholar of Trinity College, Cambridge. *Crown 8vo. 2s. 6d.*
[Classical Translations.

J. Tauler. THE INNER WAY. Being Thirty-six Sermons for Festivals by JOHN TAULER. Edited, with an Introduction. By A. W. HUTTON, M.A. *Pott 8vo. Cloth, 2s.; leather, 2s. 6d. net.*
[Library of Devotion.

E. L. Taunton. A HISTORY OF THE JESUITS IN ENGLAND. With Illustrations. *Demy 8vo. 21s. net.*
'A history of permanent value, which covers ground never properly investigated before, and is replete with the results of original research. A most interesting and careful book.'—*Literature.*

F. G. Taylor, M.A. COMMERCIAL ARITHMETIC. *Third Edition. Crown 8vo. 1s. 6d.*
[Commercial Series.

T. M. Taylor, M.A., Fellow of Gonville and Caius College, Cambridge. A CONSTITUTIONAL AND POLITICAL HISTORY OF ROME. *Crown 8vo. 7s. 6d.*
'We fully recognise the value of this carefully written work, and admire especially the fairness and sobriety of his judgment and the human interest with which he has inspired a subject which in some hands becomes a mere series of cold abstractions. It is a work that will be stimulating to the student of Roman history.'—*Athenæum.*

Alfred, Lord Tennyson. THE EARLY POEMS OF. Edited, with Notes and an Introduction, by J. CHURTON COLLINS, M.A. *Crown 8vo. 6s.*
[Methuen's Standard Library.
Also with 10 Illustrations in Photogravure by W. E. F. BRITTEN. *Demy 8vo. 10s. 6d.*
An elaborate edition of the celebrated volume which was published in its final and definitive form in 1853. This edition contains a long Introduction and copious Notes, textual and explanatory. It also contains in an Appendix all the Poems which Tennyson afterwards omitted.

MAUD. Edited by ELIZABETH WORDSWORTH. *Pott 8vo. Cloth, 1s. 6d. net; leather, 2s. 6d. net.* [Little Library.

IN MEMORIAM. Edited, with an Introduction and Notes, by H. C. BEECHING, M.A. *Pott 8vo. Cloth, 1s. 6d. net; leather, 2s. 6d. net.* [Little Library.

THE EARLY POEMS OF. Edited by J. C. COLLINS, M.A. *Pott 8vo. Cloth, 1s. 6d. net; leather, 2s. 6d. net.* [Little Library.

THE PRINCESS. Edited by ELIZABETH WORDSWORTH. *Pott 8vo. Cloth, 1s. 6d. net; leather, 2s. 6d. net.* [Little Library.

Alice Terton. LIGHTS AND SHADOWS IN A HOSPITAL. *Crown 8vo. 3s. 6d.*

W. M. Thackeray. VANITY FAIR. With an Introduction by S. GWYNN. *Three Volumes. Pott 8vo. Each volume, cloth, 1s. 6d. net; leather, 2s. 6d. net.*
[Little Library.

PENDENNIS. Edited by S. GWYNN. *Three Volumes. Pott 8vo. Each volume, cloth, 1s. 6d. net; leather, 2s. 6d. net.*
[Little Library.

F. W. Theobald, M.A. INSECT LIFE. Illustrated. *Crown 8vo. 2s. 6d.*
[University Extension Series.

A. H. Thompson. CAMBRIDGE AND ITS COLLEGES. Illustrated by E. H. NEW. *Pott 8vo. Cloth, 3s.; leather, 3s. 6d. net.*
[Little Guides.
'It is brightly written and learned, and is just such a book as a cultured visitor needs.'—*Scotsman.*

Paget Toynbee, Litt.D., M.A. See Dante.
DANTE STUDIES AND RESEARCHES. *Demy 8vo. 10s. 6d. net.*

THE LIFE OF DANTE ALIGHIERI. With 12 Illustrations. *Second Edition. Fcap. 8vo. Cloth, 3s. 6d.; leather, 4s. net.* [Little Biographies.

Herbert Trench. DEIRDRE WED: and Other Poems. *Crown 8vo. 5s.*

Philip Trevor (Dux). THE LIGHTER SIDE OF CRICKET. *Crown 8vo. 6s.*
'A wholly entertaining book.'—*Glasgow Herald.*
'The most welcome book on our national game published for years.'—*County Gentleman.*

G. E. Troutbeck. WESTMINSTER ABBEY. Illustrated by F. D. BEDFORD. *Pott 8vo. Cloth, 3s.; leather, 3s. 6d. net.* [Little Guides.
'A delightful miniature hand-book.'—*Glasgow Herald.*
'In comeliness, and perhaps in completeness, this work must take the first place.'—*Academy.*
'A really first-rate guide-book.'—*Literature.*

Gertrude Tuckwell. THE STATE AND ITS CHILDREN. *Crown 8vo. 2s. 6d.* [Social Questions Series.

Louisa Twining. WORKHOUSES AND PAUPERISM. *Crown 8vo. 2s. 6d.* [Social Questions Series.

G. W. Wade, D.D. OLD TESTAMENT HISTORY. With Maps. *Crown 8vo. 6s.*
'Careful, scholarly, embodying the best results of modern criticism, and written with great lucidity.'—*Examiner.*

Izaak Walton. THE LIVES OF DONNE, WOTTON, HOOKER, HERBERT AND SANDERSON. With an Introduction by VERNOᵃ BLACKBURN, and a Portrait. *3s. 6d.*

THE COMPLEAT ANGLER. Edited by J. BUCHAN. *Pott 8vo. Cloth. 1s. 6d. net; leather, 2s. 6d. net.* [Little Library.

Grace Warrack. See Lady Julian of Norwich.

Mrs. Alfred Waterhouse. A LITTLE BOOK OF LIFE AND DEATH. Edited by. *Pott 8vo. Cloth, 1s. 6d. net; leather, 2s. 6d. net.* [Little Library.

C. C. J. Webb, M.A. See St. Anselm.

F. C. Webber. CARPENTRY AND JOINERY. With many Illustrations. *Second Edition. Crown 8vo. 3s. 6d.*
'An admirable elementary text-book on the subject.'—*Builder.*

Sidney H. Wells. PRACTICAL MECHANICS. With 75 Illustrations and Diagrams. *Second Edition. Crown 8vo. 3s. 6d.* [Textbooks of Technology.

J. Wells, M.A., Fellow and Tutor of Wadham College. OXFORD AND OXFORD LIFE. By Members of the University. *Third Edition. Crown 8vo. 3s. 6d.*

A SHORT HISTORY OF ROME. *Third Edition.* With 3 Maps. *Cr. 8vo. 3s. 6d.*
This book is intended for the Middle and Upper Forms of Public Schools and for Pass Students at the Universities. It contains copious Tables, etc.
'An original work written on an original plan, and with uncommon freshness and vigour.'—*Speaker.*

OXFORD AND ITS COLLEGES. Illustrated by E. H. New. *Fourth Edition. Pott 8vo. Cloth, 3s.; leather, 3s. 6d. net.* [Little Guides.
'An admirable and accurate little treatise, attractively illustrated.'—*World.*

F. Weston, M.A., Curate of St. Matthew s, Westminster. THE HOLY SACRIFICE. *Pott 8vo. 6d. net.*

Helen C. Wetmore. THE LAST OF THE GREAT SCOUTS ('Buffalo Bill'). With Illustrations. *Demy 8vo. 6s.*
'A narrative of one of the most attractive figures in the public eye.'—*Daily Chronicle.*

C. Whibley. See Henley and Whibley.

L. Whibley, M.A., Fellow of Pembroke College, Cambridge. GREEK OLIGARCHIES: THEIR ORGANISATION AND CHARACTER. *Crown 8vo. 6s.*

G. H. Whitaker, M.A. THE EPISTLE OF ST. PAUL THE APOSTLE TO THE EPHESIANS. Edited by. *Fcap. 8vo. 1s. 6d. net.* [Churchman's Bible.

Gilbert White. THE NATURAL HISTORY OF SELBORNE. Edited by L. C. MIALL, F.R.S., assisted by W. WARDE FOWLER, M.A. *Crown 8vo. 6s.* [Methuen's Standard Library.

E. E. Whitfield. PRECIS WRITING AND OFFICE CORRESPONDENCE. *Crown 8vo. 2s.* [Commercial Series.

COMMERCIAL EDUCATION IN THEORY AND PRACTICE. *Crown 8vo. 5s.*
An introduction to Methuen's Commercial Series treating the question of Commercial Education fully from both the point of view of the teacher and of the parent. [Commercial Series.

Miss Whitley. See Lady Dilke.

W. H. Wilkins, B.A. THE ALIEN INVASION. *Crown 8vo. 2s. 6d.*
[Social Questions Series.

J. Frome Wilkinson, M.A. MUTUAL THRIFT. *Crown 8vo. 2s. 6d.*
[Social Questions Series.

W. Williamson. THE BRITISH GARDENER. Illustrated. *Demy 8vo. 10s. 6d.*

W. Williamson, B.A. JUNIOR ENGLISH EXAMINATION PAPERS. *Fcap. 8vo. 1s.* [Junior Examination Series.

A JUNIOR ENGLISH GRAMMAR. With numerous passages for parsing and analysis, and a chapter on Essay Writing. *Crown 8vo. 2s.* [Methuen's Junior School Books.

A CLASS-BOOK OF DICTATION PASSAGES. *Sixth Edition. Crown 8vo. 1s. 6d.* [Methuen's Junior School Books.

EASY DICTATION AND SPELLING. *Fcap. 8vo. 1s.*

E. M. Wilmot-Buxton. THE MAKERS OF EUROPE. *Crown 8vo. 3s. 6d.*
A Text-book of European History for Middle Forms.

Richard Wilton, M.A., Canon of York. LYRA PASTORALIS: Songs of Nature, Church, and Home. *Pott 8vo. 2s. 6d.*
A volume of devotional poems.

S. E. Winbolt, M.A., Assistant Master in Christ's Hospital. EXERCISES IN LATIN ACCIDENCE. *Crown 8vo. 1s. 6d.*
An elementary book adapted for Lower Forms to accompany the Shorter Latin Primer.

B. C. A. Windle, F.R.S., D.Sc. SHAKESPEARE'S COUNTRY. Illustrated by E. H. NEW. *Second Edition. Pott 8vo. Cloth, 3s.; leather, 3s. 6d. net.*
[Little Guides.

'One of the most charming guide books. Both for the library and as a travelling companion the book is equally choice and serviceable.'—*Academy.*

THE MALVERN COUNTRY. Illustrated by E. H. NEW. *Pott 8vo. Cloth, 3s.; leather, 3s. 6d. net.* [Little Guides.

Canon Winterbotham, M.A., B.Sc., LL.B. THE KINGDOM OF HEAVEN HERE AND HEREAFTER. *Crown 8vo. 3s. 6d.*
[Churchman's Library.

J. A. E. Wood. HOW TO MAKE A DRESS. Illustrated. *Second Edition. Crown 8vo. 1s. 6d.*
[Text Books of Technology.

Elizabeth Wordsworth. See Tennyson.

Arthur Wright, M.A., Fellow of Queens' College, Cambridge. SOME NEW TESTAMENT PROBLEMS. *Crown 8vo. 6s.* [Churchman's Library.

Sophie Wright. GERMAN VOCABULARIES FOR REPETITION. *Fcap. 8vo. 1s. 6d.*

A. B. Wylde. MODERN ABYSSINIA. With a Map and a Portrait. *Demy 8vo. 15s. net.*

G. Wyndham, M.P. THE POEMS OF WILLIAM SHAKESPEARE. With an Introduction and Notes. *Demy 8vo. Buckram, gilt top. 10s. 6d.*
'We have no hesitation in describing Mr. George Wyndham's introduction as a masterly piece of criticism, and all who love our Elizabethan literature will find a very garden of delight in it.'—*Spectator.*

W. B. Yeats. AN ANTHOLOGY OF IRISH VERSE. *Revised and Enlarged Edition. Crown 8vo. 3s. 6d.*

Methuen's Standard Library
Crown 8vo. 6s.

MEMOIRS OF MY LIFE AND WRITINGS. By Edward Gibbon. Edited by G. Birkbeck Hill, LL.D.

THE DECLINE AND FALL OF THE ROMAN EMPIRE. Edited by J. B. Bury, LL.D. *In Seven Volumes. Also, Demy 8vo. Gilt top. 8s. 6d. each.*

THE NATURAL HISTORY OF SELBORNE. By Gilbert White. Edited by L. C. Miall, F.R.S., Assisted by W. Warde Fowler, M.A.

THE HISTORY OF THE LIFE OF THOMAS ELLWOOD. Edited by C. G. Crump, M.A.

LA COMMEDIA DI DANTE ALIGHIERI. The Italian Text. Edited by Paget Toynbee, Litt.D., M.A. *Also, Demy 8vo. Gilt top. 8s. 6d.*

THE EARLY POEMS OF ALFRED, LORD TENNYSON. Edited by J. Churton Collins, M.A.

THE JOURNAL TO STELLA. By Jonathan Swift. Edited by G. A. Aitken, M.A.

THE LETTERS OF LORD CHESTERFIELD TO HIS SON. Edited by C. Strachey, and Notes by A. Calthrop. *Two Volumes.*

Byzantine Texts
Edited by J. B. BURY, M.A., Litt.D.

ZACHARIAH OF MITYLENE. Translated by F. J. Hamilton, D.D., and E. W. Brooks. *Demy 8vo. 12s. 6d. net.*

EVAGRIUS. Edited by Léon Parmentier and M. Bidez. *Demy 8vo. 10s. 6d. net.*

THE HISTORY OF PSELLUS. Edited by C. Sathas. *Demy 8vo. 15s. net.*

ECTHESIS CHRONICA. Edited by Professor Lambros. *Demy 8vo. 7s. 6d. net.*

The Little Library

With Introductions, Notes, and Photogravure Frontispieces.

Pott 8vo.   Each Volume, cloth, 1s. 6d. net ; leather, 2s. 6d. net.

'Altogether good to look upon, and to handle.'—*Outlook.*
'A perfect series.'—*Pilot.*
'It is difficult to conceive more attractive volumes.'—*St. James's Gazette.*
'Very delicious little books.'—*Literature.*
'Delightful editions.'—*Record.*

VANITY FAIR. By W. M. Thackeray. Edited by S. Gwynn. *Three Volumes.*

PENDENNIS. By W. M. Thackeray. Edited by S. Gwynn. *Three Volumes.*

JOHN HALIFAX, GENTLEMAN. By Mrs. Craik. Edited by Annie Matheson. *Two Volumes.*

PRIDE AND PREJUDICE. By Jane Austen. Edited by E. V. Lucas. *Two Volumes.*

NORTHANGER ABBEY. By Jane Austen. Edited by E. V. Lucas.

THE PRINCESS. By Alfred, Lord Tennyson. Edited by Elizabeth Wordsworth.

MAUD. By Alfred, Lord Tennyson. Edited by Elizabeth Wordsworth.

IN MEMORIAM. By Alfred, Lord Tennyson. Edited by H. C. Beeching, M.A.

THE EARLY POEMS OF ALFRED, LORD TENNYSON. Edited by J. C. Collins, M.A.

A LITTLE BOOK OF ENGLISH LYRICS. With Notes.

THE INFERNO OF DANTE. Translated by H. F. Cary. Edited by Paget Toynbee, Litt.D., M.A.

THE PURGATORIO OF DANTE. Translated by H. F. Cary. Edited by Paget Toynbee, Litt.D., M.A.

THE PARADISO OF DANTE. Translated by H. F. Cary. Edited by Paget Toynbee, Litt.D., M.A.

A LITTLE BOOK OF SCOTTISH VERSE. Edited by T. F. Henderson.

A LITTLE BOOK OF LIGHT VERSE. Edited by A. C. Deane.

SELECTIONS FROM WORDSWORTH. Edited by Nowell C. Smith.

THE ENGLISH POEMS OF RICHARD CRASHAW. Edited by Edward Hutton.

SELECTIONS FROM WILLIAM BLAKE. Edited by M. Perugini.

EOTHEN. By A. W. Kinglake. With an Introduction and Notes.

CRANFORD. By Mrs. Gaskell. Edited by E. V. Lucas.

A LITTLE BOOK OF ENGLISH PROSE. Edited by Mrs. P. A. Barnett.

LAVENGRO. By George Borrow. Edited by F. Hindes Groome. *Two Volumes.*

THE HISTORY OF THE CALIPH VATHEK. By William Beckford. Edited by E. Denison Ross.

THE COMPLEAT ANGLER. By Izaak Walton. Edited by J. Buchan.

MARRIAGE. By Susan Ferrier. Edited by Miss Goodrick - Freer and Lord Iddesleigh. *Two Volumes.*

SELECTIONS FROM THE EARLY POEMS OF ROBERT BROWNING. Edited by W. Hall Griffin, M.A.

ELIA, AND THE LAST ESSAYS OF ELIA. By Charles Lamb. Edited by E. V. Lucas.

A SENTIMENTAL JOURNEY. By Laurence Sterne. Edited by H. W. Paul.

A LITTLE BOOK OF LIFE AND DEATH. Edited by Mrs. Alfred Waterhouse.

MANSIE WAUCH. By D. M. Moir. Edited by T. F. Henderson.

The Little Guides

Pott 8vo, cloth, 3s.; leather, 3s. 6d. net.

OXFORD AND ITS COLLEGES. By J. Wells, M.A. Illustrated by E. H. New. *Fourth Edition.*

CAMBRIDGE AND ITS COLLEGES. By A. Hamilton Thompson. Illustrated by E. H. New.

THE MALVERN COUNTRY. By B. C. A. Windle, D.Sc., F.R.S. Illustrated by E. H. New.

SHAKESPEARE'S COUNTRY. By B. C. A. Windle, D.Sc., F.R.S. Illustrated by E. H. New. *Second Edition.*

SUSSEX. By F. G. Brabant, M.A. Illustrated by E. H. New.

WESTMINSTER ABBEY. By G. E. Troutbeck. Illustrated by F. D. Bedford.

NORFOLK. By W. A. Dutt. Illustrated by B. C. Boulter.

Little Biographies

Fcap. 8vo.   Each volume, cloth, 3s. 6d. ; leather, 4s. net.

THE LIFE OF DANTE ALIGHIERI. By Paget Toynbee, Litt.D., M.A. With 12 Illustrations. *Second Edition.*

THE LIFE OF SAVONAROLA. By E. L. S. Horsburgh, M.A. With Portraits and Illustrations.

THE LIFE OF JOHN HOWARD. By E. C. S. Gibson, D.D., Vicar of Leeds. With 12 Illustrations.

THE LIFE OF LORD TENNYSON. By A. C. Benson, M.A. With 12 Illustrations.

The Little Blue Books for Children
Edited by E. V. LUCAS.

Illustrated. Square Fcap. 8vo. 2s. 6d.

'Very elegant and very interesting volumes.'—*Glasgow Herald.*
'A delightful series of diminutive volumes.'—*World.*
'The series should be a favourite among juveniles.'—*Observer.*

1. THE CASTAWAYS OF MEADOWBANK. By T. COBB.
2. THE BEECHNUT BOOK. By JACOB ABBOTT. Edited by E. V. LUCAS.
3. THE AIR GUN. By T. HILBERT.

The Library of Devotion
With Introductions and (where necessary) Notes.

Pott 8vo, cloth, 2s. ; leather, 2s. 6d. net.

'This series is excellent.'—THE LATE BISHOP OF LONDON.
'Well worth the attention of the Clergy.'—THE BISHOP OF LICHFIELD.
'The new "Library of Devotion" is excellent.'—THE BISHOP OF PETERBOROUGH.
'Charming.'—*Record.*   'Delightful.'—*Church Bells.*

THE CONFESSIONS OF ST. AUGUSTINE. Edited by C. Bigg, D.D. *Third Edition.*

THE CHRISTIAN YEAR. Edited by Walter Lock, D.D. *Second Edition.*

THE IMITATION OF CHRIST. Edited by C. Bigg, D.D. *Second Edition.*

A BOOK OF DEVOTIONS. Edited by J. W. Stanbridge, B.D.

LYRA INNOCENTIUM. Edited by Walter Lock, D.D.

A SERIOUS CALL TO A DEVOUT AND HOLY LIFE. Edited by C. Bigg, D.D. *Second Edition.*

THE TEMPLE. Edited by E. C. S. Gibson, D.D.

A GUIDE TO ETERNITY. Edited by J. W. Stanbridge, B.D.

THE PSALMS OF DAVID. Edited by B. W. Randolph, D.D.

LYRA APOSTOLICA. Edited by Canon Scott Holland and H. C. Beeching, M.A.

THE INNER WAY. Edited by A. W. Hutton, M.A.

THE THOUGHTS OF PASCAL. Edited by C. S. Jerram, M.A.

ON THE LOVE OF GOD. Edited by W. J. Knox-Little, M.A.

A MANUAL OF CONSOLATION FROM THE SAINTS AND FATHERS. Edited by J. H. Burn, B.D.

THE SONG OF SONGS. Edited by B. Blaxland, M.A.

THE DEVOTIONS OF ST. ANSELM. Edited by C. C. J. Webb, M.A.

The Commentaries on the Revised Version
General Editor, WALTER LOCK, D.D., Warden of Keble College,
Dean Ireland's Professor of Exegesis in the University of Oxford.

THE BOOK OF JOB. Edited by E. C. S. Gibson, D.D. *Demy 8vo. 6s.*

THE ACTS OF THE APOSTLES. Edited by R. B. Rackham, M.A. *Demy 8vo. 12s. 6d.*

Handbooks of Theology
General Editor, A. ROBERTSON, D.D., Principal of King's College, London.

THE XXXIX. ARTICLES OF THE CHURCH OF ENGLAND. Edited by E. C. S. Gibson, D.D. *Third and Cheaper Edition in One Volume. Demy 8vo. 12s. 6d.*

AN INTRODUCTION TO THE HISTORY OF RELIGION. By F. B. Jevons, M.A., Litt.D. *Second Edition. Demy 8vo. 10s. 6d.*

THE DOCTRINE OF THE INCARNATION. By R. L. Ottley, M.A. *Second and Cheaper Edition. Demy 8vo. 12s. 6d.*

AN INTRODUCTION TO THE HISTORY OF THE CREEDS. By A. E. Burn, B.D. *Demy 8vo. 10s. 6d.*

THE PHILOSOPHY OF RELIGION IN ENGLAND AND AMERICA. By Alfred Caldecott, D.D. *Demy 8vo. 10s. 6d.*

The Churchman's Library
General Editor, J. H. BURN, B.D., F.R.S.E., Examining Chaplain to the
Bishop of Aberdeen.

THE BEGINNINGS OF ENGLISH CHRISTIANITY. By W. E. Collins, M.A. With Map. *Crown 8vo. 3s. 6d.*

SOME NEW TESTAMENT PROBLEMS. By Arthur Wright, M.A. *Crown 8vo. 6s.*

THE KINGDOM OF HEAVEN HERE AND HEREAFTER. By Canon Winterbotham, M.A., B.Sc., LL.B. *Crown 8vo. 3s. 6d.*

THE WORKMANSHIP OF THE PRAYER BOOK : Its Literary and Liturgical Aspects. By J. Dowden, D.D. *Second Edition. Crown 8vo. 3s. 6d.*

EVOLUTION. By F. B. Jevons, M.A., Litt.D *Crown 8vo. 3s. 6d.*

THE OLD TESTAMENT AND THE NEW SCHOLARSHIP. By J. P. Peters, D.D. *Crown 8vo. 6s.*

THE CHURCHMAN'S INTRODUCTION TO THE OLD TESTAMENT. Edited by A. M. Mackay, B.A. *Crown 8vo. 3s. 6d.*

THE CHURCH OF CHRIST. By E. T. Green, M.A. *Crown 8vo. 6s.*

The Churchman's Bible

General Editor, J. H. BURN, B.D., F.R.S.E.

Messrs. METHUEN are issuing a series of expositions upon most of the books of the Bible. The volumes are practical and devotional, and the text of the Authorised Version is explained in sections, which correspond as far as possible with the Church Lectionary.

THE EPISTLE TO THE GALATIANS. Explained by A. W. Robinson, M.A. *Fcap. 8vo.* 1s. 6d. *net.*

ECCLESIASTES. Explained by A. W. Streane, D.D. *Fcap. 8vo.* 1s. 6d. *net.*

THE EPISTLE TO THE PHILIPPIANS. Explained by C. R. D. Biggs, D.D. *Fcap. 8vo.* 1s. 6d. *net.*

THE EPISTLE OF ST. JAMES. Edited by H. W. Fulford, M.A. *Fcap. 8vo.* 1s. 6d. *net.*

ISAIAH. Edited by W. E. Barnes, D.D., Hulsaean Professor of Divinity. *Two Volumes.* 2s. *net each.* Vol. I. With Map.

THE EPISTLE OF ST. PAUL THE APOSTLE TO THE EPHESIANS. Edited by G. H. Whitaker, M.A. 1s. 6d. *net.*

Leaders of Religion

Edited by H. C. BEECHING, M.A. *With Portraits. Crown 8vo. 3s. 6d.*

A series of short biographies of the most prominent leaders of religious life and thought of all ages and countries.

The following are ready :—

CARDINAL NEWMAN. By R. H. Hutton.

JOHN WESLEY. By J. H. Overton, M.A.

BISHOP WILBERFORCE. By G. W. Daniell, M.A.

CARDINAL MANNING. By A. W. Hutton, M.A.

CHARLES SIMEON. By H. C. G. Moule, D.D.

JOHN KEBLE. By Walter Lock, D.D.

THOMAS CHALMERS. By Mrs. Oliphant.

LANCELOT ANDREWES. By R. L. Ottley, M.A.

AUGUSTINE OF CANTERBURY. By E. L. Cutts, D.D.

WILLIAM LAUD. By W. H. Hutton, M.A.

JOHN KNOX. By F. MacCunn.

JOHN HOWE. By R. F. Horton, D.D.

BISHOP KEN. By F. A. Clarke, M.A.

GEORGE FOX, THE QUAKER. By T. Hodgkin D.C.L.

JOHN DONNE. By Augustus Jessopp, D.D.

THOMAS CRANMER. By A. J. Mason.

BISHOP LATIMER. By R. M. Carlyle and A. J. Carlyle, M.A.

BISHOP BUTLER. By W. A. Spooner, M.A.

Other volumes will be announced in due course.

Social Questions of To=day

Edited by H. DE B. GIBBINS, Litt.D., M.A.

Crown 8vo. 2s. 6d.

TRADE UNIONISM—NEW AND OLD. By G. Howell. *Third Edition.*

THE CO-OPERATIVE MOVEMENT TO-DAY. By G. J. Holyoake. *Second Edition.*

MUTUAL THRIFT. By Rev. J. Frome Wilkinson, M.A.

PROBLEMS OF POVERTY. By J. A. Hobson, M.A. *Fourth Edition.*

THE COMMERCE OF NATIONS. By C. F. Bastable, M.A. *Second Edition.*

THE ALIEN INVASION. By W. H. Wilkins, B.A.

THE RURAL EXODUS. By P. Anderson Graham.

LAND NATIONALIZATION. By Harold Cox, B.A.

A SHORTER WORKING DAY. By H. de B. Gibbins and R. A. Hadfield.

BACK TO THE LAND: An Inquiry into Rural Depopulation. By H. E. Moore.

TRUSTS, POOLS, AND CORNERS. By J. Stephen Jeans.

THE FACTORY SYSTEM. By R. W. Cooke-Taylor.

THE STATE AND ITS CHILDREN. By Gertrude Tuckwell.

WOMEN'S WORK. By Lady Dilke, Miss Bulley, and Miss Whitley.

SOCIALISM AND MODERN THOUGHT. By M. Kauffmann.

THE HOUSING OF THE WORKING CLASSES. By E. Bowmaker.

THE PROBLEM OF THE UNEMPLOYED. By J. A. Hobson, B.A.

LIFE IN WEST LONDON. By Arthur Sherwell, M.A. *Third Edition.*

RAILWAY NATIONALIZATION. By Clement Edwards.

WORKHOUSES AND PAUPERISM. By Louisa Twining.

UNIVERSITY AND SOCIAL SETTLEMENTS. By W. Reason, M.A.

University Extension Series

Edited by J. E. SYMES, M.A.,
Principal of University College, Nottingham.
Crown 8vo. Price (with some exceptions) 2s. 6d.

A series of books on historical, literary, and scientific subjects, suitable for extension students and home-reading circles. Each volume is complete in itself, and the subjects are treated by competent writers in a broad and philosophic spirit.

The following Volumes are ready :—

THE INDUSTRIAL HISTORY OF ENGLAND. By H. de B. Gibbins, Litt.D., M.A. *Eighth Edition.* Revised. With Maps and Plans. 3s.

A HISTORY OF ENGLISH POLITICAL ECONOMY. By L. L. Price, M.A. *Third Edition.*

PROBLEMS OF POVERTY. By J. A. Hobson, M.A. *Fourth Edition.*

VICTORIAN POETS. By A. Sharp.

THE FRENCH REVOLUTION. By J. E. Symes, M.A.

PSYCHOLOGY. By S. F. Granger, M.A. *Second Edition.*

THE EVOLUTION OF PLANT LIFE: Lower Forms. By G. Massee. Illustrated.

AIR AND WATER. By V. B. Lewes, M.A. Illustrated.

THE CHEMISTRY OF LIFE AND HEALTH. By C. W. Kimmins, M.A. Illustrated.

THE MECHANICS OF DAILY LIFE. By V. P. Sells, M.A. Illustrated.

ENGLISH SOCIAL REFORMERS. By H. de B. Gibbins, Litt.D., M.A. *Second Edition.*

ENGLISH TRADE AND FINANCE IN THE SEVENTEENTH CENTURY. By W. A. S. Hewins, B.A.

THE CHEMISTRY OF FIRE. By M. M. Pattison Muir, M.A. Illustrated.

A TEXT-BOOK OF AGRICULTURAL BOTANY. By M. C. Potter, M.A., F.L.S. Illustrated. *Second Edition.* 4s. 6d.

THE VAULT OF HEAVEN. A Popular Introduction to Astronomy. By R. A. Gregory. With numerous Illustrations.

METEOROLOGY. By H. N. Dickson, F.R.S.E., F.R. Met. Soc. Illustrated.

A MANUAL OF ELECTRICAL SCIENCE. By George J. Burch, M.A., F.R.S. Illustrated. 3s.

THE EARTH. An Introduction to Physiography. By Evan Small, M.A. Illustrated.

INSECT LIFE. By F. W. Theobald, M.A. Illustrated.

ENGLISH POETRY FROM BLAKE TO BROWNING. By W. M. Dixon, M.A. *Second Edition.*

ENGLISH LOCAL GOVERNMENT. By E. Jenks, M.A.

THE GREEK VIEW OF LIFE. By G. L. Dickinson. *Second Edition.*

Commercial Series

Edited by H. DE B. GIBBINS, Litt.D., M.A.

COMMERCIAL EDUCATION IN THEORY AND PRACTICE. By E. E. Whitfield, M.A. *Crown 8vo.* 5s.

An introduction to Methuen's Commercial Series treating the question of Commercial Education fully from both the point of view of the teacher and of the parent.

BRITISH COMMERCE AND COLONIES FROM ELIZABETH TO VICTORIA. By H. de B. Gibbins, Litt.D., M.A. *Third Edition.* 2s.

COMMERCIAL EXAMINATION PAPERS. By H. de B. Gibbins, Litt.D., M.A. 1s. 6d.

THE ECONOMICS OF COMMERCE. By H. de B. Gibbins, Litt.D., M.A. 1s. 6d.

A GERMAN COMMERCIAL READER. By S. E. Bally. With Vocabulary. 2s.

A COMMERCIAL GEOGRAPHY OF THE BRITISH EMPIRE. By L. W. Lyde, M.A. *Third Edition.* 2s.

A PRIMER OF BUSINESS. By S. Jackson, M.A. *Third Edition.* 1s. 6d.

COMMERCIAL ARITHMETIC. By F. G. Taylor, M.A. *Third Edition.* 1s. 6d.

FRENCH COMMERCIAL CORRESPONDENCE. By S. E. Bally. With Vocabulary. *Third Edition.* 2s.

GERMAN COMMERCIAL CORRESPONDENCE. By S. E. Bally. With Vocabulary. 2s. 6d.

A FRENCH COMMERCIAL READER. By S. E. Bally. With Vocabulary. *Second Edition.* 2s.

PRECIS WRITING AND OFFICE CORRESPONDENCE. By E. E. Whitfield, M.A. 2s.

A GUIDE TO PROFESSIONS AND BUSINESS. By H. Jones. 1s. 6d.

THE PRINCIPLES OF BOOK-KEEPING BY DOUBLE ENTRY. By J. E. B. M'Allen, M.A. *Crown 8vo.* 2s.

COMMERCIAL LAW. By W. Douglas Edwards. 2s.

A COMMERCIAL GEOGRAPHY OF FOREIGN NATIONS. By F. C. Boon, B.A. *Crown 8vo.* 2s.

Classical Translations

Edited by H. F. Fox, M.A., Fellow and Tutor of Brasenose College, Oxford.

ÆSCHYLUS—Agamemnon, Choephoroe, Eumenides. Translated by Lewis Campbell, LL.D. 5s.

CICERO—De Oratore I. Translated by E. N. P. Moor, M.A. 3s. 6d.

CICERO—Select Orations (Pro Milone, Pro Mureno, Philippic II., in Catilinam). Translated by H. E. D. Blakiston, M.A. 5s.

CICERO—De Natura Deorum. Translated by F. Brooks, M.A. 3s. 6d.

CICERO—De Officiis. Translated by G. B. Gardiner, M.A. *Crown 8vo.* 2s. 6d.

HORACE—The Odes and Epodes. Translated by A. Godley, M.A. 2s.

LUCIAN—Six Dialogues (Nigrinus, Icaro-Menippus, The Cock, The Ship, The Parasite, The Lover of Falsehood). Translated by S. T. Irwin, M.A. 3s. 6d.

SOPHOCLES—Electra and Ajax. Translated by E. D. A. Morshead, M.A. 2s. 6d.

TACITUS—Agricola and Germania. Translated by R. B. Townshend. 2s. 6d.

Methuen's Junior School=Books.

Edited by O. D. INSKIP, LL.D., and W. WILLIAMSON, B.A.

A CLASS-BOOK OF DICTATION PASSAGES. By W. Williamson, B.A. *Sixth Edition. Crown 8vo. 1s. 6d.*

THE GOSPEL ACCORDING TO ST. MARK. Edited by A. E. Rubie, M.A., Headmaster of the Royal Naval School, Eltham. With Three Maps. *Crown 8vo. 1s. 6d.*

A JUNIOR ENGLISH GRAMMAR. By W. Williamson, B.A. With numerous passages for parsing and analysis, and a chapter on Essay Writing. *Crown 8vo. 2s.*

A JUNIOR CHEMISTRY. By E. A. Tyler, B.A., F.C.S., Science Master at Framlingham College. With 73 Illustrations. *Crown 8vo. 2s. 6d.*

School Examination Series

Edited by A. M. M. STEDMAN, M.A. *Crown 8vo. 2s. 6d.*

FRENCH EXAMINATION PAPERS. By A. M. M. Stedman, M.A. *Eleventh Edition.*
　A KEY, issued to Tutors and Private Students only, to be had on application to the Publishers. *Fifth Edition. Crown 8vo. 6s. net.*

LATIN EXAMINATION PAPERS. By A. M. M. Stedman, M.A. *Eleventh Edition.*
　KEY (*Fourth Edition*) issued as above. *6s. net.*

GREEK EXAMINATION PAPERS. By A. M. M. Stedman, M.A. *Sixth Edition.*
　KEY (*Second Edition*) issued as above. *6s. net.*

GERMAN EXAMINATION PAPERS. By R. J. Morich. *Fifth Edition.*
　KEY (*Second Edition*) issued as above. *6s. net.*

HISTORY AND GEOGRAPHY EXAMINATION PAPERS. By C. H. Spence, M.A., Clifton College. *Second Edition.*

PHYSICS EXAMINATION PAPERS. By R. E. Steel, M.A., F.C.S.

GENERAL KNOWLEDGE EXAMINATION PAPERS. By A. M. M. Stedman, M.A. *Fourth Edition.*
　KEY (*Second Edition*) issued as above. *7s. net.*

EXAMINATION PAPERS IN ENGLISH HISTORY. By J. Tait Plowden-Wardlaw, B.A. *Crown 8vo. 2s. 6d.*

Technology—Textbooks of

Edited by W. GARNETT, D.C.L., and PROFESSOR J. WERTHEIMER, F.I.C.

Fully Illustrated.

HOW TO MAKE A DRESS. By J. A. E. Wood. *Second Edition. Crown 8vo. 1s. 6d.*

CARPENTRY AND JOINERY. By F. C. Webber. *Second Edition. Crown 8vo. 3s. 6d.*

PRACTICAL MECHANICS. By Sidney H. Wells. *Second Edition. Crown 8vo. 3s. 6d.*

PRACTICAL PHYSICS. By H. Stroud, D.Sc., M.A. *Crown 8vo. 3s. 6d.*

MILLINERY, THEORETICAL AND PRACTICAL. By Clare Hill. *Crown 8vo. 2s.*

PRACTICAL CHEMISTRY. By W. French, M.A. *Crown 8vo. Part I. 1s. 6d.*

PART II.—FICTION

Marie Corelli's Novels.

Crown 8vo. 6s. each.

A ROMANCE OF TWO WORLDS. *Twenty-Third Edition.*

VENDETTA. *Eighteenth Edition.*

THELMA. *Twenty-Seventh Edition.*

ARDATH: THE STORY OF A DEAD SELF. *Thirteenth Edition.*

THE SOUL OF LILITH. *Eleventh Edit.*

WORMWOOD. *Twelfth Edition.*

BARABBAS: A DREAM OF THE WORLD'S TRAGEDY. *Thirty-Eighth Edition.*
　'The tender reverence of the treatment and the imaginative beauty of the writing have reconciled us to the daring of the conception. This "Dream of the World's Tragedy" is a lofty and not inadequate paraphrase of the supreme climax of the inspired narrative.'—*Dublin Review.*

THE SORROWS OF SATAN. *Forty-Sixth Edition.*
　'A very powerful piece of work. . . . The conception is magnificent, and is likely to win an abiding place within the memory

of man. . . . The author has immense command of language, and a limitless audacity. . . . This interesting and remarkable romance will live long after much of the ephemeral literature of the day is forgotten. . . . A literary phenomenon . . . novel, and even sublime.'—W. T. STEAD in the *Review of Reviews.*

THE MASTER CHRISTIAN.
　[165th Thousand.
　'It cannot be denied that "The Master Christian" is a powerful book; that it is one likely to raise uncomfortable questions in all but the most self-satisfied readers, and that it strikes at the root of the failure of the Churches—the decay of faith—in a manner which shows the inevitable disaster heaping up . . . The good Cardinal Bonpré is a beautiful figure, fit to stand beside the good Bishop in "Les Misérables." It is a book with a serious purpose expressed with absolute unconventionality and passion . . . And this is to say it is a book worth reading.'—*Examiner.*

Anthony Hope's Novels.
Crown 8vo.   6s. each.

THE GOD IN THE CAR. *Ninth Edition.*
'A very remarkable book, deserving of critical analysis impossible within our limit; brilliant, but not superficial; well considered, but not elaborated; constructed with the proverbial art that conceals, but yet allows itself to be enjoyed by readers to whom fine literary method is a keen pleasure.'—*The World.*

A CHANGE OF AIR. *Sixth Edition.*
'A graceful, vivacious comedy, true to human nature. The characters are traced with a masterly hand.'—*Times.*

A MAN OF MARK. *Fifth Edition.*
'Of all Mr. Hope's books, "A Man of Mark" is the one which best compares with "The Prisoner of Zenda."'—*National Observer.*

THE CHRONICLES OF COUNT ANTONIO. *Fifth Edition.*
'It is a perfectly enchanting story of love and chivalry, and pure romance. The Count is the most constant, desperate, and modest and tender of lovers, a peerless gentleman, an intrepid fighter, a faithful friend, and a magnanimous foe.'—*Guardian.*

PHROSO. Illustrated by H. R. MILLAR. *Sixth Edition.*
'The tale is thoroughly fresh, quick with vitality, stirring the blood.'—*St. James's Gazette.*

SIMON DALE. Illustrated. *Sixth Edition.*
'There is searching analysis of human nature, with a most ingeniously constructed plot. Mr. Hope has drawn the contrasts of his women with marvellous subtlety and delicacy.'—*Times.*

THE KING'S MIRROR. *Third Edition.*
'In elegance, delicacy, and tact it ranks with the best of his novels, while in the wide range of its portraiture and the subtilty of its analysis it surpasses all his earlier ventures.'—*Spectator.*

QUISANTE. *Third Edition.*
'The book is notable for a very high literary quality, and an impress of power and mastery on every page.'—*Daily Chronicle.*

Lucas Malet's Novels.
Crown 8vo.   6s. each.

COLONEL ENDERBY'S WIFE. *Third Edition.*

A COUNSEL OF PERFECTION. *New Edition.*

LITTLE PETER. *Second Edition.* 3s. 6d.

THE WAGES OF SIN. *Thirteenth Edition.*

THE CARISSIMA. *Fourth Edition.*

THE GATELESS BARRIER. *Fourth Edition.*
'In "The Gateless Barrier" it is at once evident that, whilst Lucas Malet has preserved her birthright of originality, the artistry, the actual writing, is above even the high level of the books that were born before.'—*Westminster Gazette.*

THE HISTORY OF SIR RICHARD CALMADY. *Seventh Edition.* A Limited Edition in Two Volumes. *Crown 8vo.* 12s.
'A picture finely and amply conceived. In the strength and insight in which the story has been conceived, in the wealth of fancy and reflection bestowed upon its execution, and in the moving sincerity of its pathos throughout, "Sir Richard Calmady" must rank as the great novel of a great writer.'—*Literature.*

'The ripest fruit of Lucas Malet's genius. A picture of maternal love by turns tender and terrible.'—*Spectator.*

'A remarkably fine book, with a noble motive and a sound conclusion.'—*Pilot.*

W. W. Jacobs' Novels.
Crown 8vo.   3s. 6d. each.

MANY CARGOES. *Twenty-Sixth Edition.*

SEA URCHINS. *Ninth Edition.*

A MASTER OF CRAFT. Illustrated. *Fifth Edition.*
Can be unreservedly recommended to all who have not lost their appetite for wholesome laughter.'—*Spectator.*
'The best humorous book published for many a day.'—*Black and White.*

LIGHT FREIGHTS. Illustrated. *Fourth Edition.*
'His wit and humour are perfectly irresistible. Mr. Jacobs writes of skippers, and mates, and seamen, and his crew are the jolliest lot that ever sailed.'—*Daily News.*
'Laughter in every page.'—*Daily Mail.*

Gilbert Parker's Novels.

Crown 8vo.   6s. each.

PIERRE AND HIS PEOPLE. *Fifth Edition.*
  'Stories happily conceived and finely executed. There is strength and genius in Mr. Parker's style.'—*Daily Telegraph.*

MRS. FALCHION. *Fourth Edition.*
  'A splendid study of character.'—
                                Athenæum.

THE TRANSLATION OF A SAVAGE. *Second Edition.*

THE TRAIL OF THE SWORD. Illustrated. *Seventh Edition.*
  'A rousing and dramatic tale. A book like this is a joy inexpressible.'—
                            Daily Chronicle.

WHEN VALMOND CAME TO PONTIAC: The Story of a Lost Napoleon. *Fifth Edition.*
  'Here we find romance—real, breathing, living romance. The character of Valmond is drawn unerringly.'—*Pall Mall Gazette.*

AN ADVENTURER OF THE NORTH : The Last Adventures of 'Pretty Pierre.' *Second Edition.*
  'The present book is full of fine and moving stories of the great North.'—*Glasgow Herald.*

THE SEATS OF THE MIGHTY. Illustrated. *Eleventh Edition.*
  'Mr. Parker has produced a really fine historical novel.'—*Athenæum.*
  'A great book.'—*Black and White.*

THE BATTLE OF THE STRONG: a Romance of Two Kingdoms. Illustrated. *Fourth Edition.*
  'Nothing more vigorous or more human has come from Mr. Gilbert Parker than this novel.'—*Literature.*

THE POMP OF THE LAVILETTES. *Second Edition.* 3s. 6d.
  'Unforced pathos, and a deeper knowledge of human nature than he has displayed before.'—*Pall Mall Gazette.*

Arthur Morrison's Novels.

Crown 8vo.   6s. each.

TALES OF MEAN STREETS. *Fifth Edition.*

  'A great book. The author's method is amazingly effective, and produces a thrilling sense of reality. The writer lays upon us a master hand. The book is simply appalling and irresistible in its interest. It is humorous also; without humour it would not make the mark it is certain to make.'—
                                    World.

A CHILD OF THE JAGO. *Fourth Edition.*
  'The book is a masterpiece.'—*Pall Mall Gazette.*

TO LONDON TOWN. *Second Edition.*
  'This is the new Mr. Arthur Morrison, gracious and tender, sympathetic and human.'—*Daily Telegraph.*

CUNNING MURRELL.
  'Admirable. . . . Delightful humorous relief . . . a most artistic and satisfactory achievement.'—*Spectator.*

Eden Phillpott's Novels.

Crown 8vo.   6s. each.

LYING PROPHETS.
CHILDREN OF THE MIST.
THE HUMAN BOY. With a Frontispiece. *Fourth Edition.*
  'Mr. Phillpotts knows exactly what school-boys do, and can lay bare their inmost thoughts; likewise he shows an all-pervading sense of humour.'—*Academy.*
SONS OF THE MORNING. *Second Edition.*
  'A book of strange power and fascination.'—*Morning Post.*

THE STRIKING HOURS. *Second Edition.*
  ' Tragedy and comedy, pathos and humour, are blended to a nicety in this volume.'—*World.*
  'The whole book is redolent of a fresher and ampler air than breathes in the circumscribed life of great towns.'—*Spectator.*

FANCY FREE. Illustrated. *Second Edition. Crown 8vo. 6s.*
  'Of variety and racy humour there is plenty.'—*Daily Graphic.*

S. Baring-Gould's Novels.

Crown 8vo.   6s. each.

ARMINELL. *Fifth Edition.*
URITH. *Fifth Edition.*
IN THE ROAR OF THE SEA. *Seventh Edition.*

MRS. CURGENVEN OF CURGENVEN. *Fourth Edition.*
CHEAP JACK ZITA. *Fourth Edition.*
THE QUEEN OF LOVE. *Fifth Edition*

MARGERY OF QUETHER. *Third Edition.*
JACQUETTA. *Third Edition.*
KITTY ALONE. *Fifth Edition.*
NOÉMI. Illustrated. *Fourth Edition.*
THE BROOM-SQUIRE. Illustrated. *Fourth Edition.*
THE PENNYCOMEQUICKS. *Third Edition.*

DARTMOOR IDYLLS.
GUAVAS THE TINNER. Illustrated. *Second Edition.*
BLADYS. Illustrated. *Second Edition.*
DOMITIA. Illustrated. *Second Edition.*
PABO THE PRIEST.
WINIFRED. Illustrated. *Second Edition.*
THE FROBISHERS.
ROYAL GEORGIE. Illustrated.

Robert Barr's Novels.
Crown 8vo. 6s. each.

IN THE MIDST OF ALARMS. *Third Edition.*
'A book which has abundantly satisfied us by its capital humour.'—*Daily Chronicle.*
THE MUTABLE MANY. *Second Edition.*
'There is much insight in it, and much excellent humour.'—*Daily Chronicle.*
THE COUNTESS TEKLA. *Third Edition.*
'Of these mediæval romances, which are now gaining ground "The Countess Tekla" is the very best we have seen.'—*Pall Mall Gazette.*

Andrew Balfour. BY STROKE OF SWORD. Illustrated. *Fourth Edition. Crown 8vo. 6s.*
'A recital of thrilling interest, told with unflagging vigour.'—*Globe.*

S. Baring Gould. See page 34.

Robert Barr. See above.

George Bartram, Author of 'The People of Clopton.' THE THIRTEEN EVENINGS. *Crown 8vo. 6s.*

Margaret Benson. SUBJECT TO VANITY. *Crown 8vo. 3s. 6d.*

J. Bloundelle Burton, Author of 'The Clash of Arms.' THE YEAR ONE: A Page of the French Revolution. Illustrated. *Crown 8vo. 6s.*
See also Fleur de Lis Novels.

Ada Cambridge, Author of 'Path and Goal.' THE DEVASTATORS. *Crown 8vo. 6s.*
See also Fleur de Lis Novels.

Bernard Capes, Author of 'The Lake of Wine.' PLOTS. *Crown 8vo. 6s.*
'The stories are excellently fanciful and concentrated and quite worthy of the author's best work.'—*Morning Leader.*
'Ingenious and original. This is a book to turn to once and again.'—*Morning Post.*

Weatherby Chesney. JOHN TOPP: PIRATE. *Second Edition. Crown 8vo. 6s.*
A book of breathless adventure.
'A rousing pleasant story.'—*Athenæum.*

THE FOUNDERED GALLEON. *Crown 8vo. 6s.*

THE STRONG ARM. Illustrated. *Second Edition.*
THE VICTORS.
'Mr. Barr has a rich sense of humour.'—*Onlooker.*
'A very convincing study of American life in its business and political aspects.'—*Pilot.*
'Good writing, illuminating sketches of character, and constant variety of scene and incident.'—*Times.*
'An ingenious tale of the sea and particularly exciting.'—*World.*
'A healthy, straightforward tale, breezy and cheerful.'—*Manchester Guardian.*

J. Maclaren Cobban. THE KING OF ANDAMAN: A Saviour of Society. *Crown 8vo. 6s.*
WILT THOU HAVE THIS WOMAN. *Crown 8vo. 6s.*
See also Fleur de Lis Novels.

E. H. Cooper, Author of 'Mr. Blake of Newmarket.' A FOOL'S YEAR. *Crown 8vo. 6s.*
'A strikingly clever story, with pictures of sporting society convincingly true.'—*Pall Mall Gazette.*

Marie Corelli. See page 32.

L. Cope Cornford. CAPTAIN JACOBUS: A Romance of the Road. *Cr. 8vo. 6s.*
See also Fleur de Lis Novels.

S. R. Crockett, Author of 'The Raiders, etc. LOCHINVAR. Illustrated. *Second Edition. Crown 8vo. 6s.*
'Full of gallantry and pathos, of the clash of arms, and brightened by episodes of humour and love.'—*Westminster Gazette.*
THE STANDARD BEARER. *Cr. 8vo. 6s.*
'A delightful tale.'—*Speaker.*
'Mr. Crockett at his best.'—*Literature.*

B. M. Croker, Author of 'Peggy of the Bartons.' ANGEL. *Second Edition. Crown 8vo. 6s.*
'An excellent story. Clever pictures of Anglo-Indian life abound. The heroine is daring and delightful.'—*Manchester Guardian.*
See also Fleur de Lis Novels.

C. E. Denny. THE ROMANCE OF UP-FOLD MANOR. *Crown 8vo. 6s.*
'A fine tragic story.'—*Weekly Register.*
'There is picturesqueness and real feeling.'—*St. James's Gazette.*

A. Conan Doyle, Author of 'Sherlock Holmes,' 'The White Company,' etc. ROUND THE RED LAMP. *Eighth Edition. Crown 8vo. 6s.*
'The book is far and away the best view that has been vouchsafed us behind the scenes of the consulting-room.'—*Illustrated London News.*

Sara Jeannette Duncan (Mrs. Everard Cotes), Author of 'A Voyage of Consolation.' THOSE DELIGHTFUL AMERICANS. Illustrated. *Second Edition. Crown 8vo. 6s.*
'A rattling picture of American life, bright and good-tempered throughout.'—*Scotsman.*
'The humour is delicious.'—*Daily Mail.*

C. F. Embree. A HEART OF FLAME. *Crown 8vo. 6s.*
'Alive with the pulsing and clamorous life of the wild folk and wild actions with which it deals. A striking, well-conceived piece of work.'—*Pall Mall Gazette.*
'An admirable story, well told. The characters are full of life, and Ramoncita is really a delicious little creature.'—*Morning Post.*
'The figure of Ramoncita, the heroine, a Mexican girl of 15, is charming—a sketch romantic and delicately drawn.'—*Manchester Guardian.*

J. H. Findlater. THE GREEN GRAVES OF BALGOWRIE. *Fourth Edition Crown 8vo. 6s.*
'A powerful and vivid story.'—*Standard.*
'A beautiful story, sad and strange as truth itself.'—*Vanity Fair.*
'A singularly original, clever, and beautiful story.'—*Guardian.*
'Reveals to us a new writer of undoubted faculty and reserve force.'—*Spectator.*
'An exquisite idyll, delicate, affecting, and beautiful. —*Black and White.*
See also Fleur de Lis Novels.

Mary Findlater. A NARROW WAY. *Third Edition. Crown 8vo. 6s.*
OVER THE HILLS *Second Edition Crown 8vo. 6s.*
See also Fleur de Lis Novels.

Tom Gallon, Author of 'Kiddy.' RICKERBY'S FOLLY.. *Crown 8vo. 6s.*

Dorothea Gerard, Author of 'Lady Baby.' THE MILLION. *Crown 8vo. 6s.*
THE CONQUEST OF LONDON. *Second Edition. Crown 8vo. 6s.*
THE SUPREME CRIME. *Cr. 8vo. 6s.*
See also Fleur de Lis Novels.

Algernon Gissing. THE KEYS OF THE HOUSE. *Crown 8vo. 6s.*
'A story of absorbing interest.'—*Liverpool Mercury.*
'The book is carefully built up, piece by piece. The figure of Brant himself moving among his people in his lonely parish of the hills is one that long remains with the reader.'—*Daily Telegraph.*

George Gissing, Author of 'Demos,' 'In the Year of Jubilee,' etc. THE TOWN TRAVELLER. *Second Edition. Crown 8vo. 6s.*
See also Fleur de Lis Novels.

Ernest Glanville. THE KLOOF BRIDE. *Crown 8vo. 3s. 6d.*
THE LOST REGIMENT. *Crown 8vo. 3s. 6d.*
THE DESPATCH RIDER. *Crown 8vo. 3s. 6d.*

Lord Ernest Hamilton. MARY HAMILTON. *Third Edition. Crown 8vo. 6s.*
'There can be no doubt that we have in "Mary Hamilton" a most fascinating story —the most stirring and dramatic historical romance that has come in our way for a long time.'—*Illustrated London News.*

Robert Hichens, Author of 'Flames,' etc. THE PROPHET OF BERKELEY SQUARE. *Second Edition. Crown 8vo. 6s.*
'One continuous sparkle. Mr. Hichens is witty, satirical, caustic, irresistibly humorous.'—*Birmingham Gazette.*
TONGUES OF CONSCIENCE. *Second Edition. Crown 8vo. 6s.*
See also Fleur de Lis Novels.

John Oliver Hobbes, Author of 'Robert Orange.' THE SERIOUS WOOING. *Crown 8vo. 6s.*
'Mrs. Craigie is as brilliant as she ever has been ; her characters are all illuminated with sparkling gems of description, and the conversation scintillates with an almost bewildering blaze.'—*Athenæum.*

Anthony Hope. See page 33.

Violet Hunt. THE HUMAN INTEREST. *Crown 8vo. 6s.*

C. J. Cutcliffe Hyne, Author of 'Captain Kettle.' PRINCE RUPERT THE BUCCANEER. With 8 Illustrations. *Second Edition. Crown 8vo. 6s.*
MR. HORROCKS, PURSER. *Crown 8vo. 6s.*
'Mr. Horrocks is a good second to the unapproachable Captain Kettle.'—*Academy.*
'Mr. Horrocks is sublime.'—*Manchester Guardian.*
'The Purser is a diverting discovery, and his adventures are related with vigour.'—*Daily Chronicle.*

W. W. Jacobs. See page 33.

Henry James, Author of 'What Maisie Knew.' THE SACRED FOUNT. *Crown 8vo. 6s.*
THE SOFT SIDE. *Second Edition. Crown 8vo. 6s.*

C. F. Keary. THE JOURNALIST. *Crown 8vo. 6s.*

Florence Finch Kelly. WITH HOOPS OF STEEL. *Crown 8vo. 6s.*
'Every chapter is filled with exciting incidents.'—*Morning Leader.*
'A daring and brilliant story of adventure. The novel teems with life and character, with life which is always within an ace of death, and character which curiously blends the ruffian and the hero.'—*Scotsman.*

Hon. Emily Lawless. TRAITS AND CONFIDENCES. *Crown 8vo. 6s.*
See also Fleur de Lis Novels.

E. Lynn Linton. THE TRUE HISTORY OF JOSHUA DAVIDSON, Christian and Communist. *Eleventh Edition. Crown 8vo. 1s.*

Charles K. Lush. THE AUTOCRATS. *Crown 8vo. 6s.*
'A clever story of American life. Its atmosphere is convincing and striking.'—*Vanity Fair.*
'Eminently readable with clever photographs of American social life.'—*Standard.*

S. Macnaughtan. THE FORTUNE OF CHRISTINA NACNAB. *Crown 8vo. 6s.*

A. Macdonell. THE STORY OF TERESA. *Crown 8vo. 6s.*
'Varied and clever characterisation and close sympathy with humanity.'—*Westminster Gazette.*
'The book is bracing as the moor itself. It has a threefold interest—its keen characterisation, its psychological insight, and its philosophy of life.'—*Pilot.*

Lucas Malet. See page 33.

Richard Marsh, Author of 'The Seen and the Unseen.' BOTH SIDES OF THE VEIL. *Second Edition. Crown 8vo. 6s.*
'Here we have Mr. Marsh at his best.'—*Globe.* See also Fleur de Lis Novels.

A. E. W. Mason, Author of 'The Courtship of Morrice Buckler,' 'Miranda of the Balcony,' etc. CLEMENTINA. Illustrated. *Crown 8vo. 6s.*
'A romance of the most delicate ingenuity and humour . . . the very quintessence of romance.'—*Spectator.*

L. T. Meade. DRIFT. *Crown 8vo. 6s.*
'Well told, and full of incident and character.'—*World.*
'A powerfully-wrought story.'—*Birmingham Post.*
'A powerful story, which treats of the drifting of a man of high intellectual gifts.'—*Court Circular.*

Bertram Mitford. THE SIGN OF THE SPIDER. *Fifth Edition.*

F. F. Montresor, Author of 'Into the Highways and Hedges.' THE ALIEN. *Second Edition. Crown 8vo. 6s.*
'Fresh, unconventional, and instinct with human sympathy.'—*Manchester Guardian.*
'Miss Montresor creates her tragedy out of passions and necessities elementarily human. Perfect art.'—*Spectator.*

Arthur Morrison. See page 34.

W. E. Norris. THE EMBARRASSING ORPHAN. *Crown 8vo. 6s.*
See also Fleur de Lis Novels.

Alfred Ollivant. OWD BOB, THE GREY DOG OF KENMUIR. *Fifth Edition. Crown 8vo. 6s.*
'Weird, thrilling, strikingly graphic.'—*Punch.*
'We admire this book . . . It is one to read with admiration and to praise with enthusiasm.'—*Bookman.*
'It is a fine, open-air, blood-stirring book, to be enjoyed by every man and woman to whom a dog is dear.'—*Literature.*

E. Phillips Oppenheim. MASTER OF MEN. *Second Edition. Crown 8vo. 6s.*

Gilbert Parker. See page 34.

James Blythe Patton. BIJLI, THE DANCER. *Crown 8vo. 6s.*

Max Pemberton. THE FOOTSTEPS OF A THRONE. Illustrated. *Second Edition. Crown 8vo. 6s.*
'A story of pure adventure, with a sensation on every page.'—*Daily Mail.*
I CROWN THEE KING. With Illustrations by Frank Dadd and A. Forrestier. *Crown 8vo. 6s.*
'A romance of high adventure, of love and war. It is a story of true love, of indomitable will, and of steadfastness that nothing can withstand.'—*Daily News.*
'A stirring tale.'—*Outlook.*

Eden Phillpotts. See page 34.

Walter Raymond, Author of 'Love and Quiet Life.' FORTUNE'S DARLING. *Crown 8vo. 6s.*

Edith Rickert. OUT OF THE CYPRESS SWAMP. *Crown 8vo. 6s.*
'A tale in which a note of freshness and individuality is struck, and the delicate question of colour is handled with originality and power. It has fine thrilling moments.'—*Spectator.*
'The whole story is admirably told. Not even in "Uncle Tom's Cabin" is there anything more exciting than the bloodhound chase after the hero.'—*Tatler.*

W. Pett Ridge. LOST PROPERTY. *Second Edition. Crown 8vo. 6s.*
'The story is an interesting and animated

picture of the struggle for life in London, with a natural humour and tenderness of its own.'—*Scotsman.*

'A simple, delicate bit of work, which will give pleasure to many. Much study of the masses has made him, not mad, but strong, and—wonder of wonders—cheerful.' —*Times.*

'A really delightful life history of a London foundling. Once more we have to thank Mr. Pett Ridge for an admirable study of London life.'—*Spectator.*

Mrs. M. H. Roberton. A GALLANT QUAKER. Illustrated. *Crown 8vo.* 6s.

'It is a strong story of love and hate, of religious excitement and calm faith.'—*Leeds Mercury.*

W. Clark Russell. MY DANISH SWEET-HEART. Illustrated. *Fourth Edition. Crown 8vo.* 6s.

Grace Rhys. THE WOOING OF SHEILA. *Second Edition. Crown 8vo.* 6s.

'A really fine book. A book that deserves to live. Sheila is the sweetest heroine who has lived in a novelist's pages for many a day. Every scene and every incident has the impress of truth. It is a masterly romance, and one that should be widely read and appreciated.'—*Morning Leader.*

W. Satchell. THE LAND OF THE LOST. *Crown 8vo.* 6s.

'An exciting story . . . the plot and passion are managed with skill, and the author shows himself a master of the art of depicting human character.' —*Glasgow Herald.*

Adeline Sergeant. Author of 'The Story of a Penitent Soul.' A GREAT LADY. *Crown 8vo.* 6s.

THE MASTER OF BEECHWOOD. *Crown 8vo.* 6s.

'A pleasant and excellently told story, 'natural and fresh.'—*Glasgow Herald.*

'A wholesome novel, with plenty of incident.'—*Spectator.*

W. F. Shannon. THE MESS DECK. *Crown 8vo.* 3s. 6d.

Helen Shipton. THE STRONG GOD CIRCUMSTANCE. *Crown 8vo.* 6s.

Annie Swan. LOVE GROWN COLD. *Second Edition. Crown 8vo.* 5s.

'One of the strongest books that the author has yet given us. We feel that the characters are taken from life. The story is told with delicacy and restraint.'—*Daily News.*

Benjamin Swift, Author of 'Siren City.' SORDON. *Crown 8vo.* 6s.

'Handled with a skill and a power

that are almost unfailing. The book is thoroughly good. It absorbs as much by its ingenuity in the use of material as by the force of its imagination.'—*Academy.*

'The author tells his story with great dramatic intentness, with simplicity, and strength.'—*Daily News.*

'A remarkable, venturesome, painful, and interesting book. The story is beautifully told ; it is rare pleasure to read such writing, so simple, finely balanced, graceful, refined, yet forcible.'—*World.*

Paul Waineman. A HEROINE FROM FINLAND. *Crown 8vo.* 6s.

'Fresh in subject and treatment.' —*Academy.*

'An idyll of country life which has the charm of entire novelty and freshness.'— *Morning Leader.*

'This tale of Russian and Finnish life is a most readable and enthralling one. The story is simple yet strong, and reveals intimate knowledge of Finnish life and manners.'—*Scotsman.*

'A delightful story.'—*Daily Express.*

'This lovely tale.' —*Manchester Guardian.*

'A vivid picture of pastoral life in a beautiful and too little known country.' —*Pall Mall Gazette.*

R. B. Townshend. LONE PINE: A Romance of Mexican Life. *Crown 8vo.* 6s.

H. B. Marriott Watson. THE SKIRTS OF HAPPY CHANCE. Illustrated. *Second Edition. Crown 8vo.* 6s.

'Mr. Watson's light touch, his genuine sense of humour, his ingenuity, and, above all, his polished and clear-cut style will provide genuine entertainment.'—*Pilot.*

H. G. Wells. THE STOLEN BACILLUS, and other Stories. *Second Edition. Crown 8vo.* 6s.

THE PLATTNER STORY AND OTHERS. *Second Edition Crown 8vo.* 6s.

Stanley Weyman, Author of 'A Gentleman of France.' UNDER THE RED ROBE. With Illustrations by R. C. WOODVILLE. *Seventeenth Edition. Crown 8vo.* 6s.

'Every one who reads books at all must read this thrilling romance, from the first page of which to the last the breathless reader is haled along. An inspiration of manliness and courage.'—*Daily Chronicle.*

Zack, Author of 'Life is Life.' TALES OF DUNSTABLE WEIR. *Crown 8vo.* 6s.

'"Zack" draws her pictures with great detail; they are indeed Dutch interiors in their fidelity to the small things of life.'— *Westminster Gazette.*

Tbe jfleur de Lis Novels

Crown 8vo.   3s. 6d.

MESSRS. METHUEN are now publishing popular Novels in a new and most charming style of binding. Ultimately, this Series will contain the following books :—

Andrew Balfour.
TO ARMS!
VENGEANCE IS MINE.

M. C. Balfour.
THE FALL OF THE SPARROW.

Jane Barlow.
THE LAND OF THE SHAMROCK.
A CREEL OF IRISH STORIES.
FROM THE EAST UNTO THE WEST.

J. A. Barry.
IN THE GREAT DEEP.

E. F. Benson.
THE CAPSINA.
DODO: A DETAIL OF THE DAY.
THE VINTAGE.

J. Bloundelle-Burton.
IN THE DAY OF ADVERSITY.
DENOUNCED.
THE CLASH OF ARMS.
ACROSS THE SALT SEAS.
SERVANTS OF SIN.

Mrs. Caffyn (Iota).
ANNE MAULEVERER.

Ada Cambridge.
PATH AND GOAL.

Mrs. W. K. Clifford.
A WOMAN ALONE.
A FLASH OF SUMMER.

J. Maclaren Cobban.
THE ANGEL OF THE COVENANT.

Julian Corbett.
A BUSINESS IN GREAT WATERS.

L. Cope Cornford.
SONS OF ADVERSITY.

Stephen Crane.
WOUNDS IN THE RAIN.

B. M. Croker.
A STATE SECRET.
PEGGY OF THE BARTONS.

Hope Dawlish.
A SECRETARY OF LEGATION.

A. J. Dawson.
DANIEL WHITE.

Evelyn Dickinson.
A VICAR'S WIFE.
THE SIN OF ANGELS.

Harris Dickson.
THE BLACK WOLF'S BREED.

Menie Muriel Dowie.
THE CROOK OF THE BOUGH.

Mrs. Dudeney.
THE THIRD FLOOR.

Sara Jeannette Duncan.
A VOYAGE OF CONSOLATION.
THE PATH OF A STAR.

G. Manville Fenn.
AN ELECTRIC SPARK.
THE STAR GAZERS.
ELI'S CHILDREN.
A DOUBLE KNOT.

Jane H. Findlater.
A DAUGHTER OF STRIFE.
RACHEL.

Mary Findlater.
BETTY MUSGRAVE.

Jane H. and Mary Findlater.
TALES THAT ARE TOLD.

J. S. Fletcher.
THE PATHS OF THE PRUDENT.
THE BUILDERS.

M. E. Francis.
MISS ERIN.

Mary Gaunt.
KIRKHAM'S FIND.
DEADMAN'S.
THE MOVING FINGER.'

Dorothea Gerard.
THINGS THAT HAVE HAPPENED.

R. Murray Gilchrist.
WILLOWBRAKE.

George Gissing.
THE CROWN OF LIFE.

Charles Gleig.
BUNTER'S CRUISE.

S. Gordon.
A HANDFUL OF EXOTICS.

C. F. Goss.
THE REDEMPTION OF DAVID CORSON.

E. M'Queen Gray.
MY STEWARDSHIP.
ELSA.

Robert Hichens.
BYEWAYS.

I. Hooper.
THE SINGER OF MARLY.

Emily Lawless.
HURRISH.
MAELCHO.

Norma Lorimer.
MIRRY-ANN.
JOSIAH'S WIFE.

Edna Lyall.
DERRICK VAUGHAN, NOVELIST.

Hannah Lynch.
AN ODD EXPERIMENT.

Richard Marsh.
THE SEEN AND THE UNSEEN.
MARVELS AND MYSTERIES.

W. E. Norris.
MATTHEW AUSTIN.
HIS GRACE.
THE DESPOTIC LADY.
CLARISSA FURIOSA.
GILES INGILBY.
AN OCTAVE.
JACK'S FATHER.
A DEPLORABLE AFFAIR.

Mrs. Oliphant.
SIR ROBERT'S FORTUNE.
THE TWO MARYS.
THE LADY'S WALK.
THE PRODIGALS.

Mary A. Owen.
THE DAUGHTER OF ALOUETTE.

Mary L. Pendered.
AN ENGLISHMAN.

Mrs. Penny.
A FOREST OFFICER.
R. Orton Prowse.
THE POISON OF ASPS.
Richard Pryce.
TIME AND THE WOMAN.
THE QUIET MRS. FLEMING.
W. Pett Ridge.
A SON OF THE STATE.
SECRETARY TO BAYNE, M.P.
Morley Roberts.
THE PLUNDERERS.
Marshall Saunders.
ROSE A CHARLITTE.
W. C. Scully.
THE WHITE HECATOMB.
BETWEEN SUN AND SAND.
A VENDETTA OF THE DESERT.
R. N. Stephens.
AN ENEMY TO THE KING.
A GENTLEMAN PLAYER.

E. H. Strain.
ELMSLIE'S DRAG-NET.
Esmé Stuart.
A WOMAN OF FORTY.
CHRISTALLA.
Duchess of Sutherland.
ONE HOUR AND THE NEXT.
Benjamin Swift.
SIREN CITY.
Victor Waite.
CROSS TRAILS.
Mrs. Walford.
SUCCESSORS TO THE TITLE.
Percy White.
A PASSIONATE PILGRIM.
Mrs. C. N. Williamson.
THE ADVENTURE OF PRINCESS SYLVIA.
X. L.
AUT DIABOLUS AUT NIHIL.

Books for Boys and Girls

Crown 8vo. 3s. 6d.

THE ICELANDER'S SWORD. By S. Baring-Gould.
TWO LITTLE CHILDREN AND CHING. By Edith E. Cuthell.
TODDLEBEN'S HERO. By M. M. Blake.
ONLY A GUARD-ROOM DOG. By Edith E. Cuthell.
THE DOCTOR OF THE JULIET. By Harry Collingwood.
MASTER ROCKAFELLAR'S VOYAGE. By W. Clark Russell.

SYD BELTON : Or, the Boy who would not go to Sea By G. Manville Fenn.
THE RED GRANGE. By Mrs. Molesworth.
THE SECRET OF MADAME DE MONLUC. By the Author of ' Mdle. Mori.'
DUMPS. By Mrs. Parr.
A GIRL OF THE PEOPLE. By L. T. Meade.
HEPSY GIPSY. By L. T. Meade. 2s. 6d.
THE HONOURABLE MISS. By L. T. Meade.

The Novelist

MESSRS. METHUEN are issuing under the above general title a Monthly Series of Novels by popular authors at the price of Sixpence. Some of these Novels have never been published before. Each number is as long as the average Six Shilling Novel. The first numbers of 'THE NOVELIST' are as follows :—

I. DEAD MEN TELL NO TALES. By E. W. Hornung.
II. JENNIE BAXTER, JOURNALIST. By Robert Barr.
III. THE INCA'S TREASURE. By Ernest Glanville.
IV. A SON OF THE STATE. By W. Pett Ridge.
V. FURZE BLOOM. By S. Baring-Gould.
VI. BUNTER'S CRUISE. By C. Gleig.
VII. THE GAY DECEIVERS. By Arthur Moore.
VIII. PRISONERS OF WAR. By A. Boyson Weekes.
IX. Out of print.
X. VELDT AND LAAGER : Tales of the Transvaal. By E. S. Valentine.
XI. THE NIGGER KNIGHTS. By F. Norreys Connel.
XII. A MARRIAGE AT SEA. By W. Clark Russell.
XIII. THE POMP OF THE LAVILETTES. By Gilbert Parker.
XIV. A MAN OF MARK. By Anthony Hope.
XV. THE CARISSIMA. By Lucas Malet.
XVI. THE LADY'S WALK. By Mrs. Oliphant.

XVII. DERRICK VAUGHAN. By Edna Lyall.
XVIII. IN THE MIDST OF ALARMS. By Robert Barr.
XIX. HIS GRACE. By W. E. Norris.
XX. DODO. By E. F. Benson.
XXI. CHEAP JACK ZITA. By S. Baring-Gould.
XXII. WHEN VALMOND CAME TO PONTIAC. By Gilbert Parker.
XXIII. THE HUMAN BOY. By Eden Phillpotts.
XXIV. THE CHRONICLES OF COUNT ANTONIO. By Anthony Hope.
XXV. BY STROKE OF SWORD. By Andrew Balfour.
XXVI. KITTY ALONE. By S. Baring-Gould.
XXVII. GILES INGILBY. By W. E. Norris.
XXVIII. URITH. By S. Baring-Gould.
XXIX. THE TOWN TRAVELLER. By George Gissing.
XXX. MR. SMITH. By Mrs. Walford.
XXXI. A CHANGE OF AIR. By Anthony Hope.

Methuen's Sixpenny Library

A New Series af Copyright and non-Copyright Books

THE MATABELE CAMPAIGN. By Major-General Baden-Powell.
THE DOWNFALL OF PREMPEH. By Major-General Baden-Powell.
MY DANISH SWEETHEART. By W. Clark Russell.
IN THE ROAR OF THE SEA. By S. Baring-Gould.
PEGGY OF THE BARTONS. By B. M. Croker.
THE GREEN GRAVES OF BALGOWRIE. By Jane H. Findlater.
THE STOLEN BACILLUS. By H. G. Wells.
MATTHEW AUSTIN. By W. E. Norris.

THE CONQUEST OF LONDON. By Dorothea Gerard.
A VOYAGE OF CONSOLATION. By Sara J. Duncan.
THE MUTABLE MANY. By Robert Barr.
BEN HUR. By Genera Lew Wallace.
SIR ROBERT'S FORTUNE. By Mrs. Oliphant.
THE FAIR GOD. By General Lew Wallace.
CLARISSA FURIOSA. By W. E. Norris.
NOEMI. By S. Baring-Gould.
THE THRONE OF DAVID. By J. H. Ingraham.
ACROSS THE SALT SEAS. By J. Bloundelle Burton.

For Product Safety Concerns and Information please contact our EU
representative GPSR@taylorandfrancis.com
Taylor & Francis Verlag GmbH, Kaufingerstraße 24, 80331 München, Germany